Praise for **Making Differentiation a Habit**

"The title of Diane Heacox's excellent new book, *Making Differentiation a Habit,* shows her philosophy and focus. Differentiation is not something to be done occasionally or when the mood strikes. Instead, it should be a habit embedded into all good teaching practices. Learning goals and standards, assessment and grading, tiered assignments, flexible grouping, and developing student responsibility and independence are all considered in this well-researched book. The author looks at all types of learning differences and gives practical strategies for dealing with both gifted students and students with learning difficulties. The book also links differentiation and RTI, showing many connections between the two. This is an important book that makes differentiation doable for all teachers in academically diverse classrooms."

Carolyn Coil, Ed.D.
Educational Consultant and Author

"*Making Differentiation a Habit* is an eminently practical book with valuable teacher assessment and reflection tools. As teachers use these tools, they will feel more in control of the diversity in readiness, motivation, and interest that confronts them.

The author has gone well beyond the marvelous path she set for us with *Differentiating Instruction in the Regular Classroom.* She has identified many clever methods to assess learning at all stages, and even cleverer ways to differentiate instruction in the heterogeneous classroom. Her examples of what all these various forms of differentiation look like are plentiful, covering every developmental level, from kindergarten through grade twelve.

The book is a wonderful synthesis of several well-respected and current resources on differentiation and assessment, all brought down to a teacher-friendly level and immediately usable in classrooms. Diane Heacox makes differentiated instruction almost fun for teachers! This is definitely a book I will require my graduate students in education to read when they take my differentiation courses."

Karen B. Rogers, Ph.D.
Professor of Education
College of Applied Professional Studies
University of St. Thomas
Minneapolis, Minnesota

Making Differentiation a Habit

How to Ensure Success in Academically Diverse Classrooms

Diane Heacox, Ed.D.

Foreword by Rick Wormeli

Library of Congress Cataloging-in-Publication Data
Heacox, Diane, 1949–
Making differentiation a habit : how to ensure success in academically diverse classrooms / Diane Heacox ; foreword by Rick Wormeli.
p. cm.
Includes bibliographical references and index.
ISBN 978-1-57542-324-1
1. Multicultural education—United States. 2. Individualized instruction. 3. Educational equalization—United States. 4. Teaching—United States. 5. Classroom management—United States. I. Title.
LC1099.3.H37 2009
371.39'4—dc22

2009001419

Cover and book design by Tasha Kenyon
Edited by Meg Bratsch

10 9 8 7 6 5 4 3 2 1
Printed in the United States of America

Free Spirit Publishing Inc.
217 Fifth Avenue North, Suite 200
Minneapolis, MN 55401-1299
(612) 338-2068
help4kids@freespirit.com
www.freespirit.com

DEDICATION

To my husband, John Bloodsworth, who is always willing to be there and take on tasks that enable me to do my "schoolwork." I wouldn't or couldn't be what I am today without his continued support and love.

To my daughter, Kylie, my very best friend. You are the light of my life and always will be.

ACKNOWLEDGMENTS

My friends in "gifted land" have continued to challenge my thinking and excite me with their innovative ideas, scholarly work, and intellect. I am grateful for their support and encouragement.

Special thanks go to Rick Wormeli, whose inspiring work and passion for teaching has resulted in new insights for educators and huge benefits for the students in their classrooms.

Thanks also go to Richard Cash, who always answers his phone when I need a word of advice or support . . . and makes me laugh! Richard's reflective thinking, in-depth knowledge, and creativity have made our collaborative work a joy.

In addition, I'd like to acknowledge Meg Bratsch, my editor, whose kind words, support, keen eye, and thoughtful, insightful work helped make this book "shine."

Finally, I extend my gratitude to all of the teachers, principals, and school leaders across the United States and Canada who have shared their enthusiasm for and commitment to doing whatever is necessary to help all students be successful in learning. You and your students will continue to be the inspiration for my work.

CONTENTS

LIST OF REPRODUCIBLE PAGES

LIST OF FIGURES

FOREWORD

BY RICK WORMELI

If, as educators, we wish to live up to the promise of differentiated schooling, we must identify the tools to use, as well as how and when to use them—no small task, as any teacher knows. Fortunately, in *Making Differentiation a Habit,* Diane Heacox has done much of the development, sorting, and explanation of the tools for us. While no single book, presenter, DVD, blog, podcast, or Web cast can provide all the strategies and structures needed to respond successfully to every unique teaching situation, this book comes closer than most. Based on current, scholarly research expertly and realistically applied in today's classrooms, *Making Differentiation a Habit* earns major credence in our profession.

Throughout the book, information is well structured, presenting flow charts and formats for purposeful teaching, versus random collections of ideas. This may be one of the book's greatest assets: It explains *when* to differentiate, not merely how.

Differentiating in the Regular Classroom, Diane's first book on differentiation, is among the go-to resources for every teacher and district implementing differentiated instruction. It is a practical volume responding effectively to teachers' requests to "show me what it looks like." With *Making Differentiation a Habit,* Diane goes further and hands us multiple, widely adaptable templates for differentiating instruction intelligently. This is not a cookbook full of passive recipes, nor is it a paint-by-numbers approach to teaching. Instead, it provides the fresh clay, the carving tools, and the spirited inspiration to form the clay to match our intent. In short, *Making Differentiation a Habit* is the thinking teacher's manual for differentiation.

In the course of the book, Diane incorporates a wide variety of subjects and grade levels, from kindergarten-level mathematics to high school-level literary and historical analysis. Educators in varied school roles will see their personal teaching scenarios in her many examples and applications. Throughout the book, information is well structured, presenting flow charts and formats for purposeful teaching, versus random collections of ideas. This may be one of the book's greatest assets: It explains *when* to differentiate, not merely how.

Among the most helpful templates in the book is the Differentiated Learning Plan (DLP). This is a user-friendly schematic that incorporates the best principles of differentiation in a step-by-step process for creating an effective lesson plan. Multiple examples of the DLP in use are also provided. Diane understands the concerns of teachers developing their first differentiated lessons as well as those who want to improve what they are already doing. She provides clear advice on tiering for readiness, interest, and learner profile; teaching gifted students; using flexible grouping for a clear purpose; and creating classroom routines that enable smooth transitions. Particularly helpful is a section of the book on how to respond flexibly to students as we learn more about them. It answers the "What do I do if . . . ?" questions all of us have as we try to meet the needs of increasingly diverse groups of students.

Much of differentiation depends on our mindset, of course, and the book prepares our minds for developing and maintaining a philosophy of differentiated instruction. It tackles misconceptions and myths regarding differentiation that still pervade our profession. It helps readers understand themselves in relation to differentiation, providing them with tools to assess their professional development, comfort zones, and places where they might push themselves. Because teachers are very conscientious and may try multiple ideas at once—which can be overwhelming—numerous reminders are provided so we don't lose track of the important elements.

Standards-based instruction stays on the radar throughout the book. Diane is adept at showing teachers the power of "Know, Understand, Do" in our objectives, and how knowledge of a developmentally appropriate curriculum serves as the launching pad for all differentiation. Recognizing the role of motivation in student learning, she shows us how to build that motivation through student choice *without* sacrificing curriculum standards. Assessment and grading practices are also addressed, with a focus on ethics, formative and summative assessments, and students' self-assessment and reflection. In addition, the chapter on Response to Intervention (RTI) is a cogent explanation of RTI and how differentiation fits into its structures and policies. Regardless of your degree of familiarity with RTI, this is an important chapter to read and consider.

Demand for teacher training in differentiated instruction has exploded in the past decade, as school districts recognize how critical differentiation is to their mission. While it's really just another name for good eclectic teaching, differentiated instruction includes some universally effective protocols that enable flexible responses to students' needs. There are some practices that are more effective than others, however, and it helps to have a trusted expert lay out the options. After reading Diane's book, no one will lack for helpful ideas or the impetus to use them. *Making Differentiation a Habit* is destined to be cover-worn, dog-eared, margin-marked, and text-highlighted by differentiation neophytes and seasoned veterans for years to come. I look forward to meeting the students of teachers who embrace its courageous and adroit pedagogy.

Rick Wormeli
Author of *Fair Isn't Always Equal* and
Differentiation: From Planning to Practice

INTRODUCTION

Making Differentiation a Habit

In the years since the publication of *Differentiating Instruction in the Regular Classroom,* I have had the privilege to work with teachers across the United States and Canada. I have also met teachers via technology in classrooms in Asia, Great Britain, Germany, India, and Singapore who use ideas and resources in the book. And regardless of where they originate from, the questions and concerns these teachers raise about differentiation seem to be similar.

"How do I make differentiation more doable given the limitations of time and resources? How do I develop greater independence and responsibility in my students so that differentiation can be more easily managed?"

"With all the 'tips and tricks' publications on differentiation, how do I know I am implementing research-based strategies in my classroom?"

"How can differentiation inform the work that I do with IDEA's Response to Intervention in my classroom?"

"Are the needs of gifted learners being appropriately addressed with classroom level differentiation?"

"Is grading different in a differentiated classroom?"

The purpose of *Making Differentiation a Habit* is to respond to the burning questions of teachers and school leaders as they work in differentiation. This book's intent is to help teachers make differentiation a routine part of their work with students. When differentiation becomes a habit, it becomes the way in which we go about "school."

When teachers effectively differentiate instruction, there is a continuous flow in the processes of teaching, learning, and assessment.

The teaching and learning process becomes fluid and flexible as we consider the differences in our classrooms and plan for them.

When teachers effectively differentiate instruction, there is a continuous flow in the processes of teaching, learning, and assessment. These components operate not as steps that we follow, but rather as a continuous cycle, each process informing the next. **Figure 1** on page 2 shows this cycle.

The purpose and goal of teaching is student learning. The cycle typically begins with formal or informal preassessment in the **assessment** phase. Based on what you learn about your students' needs, you plan and enter the **teaching** phase. At this point of the cycle, students are engaged in **learning.** As the students are engaged in learning as well as after the learning sequence, you again enter an **assessment** phase, this time using formative assessment strategies. You reflect on whether the students have accomplished learning goals. At this point in the cycle, you may need to enter another phase of teaching and learning utilizing further strategies in differentiation. Or, if goals are accomplished, you move into a new cycle with new goals. Each phase of the cycle informs your responses to and plans for your students. This book provides strategies for each of these phases.

FIGURE 1

The Cycle of Teaching, Learning, and Assessment

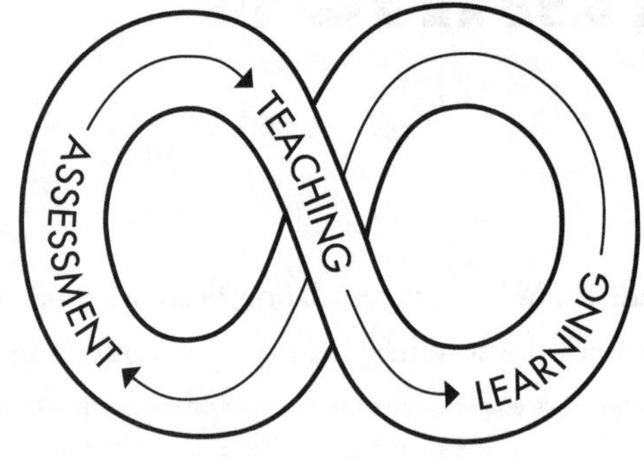

Critical Elements for Success in a Differentiated Classroom

Much has been written about differentiation as teachers take on the challenges of academically diverse classrooms. Critical to effective responses to student learning differences is an understanding of what differentiation *is* and *isn't*. It is assumed that teachers recognize that the academic diversity of their classrooms and standards/goals-based education, along with initiatives such as Response to Intervention, demand authentic differentiated approaches in order to increase the likelihood of student success in learning. But what exactly do these differentiated approaches look like? Following are the 12 critical elements for success in a differentiated classroom. These provide the framework for this book.

Authentic differentiation requires you to:

1. Identify learning goals, or KUDo's (what your students need to **K**now, **U**nderstand, and be able to **Do**).
2. Examine your professional practices in light of your students' needs.
3. Apply practical, doable, and valid assessment strategies.
4. Create differentiated learning plans.
5. Use choice opportunities to motivate student learning.
6. Prescribe tiered assignments and use flexible grouping as necessary and appropriate.
7. Maintain flexibility in your planning and teaching.
8. Develop student responsibility and independence.
9. Use ethical grading practices.
10. Differentiate instruction for gifted students with their particular and specific learning differences in mind.
11. Integrate strategies for differentiation and RTI into your classroom practices.
12. Commit to a leadership framework for differentiated classrooms in your school.

About This Book

This book provides specific ideas, strategies, templates, and formats that reflect authentic differentiation. The ideas in the book evolved from both my professional practice as a classroom teacher and facilitator of opportunities for gifted learners, and from my work with academic underachievers. Some strategies come from the practical ideas of teachers I have had the pleasure to work with. The specific goals of the book and chapter descriptions follow.

THE GOALS OF MAKING DIFFERENTIATION A HABIT

- To identify critical elements for success in academically diverse classrooms
- To distinguish authentic differentiation from random teaching tips and tricks
- To provide a format for writing learning goals that increases your clarity about what you want your students to know, understand, and be able to do

- To examine professional practices to enable educators to develop plans for the next steps in the development of the habit of differentiation
- To present practical, informal assessment strategies
- To present a differentiated learning plan that better reflects the kind of planning essential for success in academically diverse classrooms
- To examine the ways in which choice can motivate student learning
- To provide simple, timesaving techniques for designing differentiated activities, including tiered assignments
- To develop flexible lesson routines that build in responses to learning differences
- To provide strategies and routines to promote greater independence and responsibility in students
- To explore issues around grading practices in academically diverse classrooms
- To distinguish the ways in which differentiation for the gifted and talented varies significantly from strategies used for other learners
- To make clear the connections between differentiation and Response to Intervention
- To provide guidance to teacher leaders and administrators in supporting differentiation in their classrooms and schools.

Chapter 1 presents the first critical element: identifying your learning goals. The chapter describes the connections between standards-based education and differentiation. Many teachers working with state standards or provincial goals in the classroom put them into the more practical language of KUDo's, what students will *know, understand,* and be able to *do* by the end of the unit or a lesson. The how-tos of KUDo's, the critical first step in differentiation, are explained, and examples in a variety of curriculum areas are provided. Finally, a process for thinking through when and how to differentiate is presented to clarify the flow of actions in a differentiated classroom from standards to summative assessment.

The second critical element, examining your professional practices, is addressed in **Chapter 2**. In this chapter, you will thoughtfully reflect on the curriculum practices and strategies for differentiation you currently use in your classroom. You will have an opportunity to examine your practices in light of a continuum of teacher development in differentiation. You will also be provided with a survey to help you recognize the different needs of your students.

Chapter 3 addresses the critical element of assessment. A variety of practical strategies for preassessment, formative assessment, summative assessment, and student self-reflection are offered. Distinctions are made between formal and informal methods of assessment. The focus of the strategies presented in this chapter is on quick, informal assessment.

The fourth critical element, the differentiated learning plan, is introduced in **Chapter 4**. In today's diverse classrooms, the lesson plan structures developed in the 1960s and 1970s no longer work. This chapter presents a nine-step process to think through and design differentiated learning plans.

Chapter 5 extends your understandings and application of the fifth critical element: student choice. Although many formats for providing student choice are being used in classrooms, not all meet the standard of authentic differentiation. For example, distinctions must be made between a differentiated tic-tac-toe board and a randomly assembled collection of activities. Essential characteristics of differentiated choice boards are described. Additional formats and templates are introduced and ideas for best managing the use of choice in the classroom are offered.

Your understanding of and practices in tiering assignments and using flexible instructional groups will be extended in **Chapter 6**. This sixth critical element describes the most prescriptive strategy in differentiation and encourages you to try new ways to tier assignments. Two templates are offered to make designing tiered assignments quick and easy to do. Criteria for well-designed tiered assignments are also presented.

Chapter 7 describes the importance of maintaining flexibility in planning and teaching, the seventh critical element. It asks you to examine your lesson routines and then suggests ways that planning for differences can be accomplished by modifying your routines.

Increasing student responsibility and independence is a crucial endeavor in a differentiated classroom. **Chapter 8** addresses this critical element by providing procedures, management structures, tips for flexible use of space, and strategies to get your students working in ways that take less time, less direction, and less supervision from you.

Chapter 9 examines the grading dilemmas in differentiated classrooms. This critical element is discussed through responses to 10 burning questions about grading. In this chapter, you will explore your values, beliefs, and practices related to grading.

Chapter 10 explores the challenges of differentiating for gifted learners. Because of their particular and specific learning differences and needs, differentiation for gifted learners varies significantly from strategies used for most other students. Templates, formats, and strategies are offered that link best practices for gifted learners to your practices in differentiation.

Chapter 11 focuses on the eleventh critical element: examining the connections between differentiated instruction and IDEA's Response to Intervention (RTI). RTI procedures are used for students who are having difficulties academically as well as those who might be experiencing behavioral issues. The strategies of differentiation form the foundation of Response to Intervention.

Chapter 12 discusses the final critical element: providing a leadership framework for differentiated classrooms and schools. A variety of tools, including classroom walk-through protocols, are provided to allow a teacher leader or school administrator to gather specific data about differentiation. In addition, an action-planning format is offered that can be used with members of a school's faculty or with a school's leadership team.

Finally, the **Conclusion** reviews all 12 critical elements of differentiation and offers examples of ways to make differentiation a daily habit and routine.

How to Use This Book

Making Differentiation a Habit presents critical elements for success in academically diverse classrooms. Its focus is to extend the work of my previous book, *Differentiating Instruction in the Regular Classroom*, as well as to address topics that have arisen from the questions and concerns of teachers I have worked with over the past few years.

My intent is to support the work of classroom teachers, gifted and special education specialists, as well as those in school leadership positions, such as curriculum directors, building principals, teacher leaders, and professional development trainers. I also hope that the book will become a valued resource for college faculty working with preservice teachers. The habit of differentiation should begin before our first teaching position.

You may choose to go through the book chapter by chapter, examining your practices and adding new ideas and strategies. Or you may want to target a particular area for professional growth and go straight to that chapter. For example, if you want to extend your practices in tiered assignments, you may go immediately to Chapter 6.

If you are in a specialized role, you may wish to review chapters with the greatest practicality and concern for you and your school. Do you need to

Although practical in its intent, this book strives to deepen your understandings of differentiation and extend your practices to the benefit of your students.

know where and how gifted learners "fit" into a differentiated classroom? Are you wondering how RTI and differentiation can work together? Does your school need to set up a building-wide plan for moving toward a more comprehensive implementation of differentiation? Are you looking for ways to respond to some teachers' apprehension about grading in academically diverse classrooms? You will find your answers within these chapters.

Although practical in its intent, this book strives to deepen your understandings of differentiation and extend your practices to the benefit of your students. I hope it becomes a trusted resource for you as you develop the habit of differentiation. Enjoy browsing its pages for what will make differentiation more doable for you and ensure success in your academically diverse classroom!

Diane Heacox, Ed.D.

CHAPTER 1

Critical Element: Identifying Your Learning Goals

Differentiation and Content Standards

I am frequently asked how differentiation "fits into" standards-based education. Differentiation is all about working within the framework of your state's standards or province's goals. Educators recognize that not all students are at the same readiness level, or learn at the same pace or in the same way. Differentiation is what we do to enable more students to meet their state's standards or province's goals. It is the way in which we respond to learning differences as students engage in daily activities in our classroom. As such, we cannot even begin to think about differentiation (how we teach, how our students learn) without first considering our standards (*what* they will learn).

Differentiation is all about working within the framework of your state's standards or province's goals.

Therefore, any work in differentiation must begin with your state standards or provincial goals well in mind.

Know Your KUDo's

All states and provinces have some form of academic or content standards to guide the learning goals of students in their schools. Academic standards, however, are most often written in "edu-babble," the language of educators. If you are going to talk about learning goals with students and share them with parents, it is important that you put the standards into language that can be clearly understood. A learning goal should be written so that there is little room for different interpretations of its meaning.

Today, many educators are writing learning goals—whether they are at the course, unit, or lesson plan level—as "KUDo's": What do I want my students to **K**now, **U**nderstand, and be able to **Do**? All academic standards can be sorted into either *know*, *understand*, or *do* goals. Goals written as KUDo's relate the following:

Know

- What facts, vocabulary, dates, rules, people, places, etc., do I want my students to know by the end of this course/unit/lesson?
- *Knows* are usually written as a list of things we want students to memorize. They are facts related to a study.

Understand

- What concepts, principles, and generalizations will my students understand by the end of this course/unit/lesson?
- *Understandings* are typically written as sentences describing the "big ideas" of the course/unit/lesson. In writing understandings, it helps if you use the phrase "understand *that* . . ."

Do

- What will my students be able to independently do by the end of the course/unit/lesson?
- *Do's* are skills and processes. They are applications of learning and encompass both critical and creative thinking. Think of them as life skills that apply beyond this particular course/unit/lesson.
- *Do's* are written as statements beginning with a verb, usually a verb associated with Bloom's Taxonomy[1], such as compare, contrast, formulate, predict, classify, describe, summarize, or distinguish.

As an example of how to write KUDo's from academic standards, here are sample state standards and the KUDo's the teacher might write in describing the learning goals for a unit on desert biospheres.

Science Academic Standards
Grade: Elementary
Unit: Desert Biosphere

- The student will *recognize* that plants and animals have life cycles.
- The student will *understand* that organisms live in different environments.
- The student will *describe* the features of plants and animals that allow them to live in specific environments.
- The student will *recognize* that plants and animals have different structures that serve various functions.
- The student will *understand* that an organism's patterns of behavior are related to its environment.
- The student will *recognize* that changes in a habitat can be beneficial or harmful to an organism.
- The student will *recognize* that organisms interact with one another in various ways besides providing food.

1 Benjamin Bloom et al., *Taxonomy of Educational Objectives: Handbook of the Cognitive Domain* (New York: Longman, 1984).

KUDO'S FOR AN ELEMENTARY UNIT ON THE DESERT BIOSPHERE

Students will:

Know

- Plants of the desert
- Animals of the desert
- Definition of: *life cycle, habitat, environment*

Understand

- Plants and animals live in different environments.
- Desert plants and animals have particular ways of behaving that relate to their environment.
- Food chains link desert animals and plants.

Be able to

- Describe the life cycle of a desert plant and animal.
- Describe the particular characteristics (functions and structures) of desert plants and animals that allow them to live there.
- Identify how desert plants and animals interact with each other in ways other than as part of a food chain.
- Determine how changes in the desert habitat affect its animals and plants in good and bad ways.

Additional examples of KUDo's follow:

KUDO'S FOR ELEMENTARY GEOMETRY

Students will:

Know

- Definition of: *line, line segment, angle, triangle, quadrilateral*

Understand

- Geometric shapes have specific properties.

Be able to

- Identify and describe geometric shapes in their environment.
- Construct geometric shapes and identify their properties.

KUDO'S FOR HIGH SCHOOL ECONOMICS

Students will:

Know

- Definition of: *recession, depression, economic boom, monopoly, monopolistic competition, oligopoly, perfect competition, scarcity*

Understand

- Market forces affect the economy.

Be able to

- Determine how the principles of supply and demand affect the economy.
- Compare and contrast concepts of competition and monopoly and predict the consequences of each.
- Analyze the economic role of government in a free market economy.
- Determine the effects of competitive forces on businesses.
- Utilize data analysis in making decisions.

Helpful Hints for Putting KUDo's Into Practice

Be careful as you write *Do's* that you write goals, not activities. For example, "create a model of the food chain of a desert animal" sounds like a *Do,* but it is actually an activity that the students will engage in to work on an *Understanding.* When we consider the activity, we need to ask what the students will learn by making the model. Thus, the goal for this activity is: Students will understand that food chains link desert animals and plants."

Consider KUDo's a roadmap for your course, unit, or lesson. If you do not pay attention and follow your roadmap, you are not only going to lose instructional time but also move into curriculum topics or student activities not focused on your learning goals.

KUDo's enable you to critically consider the student activities you currently use in a unit and those you could potentially use. *All* student tasks within a unit must work on a goal.

1. Consider each activity.
2. Determine whether the activity works on a KUDo.
3. If it does not, eliminate the activity.

KUDo's should be shared with students and posted in the classroom.

Using this process clearly aligns all instructional activities with your unit's KUDo's. The essential first step in planning or differentiating a course, unit, or lesson must be identifying your KUDo's.

KUDo's should be shared and posted in the classroom to provide students with an understanding of the goals of a course or unit, as well as what they will be held accountable for in each unit's summative assessments. KUDo's can be shared with parents in class newsletters, conferences, or informational meetings. KUDo's are also used as a method for developing the goals for your lesson plans. Ask yourself: "By the end of today's lesson, what will my students know, understand, and be able to do?" Read more on this use of KUDo's in Chapter 4: Using a Differentiated Learning Plan.

Thinking Through the When and How of Differentiation

One of the results of standards-based education has been a greater alignment of learning goals, curriculum, assessment, and instruction. **Figure 2** shows the flow of actions from standards to summative assessment. It also shows the integration of differentiation into the flow of actions. Following is an explanation of each action.

1 Review your state or province's **academic standards.** Using your standards, establish your unit's topic or theme. Then think about "shopping" the standards in other curriculum areas for those that may also be addressed in your unit. You might collect standards from a variety of curriculum areas to create an interdisciplinary unit. Also, remember that standards in most states and provinces are the "floor" not the "ceiling" for learning goals. You must work on the prescribed standards, *but* you can also go beyond and above the standards to add more depth or challenge to your unit and to respond to the needs of the learners in your classroom.

2 Rewrite your standards as **KUDo's** to increase their clarity and provide a more accessible presentation of the goals to your students and parents.

3 Gather information about your students as it relates to your unit. Use either formal or informal **preassessment.** Also, reflect on your **students' interests** and **learning preferences** (based on the theory of Multiple Intelligences) to begin to think about the ways in which you may differentiate the unit. For examples of student inventories of interests and learning preferences, see the "Interest Inventory" and the "Projects, Presentations, Performances" forms in *Differentiating Instruction in the Regular Classroom.*[2]

4 Based on the data you have collected in Step 3, begin to **modify your unit goals.** In considering the readiness of your class, students may need to include additional goals if prerequisite content, skills, or processes are missing. You may also add more advanced or complex goals if you discover through preassessment that your students have a stronger knowledge or experience base than you expected.

You may need to consider modifying or adapting particular goals for students with special needs based on an Individual Education Plan. For gifted learners, you may replace goals they have already attained with more complex or advanced goals.

Also, revisit your students' interests. What topics will motivate their learning based on their interests? In what ways might you respond to the curiosities of your students yet keep the primary focus on the required standards/goals?

FIGURE 2

From Standards to Summative Assessment

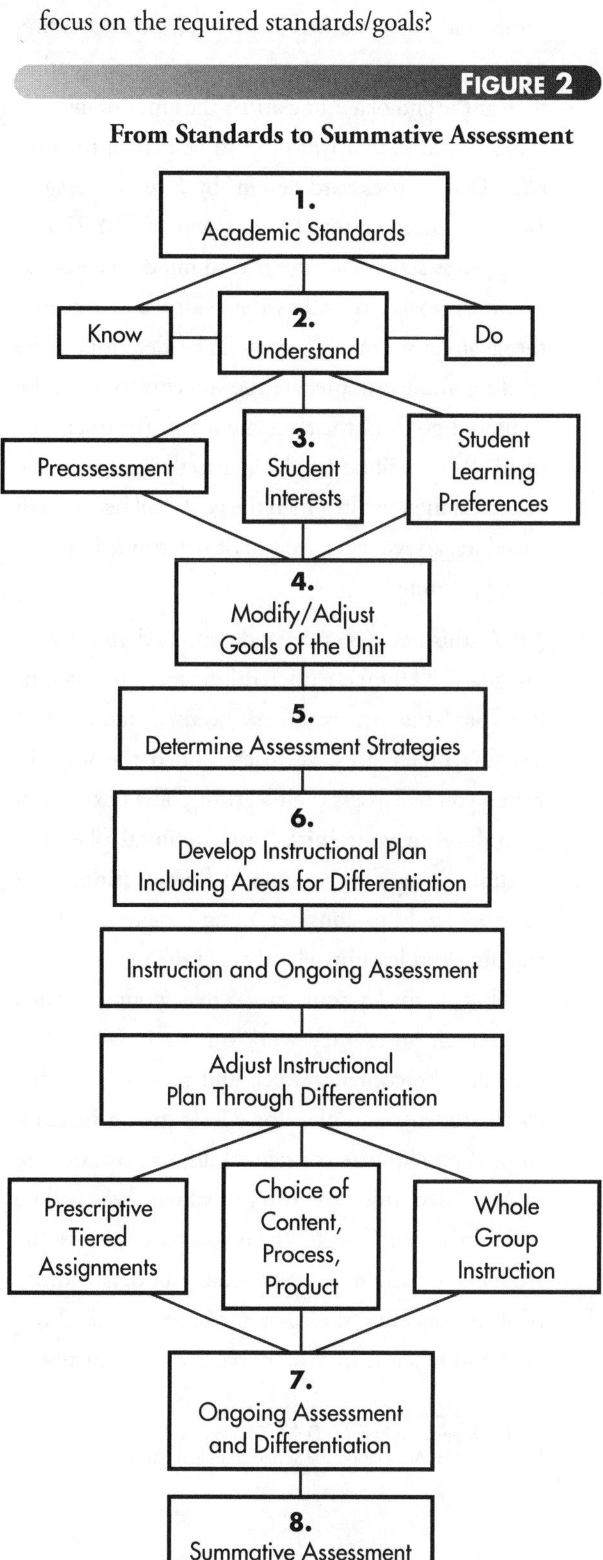

2 Diane Heacox, *Differentiating Instruction in the Regular Classroom: How to Reach and Teach All Learners, Grades 3–12* (Minneapolis: Free Spirit Publishing, 2002).

5 An early consideration in designing your unit is to **determine strategies for assessing** your students' attainment of the KUDo's. What will be evidence that the students have learned the concepts, processes, and skills outlined in your KUDo's? Deciding on assessment strategies early in your planning rather than at the end of a unit clarifies the kinds of instructional activities that will need to be part of the unit plan. Called "backward design" by *Understanding by Design* authors Grant Wiggins and Jay McTighe[3], the process starts with the end in mind (the desired results or goals), considers the evidence of reaching the goals (assessments), and finally determines the teaching needed to prepare the students to reach the goals and perform the assessment task (instructional plan). What will be taught is directly related to the goals and the ways in which the goals will be assessed; therefore, assessments need to be determined in your initial planning.

6 At this point, you have determined your learning goals (KUDo's); gathered information concerning your students' readiness needs, interests, and learning preferences; and determined the ways in which you will assess their learning. The next action is to **develop your initial instructional plan** and include areas for possible **differentiation**. You are now ready to consider, design, or redesign the teaching and learning elements of the unit.

Begin to lay out tasks that your students will engage in as they work on the KUDo's. You consider the content, skills, and processes needed by all students and plan for **whole group instruction**. If prerequisite content, skills, or processes are missing, determine the ways in which these will be retaught or reinforced. If you discover that some students already have considerable understandings of unit concepts, skills, or processes, think about how and when it may be necessary to insert **tiered assignments** and flexible instructional groups into the unit's plan. In addition, consider whether there are students who might benefit from activities above and beyond the unit because of advanced knowledge or skills.

> Differentiation is an ongoing, reflective process.

Consider how you can respond to the interests and learning preferences of your students as you design the teaching and learning activities for your unit. Will you offer some **choices** to your students? Will they have an opportunity to choose to engage in an activity that reflects their learning preferences or interests?

7 Preliminary planning of your unit and consideration of when and where differentiation may be needed is important. However, your plans must remain flexible. **Ongoing, formative assessment** of your students' learning will likely indicate instances when you need to spend more time on a concept, skill, or process; reteach in a new way; or extend/enrich learning to address the specific needs of your students. Differentiation is an ongoing, reflective process. You differentiate instruction based on student learning needs, which often emerge during the process of teaching and learning.

8 Finally, utilize **summative assessment** strategies. Analyze student results and report to your students. Based on the student results, determine the next appropriate steps in your instructional plans. Will further work be needed with some students on particular content, skills, or processes? Will the skill or process "spiral" back into the curriculum at another point so that students will have an opportunity to learn it again later on? Planning for student needs does not end with summative assessment, but rather continues to evolve based on data.

3 Grant Wiggins and Jay McTighe, *Understanding by Design* (Alexandria, VA: Association for Supervision and Curriculum Development, 1998).

CHAPTER 2

Critical Element: Examining Your Professional Practices

All teachers differentiate to a degree. Some teachers have intuitively come upon strategies that work for them. Trial and error and experience in the classroom have enabled them to figure out what works and doesn't work in helping more children learn. For some teachers, differentiation may have been a topic in a university education course. Others may have attended district professional development sessions, registered for workshops, gone to professional conferences, or joined book study groups to refine and extend their understandings of differentiation and to apply new strategies in their classrooms.

Our schools are no different than our classrooms. Teachers represent a diverse group of professionals within any one school. All teachers are in different places in developing their professional skills related to differentiation. They also have different teaching styles, so what works for one may make another uncomfortable. Then there are the students to consider. What works with one group of sixth graders may not work for another. Also, how and when teachers differentiated instruction one year is not likely to be the same in the next year because they will have different groups of students.

Know Yourself as a Teacher

It is important that you examine your current practices and identify the next step in your professional development. This chapter provides tools to help you analyze where you are in the advancement of your practices in differentiation. On pages 13–14 is a "Teacher Inventory on Differentiation Practices and Strategies." The inventory reflects practices and strategies that characterize differentiated classrooms.

As with most new practices, the key to not getting overwhelmed is to "start small but start somewhere."

It will help you identify which of these elements are used most frequently in your classroom and which are in more limited application. After reviewing the results of your inventory, your goal is to select a new strategy or two to add to your teaching repertoire. As with most new practices, the key to not getting overwhelmed is to "start small but start somewhere." Add one new differentiation strategy at a time, practice it, refine its use with your students, and only then move on to a new strategy. Look through the chapters in this book for specific ideas to extend your strategies and practices in differentiation.

Pages 15–18 present a "Continuum of Levels of Teacher Development in Differentiation." The continuum represents five domains: teaching beliefs, the role of the teacher, instructional practices, assessment strategies, and grading practices. While the "Teacher Inventory on Differentiation Practices and Strategies" enables you to critically examine the ways in which you currently differentiate, the continuum takes a more global approach. It allows you to consider your level of professional development in differentiation—from novice to expert.

Novice teachers are beginning to develop an understanding of differentiation yet show little or limited evidence of application of strategies for differentiation in their classrooms.

Practitioners are on the road to more sophisticated applications of differentiation in their classrooms. They are actively engaged in planning for differences among their students and have many strategies to choose from in their teaching repertoire.

Experts are teachers who show evidence of comprehensive differentiation in their classrooms. Their practices show both breadth and depth in understanding of the complexities of differentiation. Experts know their students deeply. They think critically about their students and their curriculum goals. They use assessment strategies to inform their instructional practices. And they teach flexibly: they respond to where their students are in their learning, and skillfully use instructional strategies to maximize learners' success.

To use the "Continuum of Levels of Teacher Development in Differentiation," consider each description across each of the three levels. Check the descriptor that best reflects your beliefs about teaching and the role of the teacher, the instructional and assessment strategies you utilize, and your grading practices. It is likely that you may be at one level in one of the domains and a different level in another. You may also find that within any one domain you may represent more than one level of development.

Once you have completed the continuum, you have a profile of the current levels of your professional development across five domains of differentiation. This information can assist you in recognizing where you are presently, and what the next steps in your development should be. The final column of the continuum provides space for you to reflect on where you are in each domain and, as appropriate, to note specifically what you might do to move to the next level of professional development in differentiation.

Professional development facilitators, school administrators, and teacher leaders may also use the completed teacher inventories and continuums in considering plans for training and development opportunities for educators. Additional information about using the tools in providing leadership for differentiation is included in Chapter 12.

Teacher Inventory on Differentiation Practices and Strategies

Check the level at which you teach.

❑ Grades K–2 ❑ Grades 3–5 ❑ Grades 6–8 ❑ Grades 9–12

Read each statement below. Circle the response that most closely describes the extent to which you use the practice in your classroom. Use the following scale:

1 = never/almost never

2 = seldom

3 = sometimes

4 = frequently, consistently

Differentiation Practices and Strategies	Level of Usage			
CURRICULUM				
1. I review my state/province's academic standards before I determine a curriculum unit's goals (KUDo's) or the goals for a lesson	1	2	3	4
2. I determine the assessments that I will use before I plan my unit activities so that there is alignment between curriculum, assessment, and instruction.	1	2	3	4
3. I ensure that all student tasks and products focus on clearly stated learning goals (KUDo's).	1	2	3	4
INSTRUCTIONAL PLANNING				
4. I preassess students to determine their readiness for each new unit or series of lessons.	1	2	3	4
5. I use ongoing (formative) assessment to adjust my instructional plans to respond to differing learning needs.	1	2	3	4
6. I use assessment data provided by my state or province or school to inform my instructional planning.	1	2	3	4
7. I gather information about my students' interests in curriculum topics.	1	2	3	4
8. I know my students' learning preferences. (Multiple Intelligences)	1	2	3	4
FLEXIBLE INSTRUCTION				
9. I use a variety of instructional strategies in my teaching.	1	2	3	4
10. I engage all my students in challenging learning experiences based on their specific needs.	1	2	3	4
11. I adjust the pace of instruction to students' learning needs, not everyone is doing the same thing on the same day every day.	1	2	3	4
12. I provide additional time, instruction, and support (e.g., scaffolding) to students based on their specific needs.	1	2	3	4

CONTINUED ➡

TEACHER INVENTORY ON DIFFERENTIATION PRACTICES AND STRATEGIES (CONTINUED)

FLEXIBLE INSTRUCTION CONTINUED				
13. I adjust curriculum topics and learning tasks to best meet my students' needs and ensure a challenging learning experience.	1	2	3	4
14. I match resources to my students' reading-readiness levels (e.g., Lexile scores).	1	2	3	4
15. I match resources to my students' level of knowledge about a curricular topic.	1	2	3	4
16. I use choice in topics, processes, or products to motivate my students.	1	2	3	4
17. I use a variety of choice formats with my students including such activities as tic-tac-toe boards, cubing, and RAFTS (Role/Audience/Format/Topics).	1	2	3	4
18. I use tiered assignments to match students with "just right, right now" tasks based on their learning needs.	1	2	3	4
19. I offer tasks reflecting my students' interests.	1	2	3	4
20. I design tasks based on student readiness; some students need more time, instruction, practice; others are "there" early.	1	2	3	4
21. I design tasks reflecting different learning preferences. (Multiple Intelligences)	1	2	3	4
22. If I use centers or stations, I either assign particular students to particular centers or match students with particular activities in each center based on their learning needs.	1	2	3	4
23. I plan and use flexible grouping in my classroom to organize students by their instructional needs.	1	2	3	4
24. I use a variety of ways to group my students (e.g., by interest, readiness, learning preference).	1	2	3	4

MY NEXT STEPS IN DIFFERENTIATION

Differentiation strategies I most frequently use:

Strategies I rarely or never use:

Circle two strategies from the bottom list that you are committed to try out in your classroom. Number them in the order you will implement them.

Continuum of Levels of Teacher Development in Differentiation

Level One: Novice
Professional practices exhibit little or limited evidence of planful differentiation.

Level Two: Practitioner
Professional practices reflect considerable evidence of active, planful differentiation.

Level Three: Expert
Professional practices reflect evidence of comprehensive differentiation. Practices suggest breadth and depth of understanding and application of best practices in differentiation.

TEACHING BELIEFS

Level One	Level Two	Level Three	Reflections *(Where am I? What next?)*
❑ Teachers control teaching and learning.	❑ Teachers share responsibility for learning.	❑ Teachers facilitate learning.	
❑ All students need to cover the curriculum, therefore, all students need to engage in the same activities.	❑ Students learn in different ways and at different paces, therefore, teachers need to plan for and offer different learning experiences to increase the likelihood of student success in learning.	❑ The student is the center of the classroom. Teachers need to know their students' readiness, learning preferences, and interests. Instruction must be consistently adjusted, modified, or adapted to specifically respond to these differences.	
❑ Success or failure in learning is "owned" by the student.	❑ Teachers can increase the likelihood of student success through differentiation.	❑ Teachers have a professional responsibility to differentiate instruction to increase student-learning success.	
❑ Students are thought of as a group (e.g., 7th graders).	❑ Students differ in learning readiness.	❑ Students differ in learning readiness, interests, and learning preferences.	

CONTINUED ➡

Continuum of Levels of Teacher Development in Differentiation (continued)

ROLE OF THE TEACHER

Level One	Level Two	Level Three	Reflections *(Where am I? What next?)*
❑ Relies on special education/gifted education faculty to address the needs of special education/GT students.	❑ Consults with special education/gifted education faculty. May collaborate with them to a limited degree.	❑ Is a partner with special education/gifted education in differentiation for special needs students.	
❑ Relies on students who master content, skills, or processes early to help/tutor those who need additional support.	❑ Offers extensions of or replaces curricular activities for those who master content, skills, or processes early.	❑ Allows for "testing out" of content, skills, or processes. Then eliminates or compacts curricular activities and provides "instead of" learning opportunities that go beyond the regular curriculum and/or capture the students' interests.	
❑ Believes lack of motivation is the students' problem.	❑ Understands the key to motivation is interest. Provides a range of activities responding to student interests and learning preferences.	❑ Gathers information about student learning preferences and their interest in unit topics. Plans for and builds interest in units based on this data.	

INSTRUCTION

Level One	Level Two	Level Three	Reflections *(Where am I? What next?)*
❑ Provides little difference between tasks assigned to students.	❑ Provides open-ended tasks in an effort to encourage students to go further.	❑ Offers tasks to match students' learning readiness, learning preferences, interests.	
❑ Paces all students together.	❑ Takes time to reteach and provide extensions of learning as necessary and appropriate.	❑ Adjusts instructional timelines and activities based on student needs.	
❑ Provides teacher-controlled learning experiences and little student independence.	❑ Plans opportunities for students that demand more independence and responsibility.	❑ Prepares students and expects that they will be responsible and independent in learning.	

CONTINUED ➡

Continuum of Levels of Teacher Development in Differentiation (continued)

INSTRUCTION (continued)

Level One	Level Two	Level Three	Reflections *(Where am I? What next?)*
❑ Follows an activity approach to learning, paying little attention to alignment of goals and instructional activities.	❑ Actively endeavors to align goals and student tasks and to decrease "sidetrips" from curricular goals.	❑ Engages in thoughtful and comprehensive planning to assure alignment of goals, student tasks, and assessment formats.	
❑ Engages most students in the same work, however, may assign additional work to challenge academically talented students.	❑ Strives to provide relevant, challenging work addressing learning goals.	❑ Engages all students in challenging, meaningful work focused on significant learning goals and their specific learning needs.	
❑ Uses mixed readiness cooperative groups, may also consider "behavior" issues when forming work groups.	❑ Uses flexible instructional grouping to match students with tasks appropriate for their learning needs.	❑ Uses flexible instructional grouping, students are grouped in a variety of ways for a variety of purposes to best meet learning goals and their needs.	
❑ Encourages students to read, do homework, or occupy their time as they choose if they finish early.	❑ Plans, presents, and posts ideas for students to engage in when they finish early.	❑ Plans, presents, and posts a "menu" of extension activities tied to curricular themes that represent a variety of learning preferences and interests for students who finish early.	
❑ Has all students engage in the same products and presentation formats.	❑ Lets students choose from a range of product and presentation formats.	❑ Plans for a range of products and presentation formats. Students are sometimes able to choose, and other times are assigned, particular products or presentation formats to either match or stretch learning preference and experience.	
❑ Provides limited or no adjustment of tasks based on needs of specific learners	❑ Uses a single strategy for tiering assignments (by readiness, challenge/complexity, learning preference, level of abstraction, learning resources, or degree of structure).	❑ Tiers assignments in a variety of ways for a variety of purposes (by readiness, challenge/complexity, learning preference, level of abstraction, learning resources, or degree of structure).	

CONTINUED ➡

Continuum of Levels of Teacher Development in Differentiation (continued)

ASSESSMENT

Level One	Level Two	Level Three	Reflections *(Where am I? What next?)*
❑ Rarely if ever uses preassessment.	❑ Relies on formal (paper/pencil) preassessment strategies. Acts on data in planning.	❑ Consistently uses both formal and informal preassessment strategies. Acts on data in planning.	
❑ Relies on daily work, homework, quizzes, and teacher observation in formative assessment.	❑ Uses a limited range of formal and informal formative assessment strategies, but consistently reflects on and acts on data when planning.	❑ Consistently utilizes a broad range of formal and informal formative assessment strategies and applies results for planning purposes.	

GRADING PRACTICES

Level One	Level Two	Level Three	Reflections *(Where am I? What next?)*
❑ Assigns grades that reflect work habits, attitudes, and behavior.	❑ Assigns grades that reflect attainment of learning goals. Reports work habits, attitudes, and behavior in another manner.	❑ Assigns grades that reflect attainment of learning goals. Learning progress, work habits, attitudes, and behavior are also reported, but in another manner.	

Know Your Students

Although some may think differentiation is just today's trendy idea, effective teachers have long been differentiating instruction, whether or not they called it such. Going forward, teachers will need the strategies of differentiation until the day they walk into classrooms where all students are at the same point of readiness, learn at the same pace in the same way, and exhibit similar interests. Obviously, this day is unlikely to arrive—which is a good thing! Today's classrooms reflect astonishing levels of academic diversity, and teachers report that the diversity of students seems to increase each year. In standards-based classrooms, differentiation is essential. It is what we do to increase the likelihood of students' success in learning.

Today's classrooms reflect astonishing levels of academic diversity, and teachers report that the diversity of students seems to increase each year.

The "Survey of Students" on page 20 enables you to think about, reflect on, and map out the differences in your classroom. Read each statement, and then list the names of the students who come to mind. If you are a secondary teacher, you may wish to think across all your courses or complete a survey for each group of students you work with during the school day. Periodically review your survey to consider any changes in your students as well as to include any new students in your reflections.

The "Survey of Students" is designed to map out the differences in readiness, interests, learning preferences, and needs as well as those affective factors that characterize your students during the school day. It is designed to help you recognize the differences among and needs of your students. Use this knowledge to guide your planning for and interactions with your students.

CREATING YOUR CLASS DIVERSITY PROFILE

Once you have completed the "Survey of Students," you are ready to consider its implications for your planning. Notice names that occur in response to several questions. Do you see a pattern of needs? Use the four tables in the "Class Diversity Profile" on pages 21–24 to identify students with related needs. List your students' names in the left-hand column on each profile table. Then review the "Survey of Students" questions. Questions are clustered on each profile table by general learning characteristic and need. For example, questions 2, 4, 6, 9, 12, and 13 all characterize students with advanced abilities. Going down the columns, check the names of students you listed for each question. When each question has been entered on the profile table, observe which students have multiple checkmarks; this indicates that the student exhibits characteristics typifying the particular kind of learner described in the table.

The "Class Diversity Profile" provides a summary of the learning differences that are represented in your classroom. As you read upcoming chapters, refer to the profiles to identify strategies that respond to the needs of particular students in your classroom.

Survey of Students

1. Who may experience difficulty with this year's curriculum because prerequisite content, skills, or processes are lacking?

2. Who generally exhibits knowledge, skills, understandings, and thinking beyond his or her age peers?

3. Who needs modifications or adaptations of work to meet the requirements of an IEP or a 504 plan?

4. Who might be a candidate for "testing" out of content or skills and replacement of regular classroom activities with more challenging work or learning opportunities reflecting their strong interests or talents?

5. Who needs tasks directed at her or his stage of English language acquisition?

6. Who doesn't need more work, but requires greater stretch or challenge in his or her work and more experiences that go beyond the regular curriculum?

7. Who needs more support when reading is required?

8. Who needs more support, scaffolding, or structure in working independently?

9. Who is capable of doing more challenging work, but instead chooses to do less demanding tasks?

10. Who needs modifications in the class environment to be able to focus on her or his work?

11. Who exhibits low value for learning, and possibly for school in general, which results in lack of motivation?

12. Who needs help with perfectionism so that she or he does not constantly stress over her or his work?

13. Who is consistently curious and inquisitive?

14. Who needs to experience more success in school and learning?

15. Who needs frequent recognition of work well done to build his or her self-confidence in doing quality work?

16. Who needs acknowledgment that she or he is making progress in learning in order to "see" herself or himself getting better?

17. Who needs to be encouraged to take a chance and take on a challenge?

18. Who prefers to work alone rather than in a group?

19. Who needs more direction on what to do and what to do next?

20. Who needs more reinforcement and attention to stay on task?

Class Diversity Profile

Profile Table #1

Multiple checkmarks indicate students with advanced abilities who need more in-depth or complex learning, as well as possible extensions or modifications of grade-level curriculum content or goals based on readiness and interests.

STUDENT NAMES	Q2	Q4	Q6	Q9	Q12	Q13

CONTINUED ➡

Profile Table #2

Multiple checkmarks indicate students who need modifications, adaptations, or greater support in learning.

STUDENT NAMES	Q1	Q3	Q5	Q7	Q8	Q20	Q21	Q22

CONTINUED ➡

Profile Table #3

Multiple checkmarks indicate students who exhibit affective needs that should be kept in mind in classroom interactions.

STUDENT NAMES	Q11 Motivation	Q14 Success Experiences	Q15 Recognition	Q17 Recognition	Q16 Confidence in Learning	Q18 Confidence in Learning

CONTINUED ➡

Class Diversity Profile (continued)

Profile Table #4

Checkmarks indicate students who may need modifications of the classroom environment.

STUDENT NAMES	Q10

CHAPTER 3

Critical Element: Applying Practical and Doable Assessment Strategies

Assessment is a critical element for success in academically diverse classrooms, because it is essential for planning for differences. A continuum of assessments should be utilized in order to successfully plan for the needs of your students. In an academically diverse classroom, assessment includes strategies that you have used in the past; however, particular kinds of assessment take a larger and more critical role.

Assessment expert Rick Stiggins and his colleagues named the specific kinds of strategies teachers must utilize to implement differentiation "assessment *for* learning," versus assessment *of* learning. Assessment is crucial in responding to the learning needs of our students. It determines when and where as well as how we might need to differentiate instruction. Therefore, the purpose of assessment in the academically diverse classroom is not only to assess the results of learning, but also to use assessment data to inform our practices in order to increase learning. The purpose of assessment *for* learning is:

- To inform instructional planning
- To actively gather information on student learning progress
- To gather information before and during, not just after, the learning process
- To enable teachers to modify learning activities based on differences and needs of students
- To support ongoing student growth
- To inform students about their learning progress and to provide direction for improvement

Assessment in an academically diverse classroom includes preassessment strategies both formal and informal, formative assessment strategies again reflecting either formal or informal methods, and summative assessments. In states and provinces, these classroom level assessments are also supplemented with competency tests both designed and scored outside the school setting.

> Assessment informs instruction; without it, purposeful differentiation is simply not possible.

In an academically diverse classroom, preassessment and formative assessment play a particularly critical role. Data from these kinds of assessment are essential to recognizing, planning for, and responding to student learning differences. **Figure 3** on page 26 outlines the flow of assessment processes in the differentiated classroom.

Systematic assessment is a critical element in making decisions about when and how you may choose to differentiate instruction. Without solid assessment plans and processes, differentiation is no more than a random instructional act. Assessment informs instruction; without it, purposeful differentiation is simply not possible.

1 Your state standards or provincial goals are always the starting point for systematic unit-level assessment. Which specific standards will be addressed in your unit? Think across curricular areas also. Although you may be an elementary teacher designing a science unit on force and motion, consider what academic standards from other curricular areas may also be included. Could the students do some explanatory writing (English/language arts)? What numerical and graphical concepts and principles are being applied in experiments and simulations (mathematics)?

2 Identifying the unit level KUDo's comes next. Write the specific learning goals for your unit based on the standards by asking yourself, "At the end of the unit, what will my students know, understand, and be able to do?" Remember, KUDo's translate standards into understandable language for your students.

3 Next, determine the summative assessment you will use to gather evidence of student learning related to the KUDo's. Apply the assessment concepts of Wiggins and McTighe[1] by beginning with the end in mind. Spend some time analyzing the assessment itself. Ask yourself, "What will my students need to know and be able to do in order for them to exhibit their learning in the way I have planned?" Your unit's instructional tasks must prepare your students to demonstrate their learning through the summative assessment. Curriculum, assessment, and instruction must be carefully aligned, or you end up with assessment "gotcha," surprising students with assessments that do not reflect the actual activities they engaged in during the curriculum unit. You don't want the assessment to be disconnected from the learning, nor do you want your assessment method to block some students' ability to show you what they know. If

1 Wiggins and McTighe, 1998.

FIGURE 3

Systematic Unit-Level Assessment Procedures

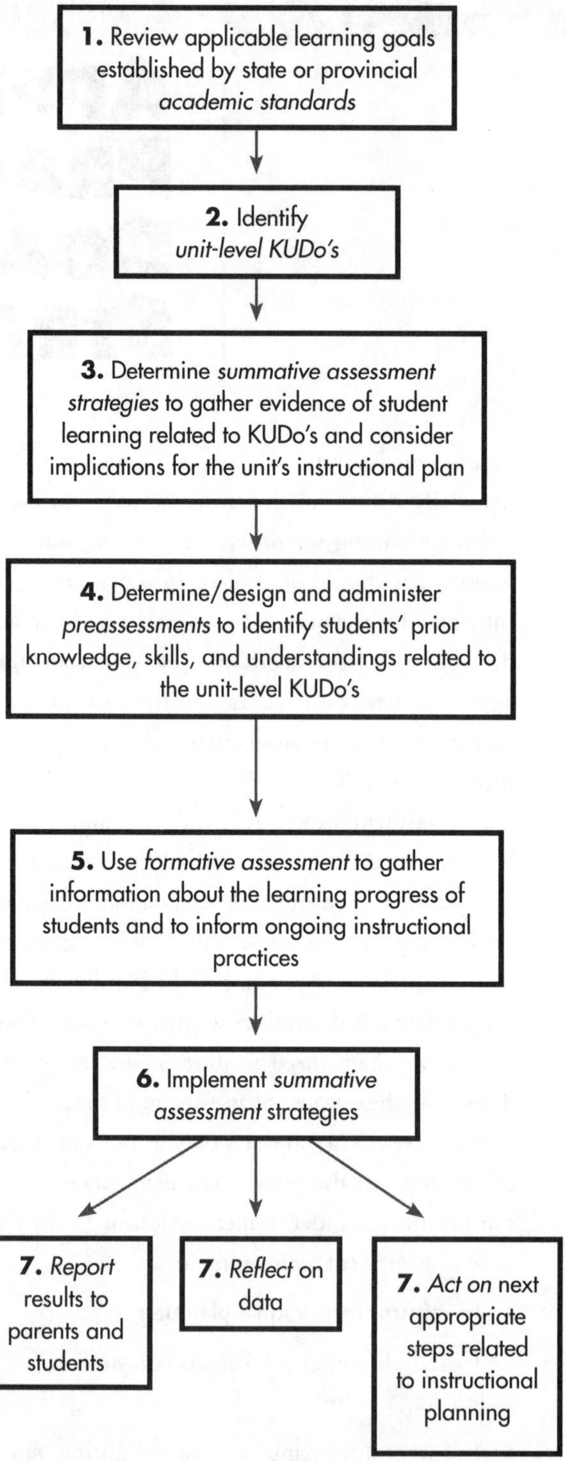

1. Review applicable learning goals established by state or provincial *academic standards*

↓

2. Identify *unit-level KUDo's*

↓

3. Determine *summative assessment strategies* to gather evidence of student learning related to KUDo's and consider implications for the unit's instructional plan

↓

4. Determine/design and administer *preassessments* to identify students' prior knowledge, skills, and understandings related to the unit-level KUDo's

↓

5. Use *formative assessment* to gather information about the learning progress of students and to inform ongoing instructional practices

↓

6. Implement *summative assessment* strategies

↓

7. *Report* results to parents and students

7. *Reflect* on data

7. *Act on* next appropriate steps related to instructional planning the summative assessment requires the student to develop a hypothesis and then design an experiment to prove or disprove it, are the students prepared to demonstrate their learning in this way? Have they had a similar experience during your unit so that the assessment truly demonstrates their learning rather than inhibits their ability to perform?

4 The next assessment process critical to differentiated units is preassessment. You need to either choose or design preassessments to identify your students' prior knowledge, skills, and understandings related to your unit KUDo's. It is not wise to assume that last year's curriculum goals were, in fact, attained by your students. Think about what prerequisite knowledge, skills, and understandings create the foundation of this year's work. Do most of the students have what it is going to take to move ahead on this year's goals? If not, your unit plans will need to be adjusted to provide the reinforcement or reteaching of whatever is missing. Differentiation of instruction now becomes critical. If the foundational skills of Algebra I are not there for the majority of Algebra I students at the beginning of the year, it makes no sense to start teaching Algebra I on the first day of class. If you do, you can bet that those behind and struggling at the beginning of the year will be the same ones behind and struggling at the end of the year. Take time to do the reteaching or reinforcement of essential foundational skills now, and you will be able to move more effectively and efficiently through your course later. Moreover, some of your students will not be doomed to fail from the first day of class.

5 Formative assessment strategies follow, and are used on a regular basis during your unit to provide information about the learning progress of your students, as well as to inform your instructional planning. It is formative assessment that provides the evidence necessary for determining whether tomorrow's lesson plan is to move on, to reteach, or to differentiate.

6 Now you are ready to administer the unit's summative assessment. Take another look at what you designed early in your planning. Does the summative assessment align with the learning goals and instructional activities that were implemented during the curriculum unit?

7 The final element in the assessment procedures used in a differentiated unit involves reporting, reflecting on, and acting on the results of the summative assessment. Report the results to students and their parents or significant adults. Then, reflect on the data in order to determine and act on next steps in instructional planning. Are students ready to move on to your next curricular topic? Or do you need to devote more time, instruction, or practice to particular skills, concepts, or understandings in this unit before most students are ready to progress? Is further differentiation necessary?

The Role of Preassessment in Differentiation

Preassessment plays a critical role in your ability to differentiate instruction. You administer preassessments before you begin the instruction in a curricular unit in order to gain an understanding of what your students know, understand, and are able to do. Without preassessment, you do not know the preparedness of your students for new learning, the specific learning differences amongst your students, or where to begin devising new curriculum goals.

When preassessing, you are "looking back" to determine the level of mastery that students bring into your grade or course. You need to know what students learned or remember from past experiences. Do the students have the essential foundational knowledge expected as they enter your grade or course? Have the students mastered the prerequisite skills and processes for success in new curriculum? You are also "looking forward" to determine what content, skills, and processes in the curriculum have already been mastered by some of your students.

You ask, "Have some students already achieved some of my learning goals?" "How and when might I differentiate the curriculum for these students so they remain challenged and engaged?"

Preassessment data assists you in determining an appropriate timeline for instruction. You find out what needs to be retaught or reinforced, what might be simply touched on or taught more quickly, and what might be eliminated within your curriculum units. The data also enables you to determine the points in a curriculum unit where flexible instructional grouping and tiered activities are best placed. Where in the unit will learning differences become obvious? Where might instructional groups based on learning differences provide students "just right, right now" activities? Who would be the members of each instructional group?

STRATEGIES FOR PREASSESSMENT

You can use either formal or informal strategies for preassessment. Formal preassessments provide information about specific students' prior knowledge and skills. They may be provided by textbook publishers as paper/pencil assessments or offered as computer software or online formats, or designed by teachers at the classroom level. Information from these assessments enables you to more specifically plan for the individual needs of your students. Tips for designing formal preassessments will be provided in the following section.

Informal preassessments are "sweeps" of your classroom to determine the general mastery level of content, skills, and processes. These strategies inform your general planning for a curriculum unit, but do not necessarily reveal specific information about individual students. Several strategies are provided in this chapter for doing quick informal preassessments that do not demand a great deal of preparation or time for analysis.

FORMAL PREASSESSMENT STRATEGIES

Formal preassessments are typically thought of as paper/pencil, online, or software formats that may be provided by textbook publishers or designed by teachers at the classroom level. However, depending on the specific curricular area, other forms of preassessment might also be appropriate; see **Figure 5.**

Formal preassessments are not graded because you are using them for diagnostic purposes only. You are seeking information to identify the entry point in learning for your students and to refine your unit plan based on student needs.

Teacher-Developed Preassessments

If you are designing your own preassessments, consider sources you may have at hand. Review your teacher editions. End-of-chapter reviews as well as end-of-unit tests are readymade preassessments.

FIGURE 4

Preassessment Strategies

FORMAL STRATEGIES	INFORMAL STRATEGIES
Publisher-developed paper/pencil, software, or online formats Teacher-developed paper/pencil or online formats Journal prompts Written responses Structured observations Student demonstrations Student interviews	Observations Conversations Directed questions Preassessment webs Walkabouts Knowledge bar graphs Check-in slips Visual organizers KWI (similar to KWL) Preassessment carousel Teacher email or text messages

If you choose to use end-of-chapter reviews or pull items from reviews, check to make sure that all critical concepts, skills, and processes in the unit are included in the items in the review. If you decide to use particular items pulled from the various sections of the unit, again make sure that key concepts, skills, and processes are represented.

You may also choose to use end-of-unit tests as preassessments. In this case, you can use the same assessment again at the end of the unit, or create another form of the test by using software provided by your textbook publisher or by creating similar but different items.

FIGURE 5

Preassessment Strategies for Specific Curricular Areas[2]

CURRICULAR AREAS	PRIMARY FOCUS OF PREASSESSMENT	PREASSESSMENT STRATEGIES
- Language arts - Social studies - World language - Humanities	- Reading, writing, and speaking skills - Understanding of concepts and generalizations - Application of critical and creative thinking skills	- Responding to journal prompts - Composing written products (paragraphs, essays, summaries) - Providing oral responses - Completing paper/pencil tests of knowledge
- Math - Science	- Understanding and application of processes, concepts, constants, and theories	- Explaining or applying processes - Reporting on observations - Solving problems - Doing demonstrations - Writing explanations or essays - Sequencing steps in a process - Determining a solution supported by a rationale or explanation - Completing paper/pencil tests of knowledge
- Music - Art - Physical education - Other performance-based curriculum	- Demonstration of technique or complex application of skills or processes	- Observing performance - Demonstrating skills - Solving problems - Sequencing steps in a process
- Technology - Industrial technology - Business applications	- Complex applications of skills to solve a problem or create a product	- Observing performance - Demonstrating skill - Solving problems - Sequencing steps in process

2 Adapted with permission from *Data Driven Instruction: A Handbook* by Lin Kuzmich (Longmont, CO: Centennial Board of Cooperative Services, 1998).

Structured Observations

Structured observations may be a preassessment strategy that works for you under particular circumstances. Think about what specifically you want to observe and then set up a learning task that will enable you to do so. For example, if you want to determine whether your students remember and can apply the scientific method, set up a lab in which you can observe them at work. Who competently goes through the process? Who struggles? Who is completely baffled?

Journal Prompts and Written Responses

Formal preassessments may also include journal prompts and written responses to questions related to a unit's content. However, keep in mind that writing skills will affect your students' ability to convey what they know and understand. If you have English language learners in your classroom, it is important to consider the stage of language acquisition of each ELL student. If the ELL students are at preproduction, early production, or the stage of early speech emergence[3], they may be better suited to preassessment using demonstrations or interviews than paper/pencil preassessments. At early stages of language acquisition, students are able to respond to "show me . . ." prompts, yes/no questions, and list or label items, and with phrases or short answers, but are not able to respond in full sentences or paragraphs.[4]

CONSIDERATIONS FOR CREATING FORMAL PREASSESSMENTS

In creating formal preassessments that provide reliable and valid data, consider the following questions:

1. Does the assessment focus on your unit's KUDo's?
2. Does the assessment provide an adequate demonstration of the concepts, skills, and processes that students are expected to acquire by the end of the unit?
3. Does the assessment allow students of a variety of learning preferences to demonstrate what they know? **Figure 6** is an example of an assessment format for a math task that allows students to demonstrate knowledge in five different ways.
4. Do English language learners have an adequate opportunity to understand and complete the assessment given language factors?
5. Do the items assess what you want to measure (the process, the content, or the product)?
6. Do the items clearly align with the end-of-unit test or culminating project to be used as a summative assessment?

INFORMAL PREASSESSMENT STRATEGIES

Not a minute is spent within a classroom when teachers are not doing assessment. You pick up a great deal simply by cruising the classroom. "Over the shoulder assessments" include the observations that you make as your students engage in activities, the conversations that you strike up which reveal students' knowledge of content both within and outside your curriculum, and the directed questions you may ask to probe their understandings.

FIGURE 6

Five Learning Preferences for a Math Task: Computing Percentiles

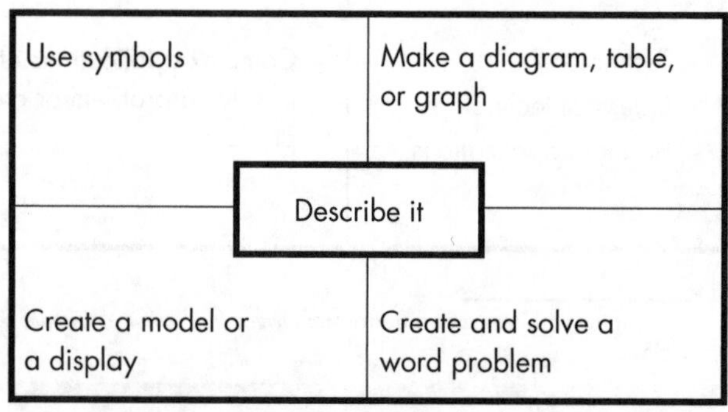

3 Stephen D. Krashen and Tracy D. Terrell, *The Natural Approach: Language Acquisition in the Classroom* (Oxford: Pergamon Press, 1983).

4 Jane D. Hill and Kathleen M. Flynn, *Classroom Instruction That Works with English Language Learners* (Alexandria, VA: Association for Supervision and Curriculum Development, 2006).

You may also notice the kinds of books or magazines students are reading, the questions posed by students that exceed your curriculum goals, and the "above and beyond" responses in class discussions as well as those responses that indicate missing background or lack of experience. Do not underestimate the importance of these informal kinds of data collection in planning for differences.

An informal preassessment "sweep" is a quick way to gather general information about what your students know and need to know about a curricular topic.

An informal preassessment "sweep" is a quick way to gather general information about what your students know and need to know about a curricular topic. These strategies do not necessarily provide specific information about what *each* child knows and doesn't know, but they do give you a general sense of where the students are before they begin a unit. "Sweeps" enable you to better plan for your students' needs. They provide information such as: "What topics could be accelerated because it appears that many students already know them? What topics appear to be new to students?"

Preassessments also inform you of the misinformation students may hold about a particular subject. Your students may believe something to be true which is not factual. Surfacing misinformation enables you to teach directly to the misconceptions and to correct them during your unit.

As is the case for all preassessments, it is important that your students understand that these tasks are not going to be graded. They are not pop quizzes! Tell your students that the information from the preassessment helps you plan their unit activities better. You want to know more about what *they* know. Emphasize that this is important work.

Topic Webs

Topic webs are a way of doing a preassessment that represents the Visual/spatial learning preference of Multiple Intelligences. Divide students into groups no larger than four and provide each group with sticky notes, markers, and a piece of flip chart paper. Lead the students through the five-step process below to complete the web.

1. All students take five sticky notes.
2. Individually, students generate at least five facts about your curriculum topic (e.g., geography). They write one fact on each sticky note. If students know more than five facts, encourage them to take more notes. Instruct students to initial each of their notes.
3. Students then label each fact using the following code:
   ! = I know this is a fact!
   ***** = I am pretty sure this is a fact.
   ? = I heard this somewhere and think it may be a fact.
4. Students share their facts in the small groups. They share one idea at a time, going around the group until all ideas have been heard.
   - If there is a fact that group consensus says is inaccurate, the group starts a pile of notes with these questionable facts.
   - Tell groups to keep duplicate facts, not to discard them.
5. Students review the facts and identify those that go together in some way. Remind them to include duplicate facts in the classification, and to keep the questionable facts in a separate pile.
6. Model the construction of a topic web using a topic and subtopics different from the ones your students are working with. Preassessment webs are also an exercise in the critical thinking skill of classification. Using their topic as a model allows them to copy rather than think! **Figure** 7 on page 32 shows an example of how a topic web is set up.

7. Now, students use markers and flip chart paper to construct a web of major topics and subtopics with their facts. They simply place their sticky notes on the flip chart paper where they fit in the web (including duplicate ideas).

8. Students post the webs in your classroom and you collect the pile of questionable facts. You may want a spokesperson for each group to report on their results, or you may wish to lead an initial discussion of the topic using the facts represented on the webs.

How is a topic web a preassessment?

1 **It represents what students know about the curricular topic.** The web reveals what topics students have thought of and know a lot about as well as what topics are not mentioned and may need more in-depth work. This information enables you to better plan your unit with a general understanding of the students' background and understandings of the topic.

2 **Misinformation is revealed.** Misinformation included on the web as well as in the pile of questionable facts tells you what you must make sure to clarify, bring to the surface, and emphasize in the unit. This is essential to prevent students from continuing to carry inaccurate understandings forward.

FIGURE 7

Sample Topic Web

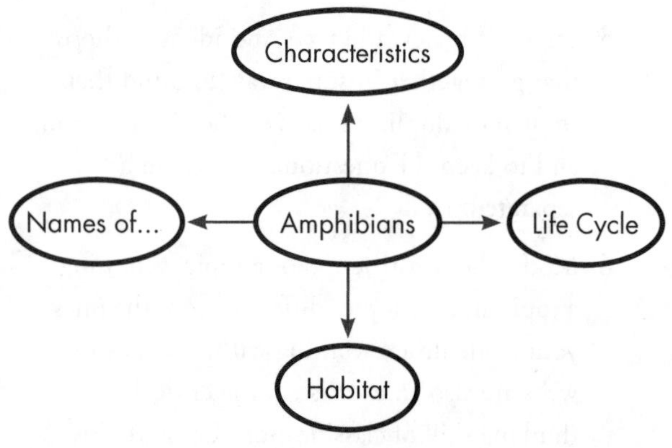

3 **Students learn from each other.** Since some students are reluctant to risk being wrong in an all-class activity, the webs allow students to share what they know in the safety of a small group setting. Secondly, the coding system (! * ?) enables all students to take a chance on ideas without risking embarrassment (e.g., "See? I put a question mark on that note because I wasn't sure about that fact.").

4 **It identifies student experts as well as those who have a more limited knowledge base to build on.** The initials on the notes enable you to notice the students who have more than five facts represented on the web. These students know a lot about the topic. If students have fewer than five ideas, it may be because they had limited information on the topic, they had ideas sent to the questionable facts pile, or they needed additional time to process and record their facts.

You may wish to keep the topic webs for reference and revision as the unit progresses, or to reflect on and revise them as a class review before summative assessment.

Tips for Using Preassessment Webs with Primary Students

Because early readers and writers will be more limited in their ability to record their ideas, the webs may be completed as a large group activity.

1. Record your students' responses on large readable cards instead of sticky notes.
2. Think ahead of time about how you will respond to inaccurate ideas when they are presented. Will you ask for a class consensus on the suggested fact? Will you create a section on your board labeled: "Let's check these out," and then do a fact search later? Or will you accept the idea and then "teach to it" later so the misinformation is corrected?
3. Once you have the ideas recorded, ask your students to help put them in groups of "like ideas." Encourage them to label each group of cards, thus creating subtopics.

4. Model the construction of a web, asking your students to help you place the cards where they belong.

Walkabout Charts

Walkabout charts are an engaging and active way to gather preassessment data in your classroom. Consider the KUDo's for your curriculum unit and design four to six tasks or questions related to the topic. Place them on a chart like this one:

FIGURE 8

Sample Walkabout Chart

Name the parts of a plant.	List the things that plants need.	Why do humans need plants?
Name two kinds of plants.	List the steps in the growth of a plant.	Name the jobs of each plant part.

Distribute charts to students and have them tour the room locating one student at a time who knows the answer to one of the questions on their walkabout charts. The student records the answer in the appropriate box and has the other student initial the box. Once a sufficient amount of time has been provided for students to gather answers, lead a class discussion about the topics on the chart. Collect the walkabout charts to review the students' understandings of and misinformation about key topics in your unit as well as to find your student experts and those students who may need additional support.

Knowledge Bar Graphs

Create the following chart on your board or on a flip chart:

FIGURE 9

Knowledge Bar Graph Template

No clue	I've heard of this.	I know a lot about this.	I'm an expert on this.

Provide a brief overview of some of the topics that will be included in your upcoming curriculum unit. You may wish to pose some questions to further clarify topics such as: Can you name the planets in order according to their distance from the sun? Can you list characteristics of different planets? Can you tell me what creates day and night? Can you describe what causes the seasons?

Next, give each student one sticky note and tell them to write their name on the back. Have students individually place their notes on the section of the chart that represents their knowledge of the new curriculum topics. By reviewing the resulting bar graph, the students recognize the variations in their experiences and differences in their knowledge bases. Later, you may review each student's self-evaluation by checking the back of the sticky notes for names.

You can also develop individual bar graphs for students to report on their levels of mastery. **Figure 10** is an example of an individual bar graph that asks students to estimate their recall of four math skills. Students color in boxes to form a bar graph indicating their level of competence in each math calculation.

FIGURE 10

Sample Knowledge Bar Graph

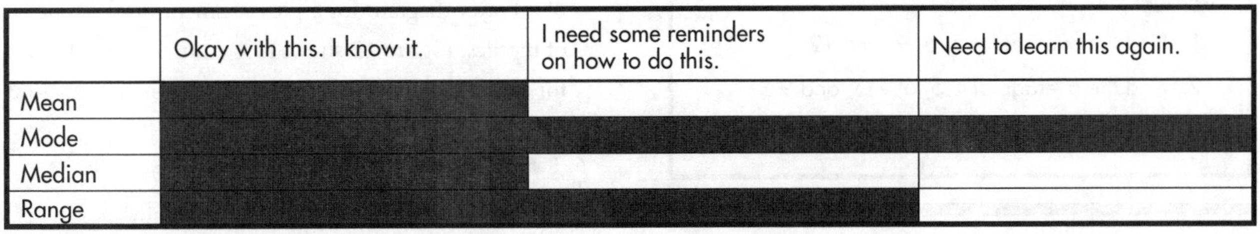

	Okay with this. I know it.	I need some reminders on how to do this.	Need to learn this again.
Mean			
Mode			
Median			
Range			

Check-in Slips

Check-in slips are a set of two to three quick questions or tasks that students complete to provide a general sense of their background knowledge on a curricular topic. Think about your KUDo's and design these questions or tasks to get a "snapshot" of student understandings. Examples of check-in slips follow.

FIGURE 11

Sample Check-in Slips

Oceans

1. Name some animals that live in the ocean.
2. What is the "geography" of oceans like?
3. Diagram a food chain for an ocean animal.

Health and Wellness

1. What things can people do to stay healthy?
2. What should and shouldn't we eat to stay healthy?
3. What risks do students your age take that can lead to illness?

The American Revolution

1. Name the leaders in the Revolutionary War.
2. Why did the colonists revolt against England?
3. Name some important events in the Revolutionary War.

Writer's Voice

1. What is writer's voice?
2. How is writer's voice used by an author to involve the reader in a story?

Averages

1. Find the average of 3, 6, 9, and 12.
2. Find the average of 2.5, 5, 7.5, and 9.
3. Find the average of 2x, 4x, 5x, and 8x.

Collect the slips and briefly scan the student responses, noting those topics that are well known and those that students seem to have little knowledge of or misinformation about. Take notice of student experts who seem to already have a depth of knowledge about the topic, as well as students who may potentially struggle with the topic and require extra assistance.

Tips for Using Check-in Slips with Primary Students

Primary teachers may wish to talk with students in a large group setting to facilitate the use of check-in slips. Ask the students questions such as:

1. What dinosaurs can you name?
2. What are the different kinds of dinosaurs?
3. Why did dinosaurs disappear?

You may also ask students to sketch versus write their ideas on check-in slips. For example, give the students a duplicated sheet of four identical drawings of bare trees placed in quadrants. Ask the students to sketch how the tree would look in fall, winter, spring, and summer. You may also encourage them to include other things in their sketches to show you what else they know about seasons.

Visual Organizers

Visual organizers combine words, symbols, arrows, and even sketches to present information. The Verbal/linguistic and Visual/spatial Multiple Intelligences are reflected in visual organizers. Visual organizers enable students to generate mental pictures to accompany information, and to create graphic representations of that information[5].

Frayer diagrams are visual organizers that were initially designed to help students discover relationships between concepts or ideas, but can also be used as a preassessment strategy. **Figure 12** shows one use of a Frayer diagram for a preassessment on the topic of reptiles. **Figure 13** shows four common templates for Frayer diagrams utilized for preassessment.

5 Robert J. Marzano, et al., *Classroom Instruction That Works: Research-Based Strategies for Increasing Student Achievement* (Alexandria, VA: Association for Supervision and Curriculum Development, 2001).

Visual organizers such as charts, timelines, and storyboards can also be used as preassessments. Provide students with the formats and ask them to complete as much of the information as possible. Collect and scan the students' work to inform your unit planning.

Second copies of the visual organizers can be provided for students to complete as the unit progresses. Initial preassessment copies could also be returned to students at the end of the unit for revision and completion prior to the summative assessment.

KWI

KWI is my version of a strategy that many teachers use called KWL. KWL stands for a set of questions asked of students: What do you **k**now about ______? What do you **w**ant to know about ______? What did you **l**earn about ______? Alternately, KWI stands for the following questions: What do you **k**now? What do you **w**ant to know? What are you ***interested in learning*** about this topic?

Used in a science unit on the rainforest ecosystem the questions would be:

- What do you know about rainforests?
- What do you want to know about rainforests? (What specific questions do you have?)
- What are you interested in learning about rainforests? (What are you most curious about?)

The "K" part of KWI is a natural way to gather preassessment data on a topic to determine your students' prior knowledge as well as any misinformation they may hold to be true. The "W" generates questions to be answered during the unit. However, if the key to motivation is interest, the way to really hook students into the unit is to find out what specifically they are interested in learning about the topic: the "I." We never have enough time to teach all we need to teach. Why not eliminate or just touch briefly on those topics that students already know a lot about, make sure you address the questions they have, and spend more time on the topics that they are interested in? Remember, however, that your KUDo's guide your instruction. If a topic or activity does not work on a KUDo, do not do it!

FIGURE 12

Sample Frayer Diagram

Definition of a Reptile An animal with dry skin.	**Facts About Reptiles** Covered with scales Vertebrate Shed skin Cold blooded
Examples of Reptiles Lizards Snakes Crocodiles	**Examples of Non-Reptiles** Frogs Toads Tigers Hawks

FIGURE 13

Common Frayer Diagram Templates[6]

Facts	Words to Describe
Pictures, Sketches or Diagrams	Questions

Definition	Facts
Examples (What it is)	Non-Examples (What it isn't)

Words	Sketches

Definition	Facts
Sketches or Diagrams	Personal Experiences

6 Dorothy Ann Frayer, et al., *A Schema for Testing Level of Concept Mastery* (Technical Report No. K16, University of Wisconsin, 1969).

Preassessment Carousel

Preassessment carousels rotate student groups through a set of posted topics or questions related to your curriculum unit. As students rotate to each workstation, they list what they already know about the topic. To set up your carousel follow these steps:

1. Identify four or five major topics or ideas included in your unit. For a social studies unit on your state or province, the topics might be: 1. Geography and climate, 2. Economics, 3. Government and leadership, and 4. Important people and events in our history.

2. On separate sheets of flip chart paper, write the number and the topic at the top (e.g., **1. Geography and climate**). Depending on the size of your class, you may wish to make two sets of these charts so that students can be divided into smaller working groups.

3. Assign students to groups of no larger than four members. Provide each group with a different color marker to distinguish that group's responses on the charts.

4. Create workstations by posting the charts in numerical order on the walls of your classroom, or placing them on tabletops or desks.

5. Have students rotate through the workstations as directed by you. Assign each group a workstation to begin their rotation.

6. When students reach a station, direct them to read what has been listed previously and then add new information. If something has been listed previously that the group does not believe is a fact, have them put a question mark next to the item.

7. Direct students to remain at a workstation until directed by you to rotate to the next. Watch student groups to determine when it appears they are ready to rotate. By the fourth rotation to a workstation, students may have exhausted all ideas!

Once the rotations are complete, you may wish to have spokespeople report on what was entered at each workstation. You will also want to clarify any items coded with question marks, or extend other ideas as necessary and appropriate.

Carousels can also be used at the end of a curriculum unit to review factual information before a summative assessment.

Teacher Email or Text Message

Ask students to write and send an email or text message (text language can be creative and fun!) to you about the upcoming unit. Select from the following prompts or come up with ideas of your own:

- I know that . . .
- I learned about this by . . .
- This makes me think of . . .
- I am not sure about . . .
- By the end of the unit, I'd like to know . . .
- I'd enjoy this unit most if . . .
- On a scale of 1 to 4, my interest in this unit is probably a ______ because . . .
- I think this topic is important to learn about because . . .

You may select particular prompts for all students to respond to, let the students choose from a list of prompts, or ask each student to respond to a particular number of prompts (e.g., ask them each to choose two).

PREASSESSMENT REMINDERS

1. **Preassessments must be clearly and specifically tied to KUDo's.** Their purpose is to provide information related to what your students already know, understand, and are able to do before the curriculum unit is underway.

2. **Use formal or informal preassessment at least two weeks before your class begins a unit.** Preassessments assist you in modifying or adapting your initial instructional plans in response to your students' needs. Give yourself time to think through what you have learned from the preassessment and to take action on modifications in your planning or

timeline for the unit. If you wait to do the preassessment on the first day of the unit, it may be too late or too discouraging to change some of your plans.

3 **Preassessments preview unit topics for your students.** Learners move into new curriculum units not only with a better idea about the topics that will be addressed, but also with an affirmation of what they already know about the curriculum topics.

4 **Preassessments may reveal insightful responses from some students.** As you review preassessments, look for those students who might be thinking above and beyond others in your classroom. Wiggins and McTighe[7] suggest that teachers look for:

- New, novel, or original ways of looking at a topic, problem, or issue
- Evidence of a more powerful principle than what is being taught
- A leap in intuition
- More analytical responses rather than "just the facts"
- Novel implications
- Knowledge or understandings beyond what is addressed in the curriculum

Such responses to a preassessment strategy suggest that you need to consider whether your curriculum goals provide enough rigor and complexity for these learners. Differentiation for gifted learners may take them into advanced learning goals that would be inappropriate for other students in your classroom. Specific strategies for meeting the needs of gifted and academically talented students are offered in Chapter 11.

5 **Preassessment is critical to effective instructional planning.**

- Preassessment data influences the timeline for the unit. What might you need to reteach or reinforce before you move on to new content, skills, or processes? What do students already know so you can move more quickly through the unit?
- Secondly, preassessment data reveals topics that might be addressed with greater depth or complexity based on the students' prior learning and experiences.
- The data also provide guidance on what topics might need to be emphasized to correct student misinformation.
- Finally, the preassessment data helps you predict those points in the unit at which tiered activities are likely to be necessary, when student learning needs appear to be distinctly different based on prior knowledge, skills, and processes.

Formative Assessment

Formative assessments are the tools that teachers use to gather information about student learning progress as well as to inform instructional planning. The information from formative assessment practices is critical to diagnosing student learning needs. Formative assessment identifies which of your students have reached learning goals and which need additional time, practice, and instruction. This information allows you to guide instruction in response to learning differences, which is central to differentiation. Such ongoing assessment also indicates when tiered assignments and flexible instructional groups are the most appropriate strategy for use the next day.

Formative assessment practices can be either formal or informal in design, and must be used on a consistent basis. Such practices are checkpoints in the cycle of teaching and learning that enable you to gather specific information on student progress. Whether you use informal or formal methods, it is critical that you think about and reflect on your students' work. Scans of their work provide guidance for tomorrow's differentiation. As you review student work consider the following:

1. What student understandings are evident in the work?
2. What misunderstandings or misinformation are evident in the work?

7 Wiggins and McTighe, 1998.

3. Have any students approached the work in a striking or unusual manner?
4. What additional instruction or clarification is necessary based on the evidence of learning presented in the work?
5. What specific patterns of problems appear in the work?
6. Do any students need additional time, instruction, or practice in the concepts, skills, or processes?

DESCRIPTIVE FEEDBACK

When teachers use assessment *for* learning, students benefit from the descriptive feedback[8]. Descriptive feedback, in contrast to evaluative feedback such as grades, enables your students to learn through the assessment process. Evaluative feedback focuses on what the student failed to do rather than what he or she succeeded in doing. It sends a message to the student that may be interpreted as blame, "you should have . . ." Descriptive feedback is constructive, helpful information that clearly addresses answers, "How can I do better?" Think of it as coaching rather than critiquing. In a differentiated classroom, descriptive feedback is essential since it provides specific guidance to the student for improved performance.

Descriptive feedback:

- Confirms whether or not responses are correct
- Describes why an answer is correct
- Enables the student to see what has and has not been achieved
- Provides a "better way" to do or approach something
- Suggests specific ways in which students might improve their performance[9]

Descriptive feedback affects both performance and motivation.[10] Because it provides specific information on "how to get better," students are more motivated to improve their performance because they know what to do next. It is critical for students to be able to answer: "Where am I? What did I do well? Where or how did I fall short? How can I improve my work? What next?" Descriptive feedback also fosters greater interest in the task for its own sake rather than just for a grade.[11] This is key for developing self-regulated learners.

Also keep in mind that not everything needs to be graded. Research on descriptive feedback indicates that if teachers provide both feedback and a grade on student work, the students focus on the grade rather than on the feedback. When grades and feedback are used together, the students view the feedback as comments on their *grade* rather than their *performance*.[12] For the greatest effect, use descriptive feedback without grades.

Ways to Provide Descriptive Feedback

Make comments directly on the student's work beside the relevant content. You may want to ask students to increase their margins in writing tasks to allow room for comments.

- Provide specific detail related to their work beside the rubric or checklist item given to the students. For example, if a student's explanation of a process lacked detail, note the specific ways he or she could increase detail next to the rubric item.
- Use sticky notes to comment on particular elements in a paper or project.
- Pose questions to prompt students to reflect on their work more deeply. (What additional avenues might have been taken during this national crisis? What other perspectives might be considered in this situation?)

8 Lorna M. Earl, *Assessment as Learning: Using Classroom Assessment to Maximize Student Learning* (Thousand Oaks, CA: Corwin Press, 2004).

9 Caroline Gipps et al., *What Makes a Good Primary School Teacher? Expert Classroom Strategies* (London: Routledge Falmer, 2000).

10 Susan M. Brookhart, *How to Give Effective Feedback to Your Students* (Alexandria, VA: Association for Supervision and Curriculum Development, 2008).

11 Brookhart, 2008.

12 R. Butler and M. Nisan, "Effects of No Feedback, Task-Related Comments, and Grades on Intrinsic Motivation and Performance," *Journal of Educational Psychology* 78 (1986): 210–216.

- Provide oral feedback by simply stopping by students' desks.
- Provide oral feedback by setting aside some class time for face-to-face conferences at a table in your classroom, or by establishing office hours to work with students one-on-one.
- Use student workfiles for works-in-progress. Provide a file folder for students to submit their work for review. Make your comments on the file folder itself or on a log inserted into the workfile. Be sure to date your comments so students can follow the sequence of your feedback. You may also code items for student reference. For example, if you are coaching the student on clarity in sentence structure, in the file folder comments refer the student to the sentences noted with an asterisk (*) in their text.

STRATEGIES FOR FORMATIVE ASSESSMENT

Just as in preassessment, there are both formal and informal strategies for formative assessment. Formal formative assessments typically demand teacher time to prepare, analyze, review, or grade, and they provide a more comprehensive review of student progress and more substantive evidence of learning. In contrast, informal strategies are quick, on-your-feet methods of data collection. They demand little or no teacher preparation or time for scoring or entering of data. Informal formative assessments are simply quick checks for understanding, but they have the same effect on your instructional planning. **Figure 14** provides ideas for both formal and informal formative assessment.

FORMAL STRATEGIES FOR FORMATIVE ASSESSMENT

Many of the formal strategies listed for formative assessment in the chart below commonly used by teachers. Quizzes, daily work, first drafts of writing, science logs, records of observations or readings, and journal entries are used with regularity in most classrooms.

In differentiated classrooms, however, student work is first analyzed critically and then used to make instructional decisions. The purpose of the work is not to simply have one more thing to put in the grade book. Its purpose is to enable you to critically reflect on student learning progress and decide whether to move on in the curriculum; reteach or reinforce content, skills, or processes; or whether your next instructional course of action is differentiation. Formal formative assessment strategies are purposefully integrated into lessons in order to gather specific information on student learning progress.

Demonstrations

Teachers may set up opportunities for students to demonstrate their learning. For example, you might:

- have students develop and test a hypothesis, and then review their lab reports
- collect work samples such as initial sketches of a poster advocating for a political position on a current issue, in order to reflect on the students' accurate application of methods of persuasion
- collect and review writing samples to determine whether your students have mastered the topic sentence

FIGURE 14

Formative Assessment Strategies

Formal Strategies	Informal Strategies
Quizzes	Directed questions
Daily work	Systematic observation
Demonstrations	Discussion reflections
Work samples	Homework scans
Portfolio reviews	Grade scans
Sketches, drawings, diagrams	"Thumbs" assessment
Logs, records, journals	Card signals
Drafts	White board demonstrations
Graphic organizers	Critical reflection stems
Exit slips	Student self-evaluation with rubrics/checklists
Preview/review	

FIGURE 15

Sample Graphic Organizer: Events in the Civil War

EVENT	FACTS	SIGNIFICANCE
Battle of Antietam		
Emancipation Proclamation	*Announced Sept. 22, 1862.* *Lincoln is the author.*	Effects on North: Effects on South:
Battle of Fredricksburg		
Chancellorsville		
Battle of Gettysburg		
Battle of Vicksburg		
Battle of Chattanooga		*Split Confederates' only east/west rail line.*
Grant given control of the Union Army	Grant's Battle Plan:	
Sherman's march through Georgia		Results:
Confederate surrender at Appomattox Courthouse	Surrender terms: 1. 2. 3. 4.	

Portfolio Reviews

Portfolio reviews provide concrete information about student applications of learning. Determine what you are specifically looking for, and then review the portfolio with that specific criteria in mind. Keep notes on who is "there," and who needs more time or instruction to get "there."

Sketches, Drawings, and Diagrams

You also may ask students to do sketches, drawings, or diagrams to illustrate what they have learned. For example, you may expect students to diagram and label the steps in photosynthesis. You then review their sketches for accuracy and evidence of understanding.

Graphic Organizers

Graphic organizers can be completed to check student understanding of curriculum content or to ask students to engage in critical thinking related to curriculum topics. **Figure 15** shows a "fact trapper" graphic organizer to determine student understanding of important events in the Civil War.

Notice there are sample entries in italics in the "Facts" and "Significance" columns to model the kinds of responses that should be written in each. In some cases, additional specific details are indicated to guide student responses, such as noting that the effects of the Emancipation Proclamation on the North and the South need to be detailed.

Figure 16 is a sample of a graphic organizer engaging students in analyzing environmental issues. It requires them to apply their knowledge of an issue to a decision-making process. Students must have the foundational knowledge about the issue in order to successfully complete the process. In using the organizer, students first recall up to three different positions on the issue and describe these positions at the top. Next, students consider the positives and negatives of each position. The third step in the process requires students to reflect on their beliefs and values related to the issue. Finally, they determine which position best reflects their beliefs and values, and provide a rationale for their decision.

INFORMAL FORMATIVE ASSESSMENT STRATEGIES

Informal strategies gather information about students' understandings and learning progress, but demand little teacher preparation or analysis time. Teachers may direct specific questions to all or some students to check their understandings. You may set up a learning activity for purposes of systematically observing the students in order to determine their competencies. For example, you might set up a battery and bulb lab to observe whether students understand the principles of circuitry. In addition, you reflect on student responses during a class discussion. Who seemed confident in their understandings? Who clearly seemed "lost" or unprepared for the discussion? Such informal formative assessment strategies and our mental note-taking or jotted-down comments provide information that influences our subsequent lesson plans.

Homework and Grade Scans

You may also use scans of homework to sort out where students are in their learning. Who accomplished the day's learning goal? Who didn't? Or you may refer to your online or paper grade book to remind yourself about how particular students performed the last time you worked on either this skill or a prerequisite skill or process. Who was there? Who needs more time, instruction, or practice?

"Thumbs" Assessment

Teachers also may ask students to be actively engaged in providing formative assessment information. "Thumbs" assessment is such a strategy. After you have completed direct instruction and you question whether the students are ready to move on to a new concept or to independent work, simply ask "Where are you on this?" Students signal to you by placing their thumb chest-high to indicate:

- thumb up — "I've got it"
- thumb sideways — "Teach me a little more, give me a couple more examples, I'm almost there"
- thumb down — "I'm confused, I don't get it, teach me more"

"Thumbs" assessment provides on-the-spot information about where to go next in your lesson. You may also use it as a way to dismiss students to independent work. The "thumbs up" students move on to their assignment, while the "thumbs sideways" or "thumbs down" kids stay with you for more

FIGURE 16

Sample Graphic Organizer: Positions on an Environmental Issue

Issue: ______________________

Position 1:		Position 2:		Position 3:	
+	–	+	–	+	–
[positives]	*[negatives]*				

Criteria for My Selection:

My Decision and Rationale:

instruction, practice, or examples. Keep in mind that your students need to know that "thumbs up" means they are confident going on independently, and you will not be going back to their desks to do one-on-one reteaching with them. If you do not hold fast to this guideline for the strategy, it will not work for dismissal to independent work.

Some teachers do a variation of the "Thumbs" strategy using colored cards or yes/no cards. Students are given red and green cards or yes/no cards that they use to signal to the teacher when asked the question, "Where are you on this?" You decide which strategy might work best for your students.

Whiteboard Demonstrations

Many teachers use individual whiteboards in their classrooms and consider student responses to questions, math problems, definitions, and true/false statements as quick checks for understanding. Pose the question, give students time to respond, and ask them to turn their boards over when they are done. Then, tell them to display their boards in unison when you say "go" or countdown from four. If students display their boards as they finish, some are doing the thinking while others are merely copying! If you are to consider this a check for understanding, they *all* need to do the thinking. A scan of their responses tells you if students are ready to move on, if more instruction and modeling are needed, or if you need to differentiate by having some students stay with you a little longer and others move on to independent work.

Critical Reflection Stems

Critical reflection stems are open-ended questions or tasks that require students to reflect on their learning. You can make them as structured or unstructured as you wish. Critical reflection is used after some direct instruction, when you want to check where students are in their learning. Students typically write responses, but you may also encourage them to draw, sketch, or diagram. Frayer diagrams can also be used as formative assessment templates (Figures 12 and 13 on page 35). Following are some samples of critical reflection stems that could be posed to your students:

1. What did you learn or discover?
2. Why is this important to know?
3. Summarize the key ideas.
4. Add your own ideas, insights, and perspectives.
5. What else do you know about what we talked about today?
6. What new questions do you have about this topic?
7. What is still confusing to you?
8. What do you want to learn next about the topic?

Student Self-Evaluation

Students are also able to actively engage in formative assessment when teachers provide rubrics or checklists for their work. Make sure that the language in the rubric or checklist is kid-friendly, using the same words and language you used with students in instruction. In designing rubrics, avoid "edu-babble" that we educators use but that does not convey clear meaning to students.

> When students chart or graph their progress, a greater sense of success results. They also become more motivated to strive for improvement because they can see their learning progress over the course of the term.

Students may also chart or graph formative assessment results, which enable them to see their own improvement. For example, have students complete week-by-week line graphs to show spelling or vocabulary test results. Rick Stiggins[13] suggests that when students chart or graph their progress,

13 Richard J. Stiggins et al., *Classroom Assessment for Student Learning: Doing It Right—Using It Well* (Portland, OR: Assessment Training Institute, 2004).

a greater sense of success results. They also become more motivated to strive for improvement because they can see their learning progress over the course of the term.

Exit Slips

Exit slips are a quick way to check for understanding. At the end of a class or instructional period, the teacher poses a question or presents a quick task to determine whether students have met the goals for the day's lesson. Students record their responses on their own paper, including their name at the top. Exit slips are typically used when you have just completed some instruction and you are not sure whether the students are ready to move on to a new topic the next day. The purpose of the slips is to gather information to determine what the next day's plan will be. Why wait until tomorrow to review homework when you can get the information right now?

Exit slip questions or tasks reflect that day's learning goals. For example, you might ask students to:

- Solve a math problem applying a process just taught
- Summarize the rotation and revolution of Earth and its effects
- Write a quick definition of a metaphor and a simile
- Sketch out the process of passing a bill into law
- Make a list of examples of synonyms and antonyms

Exit slips should reflect the KUDo's for your lesson. Therefore, you might choose to design them around *know*, *understand*, and be able to *do* as in **Figure 17,** an example of exit slips for a lesson on climate and weather. The exit slip questions and tasks are in bold.

Keep in mind that exit slips are *not* pop quizzes. They are not graded or recorded. After collecting the slips, you breeze through them scanning for accuracy. Then, make three piles: one pile for those students who are clearly "there" and understand the concept, skill, or process; another pile for the students who are "almost there" and need just a few more examples or a little more instruction; and a third pile for the students who are clearly "not there" and need more time, instruction, and practice to get them to mastery.

Your three piles determine the next day's lesson plan. If most of your students are in the "there" and the "almost there" piles, you can reasonably move on the next day. However, you need to find the time to pull those students together who need a little more instruction, modeling, or practice. Think about using independent work time the next day to reinforce their learning.

If most of your students are in the "not there" and the "almost there" piles, it is best to return to the content, skill, or process and use a different instructional strategy to reteach the next day. If your exit slips are spread among all piles *or* split between the "there" and the "not there" piles, you should plan for tiered assignments and flexible instructional groups the next day.

FIGURE 17

Sample Exit Slip

Know: Understand the kinds of precipitation.

Name the kinds of precipitation.

Understand that: The water cycle represents a system of interactions on Earth and in its atmosphere.

How is the water cycle a system of interactions? Describe this system in a paragraph or create a labeled diagram to share your ideas.

Be able to do: Distinguish the ways in which climate and weather are interrelated.

How are climate and weather interrelated?

Your students need to understand that although exit slips are not graded they are important work. Appeal to them by explaining how the slips will help you plan what will happen in class the next day. Exit slips will also determine their tasks and groups they may work in. If students fail to turn in an exit slip, automatically place them in the reteach/reinforce group should tiered assignments and flexible groups result from the data collected, as you have no evidence of their knowledge of the topic.

If you are a secondary teacher, you may choose to put a box by your door that students can drop slips into as they exit the classroom. Make sure to scoop them up before the next group comes in so that you do not have to sort them out by class period later in the day.

Preview/Review (PR)

The preview/review or PR strategy has elements of both preassessments and formative assessments. Teachers develop a list of 10 statements related to a topic that will be addressed in a mini-lecture or direct instruction lesson, or that the students will read about during the class period. Some of the written statements are true and some are false (see **Figure 18**). In the preview phase, students read the list and mark each statement as true or false on the left side of the statement. Then the students engage in the lesson. In the review phase at the end of the class period, students return to the PR, read the statements again, and mark each true or false on the right side of the statement.

In previewing the statements, students are given an overview of the topics for the day. They receive affirmation for the things they might know already ("I *do* know something about this!"), but also clear indications of what to listen or read for ("I *didn't* know this!"). Previews highlight the important points of the day's lesson.

Collect the PRs at the end of the period to determine which students knew considerable content before the lesson (little change in responses from preview to review) and which students failed to capture key concepts and ideas by the end of the lesson (no correction of incorrect responses from preview to review). PRs provide formative assessment information to guide your lesson plans for the following day.

Summative Assessment

Although we may think of summative assessment as the last component in our work with students in a curricular unit, in a differentiated classroom it continues to guide our planning. The purpose of summative assessment is to provide information about whether our students have met our unit's goals (KUDo's). In a differentiated classroom, it means that we critically reflect on the results, both of the class as whole as well as on individual students' performances. Based on your students' results, you may decide that you are ready to move on to your next curricular unit. Or you may decide to devote

FIGURE 18

Sample Preview/Review

Preview/Review on Simple Machines	
Preview	**Review**
1. ___ There are seven simple machines.	1. ___
2. ___ A stapler is a compound machine.	2. ___
3. ___ The shape of a wedge effects its ability to do its work.	3. ___
4. ___ Force influences the effectiveness of machines.	4. ___
5. ___ A fulcrum is part of an inclined plane.	5. ___
6. ___ A simple machine must have at least one moving part.	6. ___
7. ___ A screw is an inclined plane.	7. ___
8. ___ A pulley is used to hold two or more things together.	8. ___
9. ___ A baseball bat works as a lever.	9. ___
10. ___ A wheel and axle is a compound machine.	10. ___

more time, instruction, and practice to particular skills, concepts, or understandings with all or some of your students. Summative assessment is a part of the continuous feedback loop on learning you engage in within a differentiated classroom. As Stiggins notes, "assess accurately and use assessment to benefit students."[14]

In considering the learning differences in your classroom, it is important that summative assessment take a variety of forms. Teachers should vary assessment formats while gathering evidence of student learning in reliable and valid ways. The assessments in **Figure 19** are divided into those completed by students independently and those directly facilitated by teachers.

Summative assessment is typically used to measure knowledge, reasoning abilities, performance skills, or the ability to create products to demonstrate attainment of learning goals.

- Assessments that measure ***knowledge*** seek to determine the degree to which students have mastered factual information such as definitions and vocabulary.
- Assessment of ***reasoning*** considers thinking skills such as the ability to analyze, evaluate, and infer, as well as processes such as problem solving and decision-making.
- Assessment of ***performance skills*** determines the degree to which students can demonstrate their knowledge and reasoning by "doing." These assessments ask students to observe, perform, demonstrate, apply, model, and/or use their knowledge.
- The final assessment method seeks to measure the students' ***ability to create a product to demonstrate their learning***. Final products reflect the students' ability to apply knowledge, reasoning, and performance skills. Students are asked to design, create, develop, or construct a product representing their learning.[15]

14 Stiggins et al., 2004.

15 Stiggins, et al., 2004

INDEPENDENT SUMMATIVE ASSESSMENTS

A variety of assessment methods are available for students to complete independently. These methods include selected response, extended written response, and various performance assessments. Selected response formats include true/false, multiple choice, matching, short answer, and fill-in paper/pencil, software, or online assessments. Extended written response formats engage students in responding to questions as well as composing brief, one-page essays. Performance assessments reflect application of learning in the creation of a product. Projects, demonstrations, presentations, exhibits, and performances represent student learning. Assessment is often based on both teacher observation and the use of a rubric or checklist detailing specific quality criteria for use in evaluating the product.

Stiggins suggests that teachers consider which assessment method is the most appropriate, accurate, and efficient in measuring particular learning goals. He provides the following guidance:[16]

16 Richard J. Stiggins, *Student-Involved Classroom Assessment*, 3rd ed. (Upper Saddle River, NJ: Prentice Hall, 2000).

FIGURE 19

Independent and Teacher-Facilitated Assessments

Independent Assessments	Teacher-Facilitated Assessments
Paper/pencil, software, or online format	Interviews
Selected response	Conferences
Extended writing	Question/answer
Demonstrations	Oral examinations
Projects/products/ performances	One-on-one "staged" tasks
Presentations/exhibits	Structured observations

To assess **knowledge mastery** use:

- **Selected response tests** including multiple choice, true/false, matching, and fill-in responses to assess mastery of content.
- **Essays** that ask students to convey their understanding of relationships among elements of knowledge.

To assess **reasoning** use:

- **Selected response tests** to reveal basic patterns of reasoning.
- **Essays** that ask students to describe complex problem solutions.
- **Performance assessment** to enable teachers to observe students engaged in tasks and make inferences related to their reasoning skills based on their performance.

To assess **performance skills** use:

- **Performance assessment** to enable teachers to observe and evaluate skills used in the performance of the task.

To assess students' **ability to create a product** using knowledge, reasoning, and performance skills use:

- **Performance assessment** to enable teachers to assess the students' proficiency in carrying out steps in a task. Rubrics also enable teachers to assess the degree to which the product reflects particular attributes.

Matching what you are assessing with the most appropriate, accurate, and efficient assessment tool is critical in gathering the evidence of learning you need to guide planning in a differentiated classroom.

TEACHER-FACILITATED SUMMATIVE ASSESSMENTS

In addition to assessments that engage students independently, there are also teacher facilitated assessment formats. These assessments include teacher interviews, conferences, question/answer sessions, one-on-one "staged" tasks, and structured observations.

Interviews, Conferences, and Question/Answer Sessions

Teachers conduct interviews, conferences, and question/answer sessions to evaluate students' knowledge, as well as understandings of key facts, concepts, and principles related to a particular study. These one-on-one sessions allow you not only to consider what students know and understand, but also enable you to prompt for additional information or clarification. There may be students, such as those with particular disabilities, learning preferences, or at a particular stage of English language acquisition, who can better *tell* you what they know than demonstrate it on selected response or extended writing exams.

Question/Answer Sessions

Teacher facilitated assessments also include one-on-one or small group question/answer sessions. Carefully constructed questions allow students to engage in conversations about their learning. Students may form a small group to discuss a common reading. Gifted students may discuss the results of an independent investigation of a topic beyond the scope of the curriculum. For some students, the "safety" of one-on-one's or small group sessions increases their willingness and comfort in responding to questions posed by the teacher. Using this format, you are also able to better tailor the questions to the particular needs of the students.

Teacher facilitated assessments are important in evaluating English language learners who are at beginning stages of language acquisition. Consider the characteristics of students at each stage of language acquisition. Use prompts reflecting the student's stage of language acquisition when doing a one-on-one assessment. **Figure 20** suggests teacher prompts that are most appropriate at early stages of language acquisition.

FIGURE 20

Assessing English Language Learners in Teacher Facilitated Assessments[17]

STAGE	CHARACTERISTICS	TEACHER PROMPTS
Preproduction (0–6 months)	- Minimal language comprehension - Does not verbalize - Nods "yes" and "no" - Draws - Points	- Show me . . . - Circle the . . . - Where is . . . - Who has . . .
Early Production (6 months–1 year)	- Limited comprehension - One- or two-word responses - Uses key words and familiar phrases - Uses present tense verbs	- Yes/No questions - Either/Or questions - One- or two-word answers - List . . . - Label . . .
Speech Emergence (1–3 years)	- Good comprehension - Produces simple sentences - Makes errors in grammar and pronunciation	- Why . . . ? - How . . . ? - Explain . . . - Phrase or short-sentence answers

17 Adapted with permission from *Classroom Instruction That Works with English Language Learners* by Jane D. Hill and Kathleen M. Flynn (Alexandria, VA: Association for Supervision and Curriculum Development, 2006).

One-on-One "Staged" Tasks

You may also stage particular tasks to enable your students to individually demonstrate their learning for you. Primary teachers may meet with individual students and ask them to continue a pattern of manipulative figures. Secondary teachers may ask students to demonstrate their ability to apply an algorithm as the teachers observe their work.

Structured Observations

Finally, you may identify a particular skill or process you wish to observe while students are engaged in a task. A structured observation goes beyond simply walking the classroom when students are working. You identify specific skills or processes to evaluate and then set up a learning task that enables you to observe students engaged with this skill or process. You may use a class checklist to note observations of individual students, or you might make notations about specific students on sticky notes and place them in their student file folders for reference.

Regardless of whether you choose to use independent or teacher facilitated formats, there are particular characteristics of summative assessment that you should keep in mind.

Nonnegotiable Characteristics of Summative Assessments[18]

A high-quality classroom-level summative assessment:

- Provides clear, consistent, accurate evidence of student learning
- Reflects the KUDo's of the unit
- Utilizes a format similar to what the students have experienced during the unit
- Advances learning rather than simply documenting it
- Is developmentally appropriate
- Requires an appropriate level of challenge for all students
- Avoids sources of bias
- Enables teachers to diagnose and respond to student needs based on data
- Measures what it intends to measure (e.g., if the intent is to measure content, the assessment is not influenced by process or product results)
- Is modified or adapted as required to address the needs of special education and ELL students

18 Ken O'Connor, *How to Grade for Learning: Linking Grades to Standards* (Thousand Oaks, CA: Corwin Press, 2002); Stiggins, 2004; Cindy Strickland, *Tools for High Quality Differentiated Instruction: An ASCD Action Tool* by (Alexandria, VA: Association for Supervision and Curriculum Development, 2007); Wormeli, 2006.

Should I Differentiate Assessments?

Some teachers extend the practices of differentiation to the assessments they use in their classrooms. For example, you may:

- Use the same assessment for all students
- Use the same assessment for all students, but include a component that allows for student choice
- Offer student choice of different assessment formats
- Prescribe assessment formats based on student needs

GUIDELINES FOR DIFFERENTIATING ASSESSMENTS

Here are important guidelines to keep in mind as you consider differentiated assessments.

Differentiated Assessment MUST:

- Measure identical learning goals or standards
- Keep the element being measured (content, process, or product) the same in each format
- Enable students to demonstrate full proficiency in the goal or standard
- Require an appropriate level of challenge for all students

Differentiated Assessment MIGHT:

- Offer different products (unless the product is also a learning goal) based on learning preference
- Reflect lesser or greater levels of challenge or complexity
- Offer concrete or abstract applications
- Provide structured or open-ended tasks
- Provide different levels of support or scaffolding

WHEN TO DIFFERENTIATE ASSESSMENTS

In considering whether to differentiate an assessment, ask yourself the following questions:

- What components of an assessment (content, process, or product) could be modified based on the goals I want to measure?
- What components of an assessment need to be maintained to ensure their alignment with the learning goal?
- Is the format of the assessment related to a learning goal, or can students show their learning in a variety of formats?
- Is it possible to provide student choice in one of the components without affecting the focus of the assessment?
- Might I need to prescribe particular formats to particular students based on learning differences?
- Is the assessment a "test prep" experience? If so, all students need to do the same assessment so all are equally prepared when this format is presented in the future.
- Will a particular product prevent some students from effectively demonstrating their learning?
- Will offering student choice in the content, process, or product components of the assessment inhibit my ability to effectively assess student learning?

HOW TO DIFFERENTIATE ASSESSMENTS

1. First, determine whether you are assessing **content** (knowledge), **process** (reasoning abilities, performance skills), or the ability to create a particular **product** to demonstrate learning.
2. **Vary** assessment formats on a continuum as appropriate to your assessment goals by:
   - Demanding lesser or greater levels of task challenge (See Bloom's Taxonomy on page 144)
   - Demanding lesser or greater levels of application complexity
   - Providing greater task structure (specific guidelines) or more open-endedness (ability to create direction with the work)
   - Requiring concrete or more abstract applications
   - Providing more or less support or scaffolding (e.g., templates, graphic organizers, word banks)

3. Consider whether **student choice** will be provided in the assessment. Determine which element (content, process, or product) might include choice in light of the goal you are assessing. If products are open to choice, they may represent the various learning preferences.
4. Consider whether you will match students with a particular assessment or if you will allow students to choose which assessment format they will engage in.

USING VARIED FORMATS IN DIFFERENTIATING ASSESSMENTS

Once you have determined whether you are assessing content, process, or product, you begin designing your assessment format, varying tasks by levels of concreteness, complexity, structure, scaffolding, and learning preference. The first "tier" of the assessment is the task that will be appropriate for most of your students. This task or series of questions, problems, or selected response statements needs to clearly determine the students' proficiency with the standard(s)/goal(s) you are assessing. Then, think of moving that task along a continuum to create a more advanced assessment task or to modify a task based on the needs of special learners. Consider: Where's the starting point on the continuum for *most* learners? Then move the task along the continuum in the design process. Do not assume that special needs students or students engaged in RTI processes will necessarily only engage in tasks representing the left side of the continuum. Their most appropriate task may be a modification of a task on the right side of the continuum.

Consider the continuum in **Figure 21**.

Basic to Challenging Tasks

Figures 22 to 24 present sample assignments including tasks that range from basic to challenging.

Simple to Complex Applications

Figures 25 to 27 present sample assignments including tasks that involve applications ranging from simple to complex.

Structured to Open-Ended Tasks

Figures 28 to 30 present sample assignments including tasks that range from structured to open-ended.

FIGURE 21

Task-Application Continuum

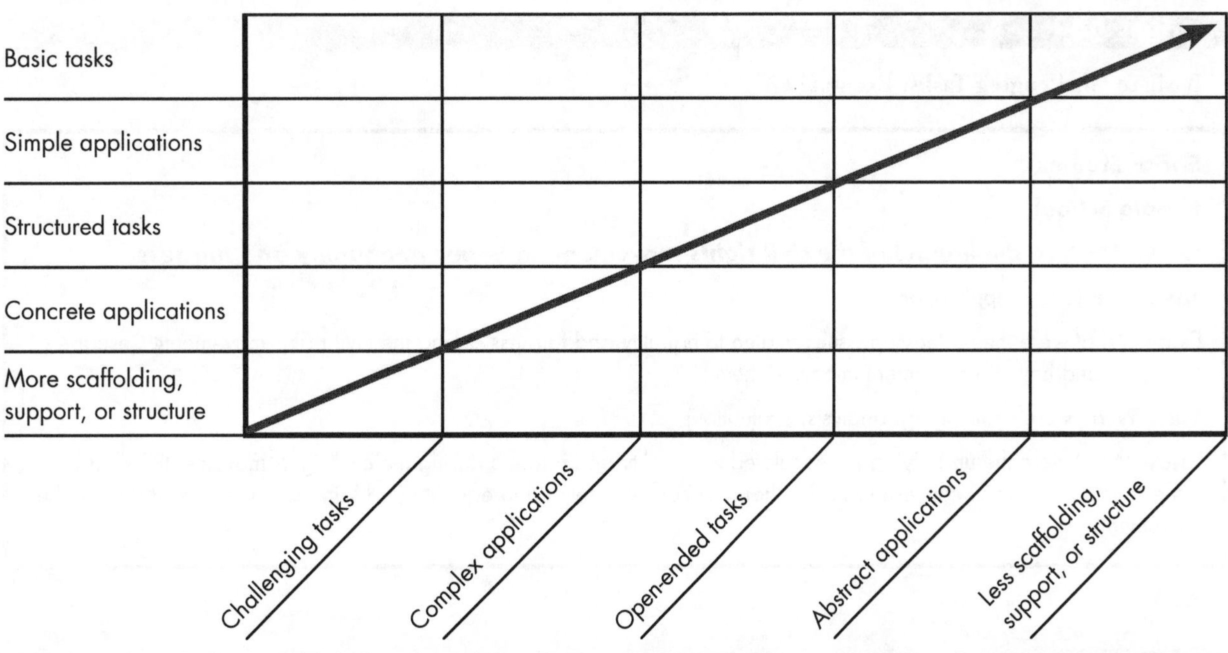

FIGURE 22

Basic to Challenging Tasks: Example #1

Biology
Elementary
Goal: Distinguish characteristics of various plant seeds

All students are given a packet of two different kinds of seeds.

Task One (Basic: application)

Students categorize the seeds and then list characteristics of each on a chart provided by the teacher.

Task Two (More challenging: analysis)

Students categorize the seeds and then compare and contrast their characteristics on a chart of like and different.

FIGURE 23

Basic to Challenging Tasks: Example #2

Family and Consumer Science
Middle School
Goal: Determine job requirements for career clusters

Task One (Basic: application, synthesis)

Diagram a career cluster. Identify the particular interests, abilities, aptitudes, skills, and personal characteristics necessary for success in these jobs by writing a classified ad for someone well suited for such positions.

Task Two (More challenging: analysis, evaluation, synthesis)

Diagram a career cluster. Consider the degree to which you possess the particular interests, abilities, aptitudes, skills, and personal characteristics necessary for success in these jobs. Write a letter to an employment agency or "headhunter" describing why you are suitable for a position in this career cluster. Use the job's necessary interests, abilities, aptitudes, skills, and personal characteristics as a way to analyze your potential for the position.

FIGURE 24

Basic to Challenging Tasks: Example #3

Social Studies
Middle School
Goal: Analyze the impact of the civil rights movement on issues of equality and fairness

Task One (Basic: application)

Essay: What were the underlying issues related to equality and fairness during the civil rights movement? Describe the issues and how the movement impacted them.

Task Two (More challenging: analysis, evaluation)

Essay: What were the underlying issues related to equality and fairness during the civil rights movement? What issues continue to be of concern today? What new concerns related to equality and fairness have emerged since the movement?

FIGURE 25

Simple to Complex Applications: Example #1

Social Studies

Elementary

Goal: Determine characteristics of urban and rural communities

Task One (Simple)

Divide your paper into two sides. Label one side "City" and the other side "Country." Use pictures, sketches, or words to show things you find only in the country or only in the city. *For example:* a car could be found in the city or in the country so it would not be on your chart.

Task Two (More complex)

Create a Venn diagram showing how cities and the country are alike and different.

Task Three (Most complex)

Think of what makes a city a special place and what makes the country a special place. Divide a piece of poster paper into two sides. On one side use characteristics of the country to demonstrate that it is the best place to live. On the other side list characteristics to demonstrate that cities are the best places to live.

FIGURE 26

Simple to Complex Applications: Example #2[19]

Math

Elementary

Goal: Calculate fractional parts of numbers

Task One Problems (Simple)

1. Abby had $15. She needed to spend $\frac{4}{5}$ of it on a flash drive for her computer. How much money did she have left after her purchase?
2. There are 45 students from your school at the new action movie. $\frac{4}{9}$ of them are girls. How many boys are attending the movie?
3. $\frac{3}{7}$ of the pens in a box are black. The rest are blue. There are 24 blue. How many pens are there all together?
4. Carlos had some CDs he didn't want anymore. He sold $\frac{4}{5}$ of them. If he sold 40 CDs, how many did he have to begin with?

Task Two Problems (More complex)

1. Marcus got $200 for work he did for his neighbors. He spent $\frac{2}{5}$ of it on a portable DVD player and $\frac{1}{4}$ of the remainder of the money on DVDs. How much money did he have left after shopping?
2. Cherise's parents want her to save some of the money she gets for baby-sitting during the summer. She put $\frac{1}{2}$ of her money in the bank and spent $\frac{1}{2}$ of the remainder. If she had $50 left after shopping, how much money did she make during the summer baby-sitting?
3. Libby works at a State Fair food booth. The booth had 1,280 corn dogs to sell. On Friday, $\frac{3}{5}$ of them were sold. On Saturday, $\frac{1}{4}$ of the remainder were sold. How many corn dogs are left to sell on Sunday?
4. Kei needs to read a book for his English class by Tuesday. He read $\frac{1}{4}$ of the pages on Saturday, and $\frac{2}{5}$ of the remaining pages on Sunday. If he still has 18 pages left to read before class, how many pages were in his book?

19 Provided courtesy of Douglas Springer, Marshall Elementary; Marshall, WI. Used with permission.

FIGURE 27

Simple to Complex Applications: Example #3[20]

Biology

High School

Goal: Conduct laboratory experiments to gather and analyze data

Task One (Simple)

Lab A

- Complete the lab "A study in osmosis: Potato cores in solutions."
- Analyze the data and calculate the mass change and volume change that occurs from day one to day two.
- Organize the data into two scatter plot graphs: the first showing solution concentration vs. mass change; the second showing solution concentration vs. volume change.
- Compare and contrast the two data sets.
- Deduce the relationship between the solutions the potato core was placed in, and the kind of mass change or volume change observed.
- Infer what the concentration of solution in a potato cell will be.

Lab B

- Complete the lab "Eggmosis."
- Make predictions as to what is going to happen each day of the lab.
- Collect daily data and produce an organized table for each day of the experiment.
- List mass change from day to day.
- Explain the changes with regard to diffusion, osmosis, and type of solution.
- Draw diagrams of each day's procedure.
- Draw before and after diagrams of the egg for each day.

Choose one of the extensions below:

1. Eggmosis Extension

- After completing the "Eggmosis" lab, write an introduction that includes background information on the lab.
- Discuss ways to improve the lab.
- Summarize the data, explaining not just what happens, but *why* it happens.
- Report on ways the techniques or information acquired from the lab is used in everyday life. For example, why doesn't honey or syrup require refrigeration, but fruit juice does?
- Produce a formal lab procedure for making measurements more quantitative for doing the lab. This can include using a variety of solution concentrations and extending the lab over several days, or using several eggs and measuring their changes in a variety of treatments.

2. Potato Cores Extension

- After completing the "Potato cores" lab, write an introduction that includes background information on the lab.
- Using data from the entire class, create two scatter plot graphs: one showing mass change, the other volume change.
- Analyze the two data sets to determine which will yield the most reliable and reproducible information. Justify why that data set will be more accurate.
- Discuss ways to improve the lab.
- Summarize the data, explaining not just what happens, but *why* it happens.
- List three ways the techniques or information acquired from the lab is used in everyday life. For example, why doesn't honey or syrup require refrigeration, but fruit juice does? Or, how is knowledge of diffusion and osmosis applied to delivery of intravenous medicine?

Task Two (More complex)

- Write a procedure for doing an experiment that will measure the effect of a cell's volume on diffusion. You may research some suggested investigations that cover these topics online or in books.
- Perform the lab and record your data.
- Write an analysis of the results.
- Discuss what you thought of the lab and list three ways to improve it.
- Describe what you learned and evaluate the usefulness of doing this lab in future biology classes.
- Summarize the data, explaining not just what happens, but *why* it happens.
- List three ways the techniques or information acquired from the lab is used in everyday life.

20 Provided courtesy of Quentin Cartier, Arrowhead High School; Hartland, WI. Used with permission.

FIGURE 28

Structured to Open-Ended Tasks: Example #1

English/Language Arts

Elementary

Goal: Distinguish characteristics of book characters

Task One (More structure)

Choose four of the adjectives below that describe your character. Give examples from the book to show each characteristic.

aggressive	cheerful	strong	helpful	confused	caring	careless
angry	hardworking	fearful	optimistic	jealous	hopeful	disappointed

Task Two (More open-ended)

Select four or five adjectives to describe your character. Provide examples from the book that show these characteristics.

FIGURE 29

Structured to Open-Ended Tasks: Example #2

Geography

Elementary

Goal: Analyze the interrelationship of population centers and geography

Task One (More structure)

Study the U.S. topographic map you are given with population centers noted. Based on geography, identify why the population centers are located in each area.

Task Two (More open-ended)

Study the topographic map you are given. Place population centers where you predict they will develop. Provide a rationale for their placement.

FIGURE 30

Structured to Open-Ended Tasks: Example #3

Biology

Middle School

Goal: Identify cell parts and functions

Task One (More structure)

Identify animal cell parts on a diagram. List the functions of each.

Task Two (More open-ended)

Create an analogy between an animal cell and its parts and functions, and a business, home, or factory and its parts and functions.

More or Less Scaffolding

Figures 31 and 32 present sample assignments including tasks that involve different levels of scaffolding.

USING STUDENT CHOICE IN DIFFERENTIATING ASSESSMENTS

You may decide to include student choice in one of the elements of your assessment. Remember, however, that the choice cannot affect your ability to reliably assess the standard or KUDo. For example, if you are assessing the students' ability to create a timeline, you could provide choice in content (what the timeline is about) but would need to have all students create the same product (the timeline). **Figure 33** shows an example of a task for order of operations, in which the content remains the same but the students choose how to show what they have learned (product) based on learning preference.

In **Figure 34,** a world language assessment, the content (subject pronouns) remains constant in all three tasks, however, the students are given a choice in how to represent this information (product) based on learning preference.

FIGURE 31

More or Less Scaffolding: Example #1

English/Language Arts
Elementary
Goal: Retell a story

Task One (More scaffolding)
Listen to the story your teacher reads aloud. Fill in the blanks in the story below.

First, the _____ went to the _____ house of the first pig. He blew and blew and _____. Then he went to the _____ house of the second pig. He blew and blew and _____. Finally, he went to the _____ house of the third pig. He blew and blew and _____. In the end, the wolf _____ and the pigs _____.

Task Two (Less scaffolding)

Listen to the story your teacher reads aloud. In the graphic organizer below, you may draw pictures or list words in each box to recall the elements of the story. Then, write a summary of the story in at least one sentence.

Characters	Setting
Problem	Solution

Summary:

FIGURE 32

More or Less Scaffolding: Example #2

World Language
Elementary/Middle School
Goal: Categorize Spanish vocabulary words

All students are given the same list of vocabulary words.

Task One (More scaffolding)

Categorize the vocabulary words into seven categories: *Los Adjetivos, La Familia, Los Números, El Calendario, La Comida, Los Verbos,* and *La Escuela.*

Task Two (No scaffolding)

Categorize the vocabulary words into groups. Label each group with an appropriate title.

FIGURE 33

Task Involving Student Choice: Example #1

Math
Elementary/Middle School
Goal: Describe the procedures in order of operations

Task One (Logical/mathematical)

Construct an illustrated flow chart to help you remember order of operations.

Task Two (Verbal/linguistic)
Write a text message to a classmate explaining order of operations. Include clear directions. You may use abbreviations from a text messaging online dictionary or come up with your own creative abbreviations.

FIGURE 34

Task Involving Student Choice: Example #2

World Language
Middle School
Goal: Demonstrate the meaning of subject pronouns in Spanish

Task One (Visual/spatial)

Create an illustrated poster to show the meanings of the subject pronouns.

Task Two (Musical)

Compose a rhyme, poem, or rap to help you remember the meanings of the subject pronouns.

DIFFERENTIATING A COMPONENT OF AN ASSESSMENT: TOTALLY 10

Carissa Smith, a teacher in Fargo, North Dakota, uses the strategy "Totally 10" from *Differentiating Instruction in the Regular Classroom*[21] as a method for differentiating Earth Science tests. Totally 10 is used to design student tasks at different levels of challenge and complexity. Tasks are assigned different values related to Bloom's challenge levels. Students must select and complete tasks to equal a value of 10. The following value pattern is used:

Score 2

Tasks at the knowledge, comprehension, and application Bloom's levels

Score 4

Tasks at the application and analysis levels

Score 6

Tasks at the analysis, evaluation, and synthesis levels

Score 10

Tasks at a higher level of complexity as well as challenge (think Bloom's), a more comprehensive representation of the standards or KUDo's

Since many students think "less is better," they are more likely to select the more challenging activities with the higher point values so they reach a score of 10 by doing fewer tasks. In this way, Totally 10 nudges students toward choosing challenge over "quick and easy."

21 Heacox, 2002.

Carissa asks her students to complete a paper/pencil test on her unit's content and then adds the Totally 10 component at the end of the test. She directs students to choose questions/problems from any of the four categories, but limits them to only two questions from the Score 2 category. **Figure 35** shows the choice component of Carissa's test on the topic of the ocean.

Assessments Modifications for Special Needs Students

There may be times in an inclusion classroom when modifications of assessment tasks are necessary. In these cases, in addition to basic (on-target) tasks appropriate to most students in your classroom and extended tasks for students who need additional challenge or complexity, a third assessment format emerges: modified tasks. Modified tasks may provide more support or scaffolding in order for students to successfully demonstrate their learning. The three tasks are modeled in the following science assessment on global warming. All tasks are focused on assessing the same learning goal: Students will be able to analyze different perspectives on global warming.

The on-target **basic task** used by most students in the classroom:

- Analyze two perspectives on global warming. Summarize the perspectives presenting critical facts for each.

An **extended task** is directed to those students who can benefit from more complex tasks:

- Analyze two perspectives on global warming. Create an argument for each perspective summarizing critical facts for each.

A **modified task** is provided for those students who need more support and/or different methods for demonstrating their knowledge. The student's specific learning issues determine the way in which an assessment task would be modified. Examples of a modified task for this assessment might be:

- Complete the graphic organizer to present two perspectives on global warming.

- Create a visual representation of two perspectives on global warming.

Differentiated Grading on Differentiated Assessments

Much has been written and discussed about grading in a differentiated classroom. Ethical practices suggest that if students are assigned particular assessments in light of their learning needs, each student is eligible for an identical range of points (e.g., 0–75 points) and the same range of grades (F to A). In independent assessments, accuracy of responses would determine grades even if students are engaged in different test formats. Performance assessments are evaluated based on a checklist or rubric detailing specific criteria for each assessment format. See Chapter 9 for a detailed discussion of ethical grading practices in a differentiated classroom.

FIGURE 35

Totally 10 Example[22]

Ocean Test

Directions: You may choose questions from any category to total a score of 10. You may pick only two questions from the Score 2 section.

Score 2

1. Does the Red River have any impact on oceans? Why or why not?
2. Define *gyres*. Draw a picture of the movement of a gyre in the Northern Hemisphere.
3. Define a *neap tide*. Draw the position of the earth, moon, and sun during a neap tide.

Score 4

1. Draw a wave. Label these features: wave length, wave height, crest, trough.
2. Determine how the following liquids would layer in a container. Number them 1 to 4, with 1 being the top layer and 4 being the bottom layer. Explain your decisions with facts about liquids.

   __ ice cold saltwater

   __ ice cold freshwater

   __ hot saltwater

   __ hot freshwater

Score 6

1. Compare *El Niño* to *La Niña*. Consider differences in ocean temperature, air temperature, and precipitation. Write your comparisons in a paragraph or construct a chart to share your ideas.
2. Predict what would happen if freshwater was placed on a hot plate. What would cause the freshwater to layer? Explain why this happens in terms of density changes, heat transfer, and convection.

Score 10

1. Imagine that an oil spill occurs off the southern tip of Florida. The governor of Florida has decided that money does not need to be spent to clean up the oil spill. It will not affect the marine organisms around Florida or along the eastern coast of the United States. Why would the governor believe this to be true?
   A. Draw a picture showing the location of the oil spill. Include the name of the ocean and label the three nearest continents.
   B. Draw the path the oil spill will take.
   C. Determine the relevant currents located in this area. Draw the currents, label them, add arrows showing their paths, and tell whether they are warm or cold currents.
   D. After completing the diagram, justify the governor's response to the oil spill.
2. Create a plan for determining the composition of the Pacific Ocean's floor. In your plan do the following:
   A. Draw a map of the Pacific Ocean. Label the four continents that border it and Hawaii.
   B. Mark where you will collect samples. Explain why you selected those locations.
   C. Explain how surface currents will affect your routes to collection sites.
   D. Explain why collecting all of your samples by Hawaii would create an inaccurate conclusion of the composition of the Pacific Ocean floor.

22 Provided courtesy of Carissa Smith, Fargo Public Schools; Fargo, ND. Used with permission.

CHAPTER 4

Critical Element: Using a Differentiated Learning Plan

Today's classrooms reflect growing diversity in student learning needs, preferences, interests, and readiness. However, many teachers were initially introduced to lesson plan structures based on effective schools research conducted in the 1960s and 1970s.[1] Such structures emphasize direct instruction and include the following phases in the lesson: student orientation to the lesson; initial instruction on concepts, skills, or processes; teacher-guided practice; student independent practice; and checks for understanding. Students tended to march through the phases of the lesson as a group with limited preplanning for differences.

Research on these lesson plan structures was conducted during a time when the range of academic diversity in the classroom was fairly narrow and Public Law 94-142 (IDEA) was not yet implemented. Thus, special needs students were excluded from much of the research.[2]

Although these lesson plan structures were designed to maximize instructional time, they did not recognize that not all students learn in the same way and at the same pace. Therefore, teachers may struggle with a lesson plan structure that no longer works efficiently or effectively for them. Today, the work of lesson plan design is an exercise in planning activities for various groups of students with different learning preferences, interests, and readiness levels. As such, teachers need a lesson plan structure that walks them through a process that enables them to examine learning differences and plan accordingly.

"The Differentiated Learning Plan" (or DLP) on page 58, is designed to enable teachers to thoughtfully develop lessons responding to differences in their classrooms. As a planning tool, it recognizes that there is more than one way to differentiate a lesson. The nine-step process encourages educators to put students at the center of the planning and respond specifically to their needs.

Differentiation is not just a set of strategies that we "plug in" randomly; it is a planful process.

The DLP guides the teacher step-by-step in examining possibilities for differentiating a lesson, but does so flexibly. Not all lessons are differentiated at the same point or in the same way.

Differentiation is not just a set of strategies that we "plug in" randomly; it is a planful process. We consider what we teach, how we teach it, how the students will engage in the learning, and how they will demonstrate their attainment of the lesson's goal. At each phase of this process, we need to consider where differences among our students emerge and how we will preplan for them.

1 William N. Bender, *Teaching Students with Mild Disabilities* (Boston: Allyn & Bacon, 1996).

2 William N. Bender, *Differentiating Math Instruction: Strategies That Work for K–8 Classrooms!* (Thousand Oaks, CA: Corwin Press, 2005).

DIFFERENTIATED LEARNING PLAN

* indicates a strategy for differentiation

1. Standards/KUDo's:

2. Preassessment/Formative Assessment Notes:

3. Hook:

4. Content Delivery (WHAT they will learn)

___ same resources

___ different resources (e.g., leveled)*

___ same goal for all

___ advanced goal for some*

___ modified goal for some*

Notes:

5. Direct Instruction/Modeling

(HOW they will learn it)

___ single strategy that engages all

___ more than one learning preference (based on Multiple Intelligences)*

___ more than one modality (e.g., auditory, visual, kinesthetic)*

Notes:

6. Application Activities

(HOW they will learn it)

___ same for all

___ tier by learning preference (based on Multiple Intelligences)*

___ tier by readiness*

___ tier by challenge/complexity*

Notes:

7. Independent Application (How they will DEMONSTRATE their learning)

___ individual work

___ with a partner

___ in a small group (based on Multiple Intelligences)*

___ tier by readiness*

___ tier by challenge/complexity*

___ student choice based on interest*

Notes:

8. Closure: Activity/Question and Answer/Sharing of Products/Exit Slip/Review/Critical Reflection/Question Posing

Notes:

9. What next?

Formative Assessment Notes:

The planning process begins with academic standards and learning goals. Preassessment and formative assessment data is actively utilized in directing the plan. Information about learning preferences (based on Multiple Intelligences), interests, and readiness is integral to creating plans that increase the likelihood of student success. Phases 4–7 of the planning process ask teachers to consider integration of particular elements of differentiation and provide opportunities to plan for differences: Content delivery, Instruction/modeling, Application activities, and Independent application. It is not suggested or even recommended that teachers differentiate at each phase of the DLP. It is recommended that teachers commit to differentiating *at least one* phase of the learning plan.

The Nine Phases of Using the Differentiated Learning Plan

❶ Standards/KUDo's

The first phase requires you to list the specific learning goals for the lesson. These goals reflect your state or provincial academic standards. You may write your lesson as stated by the standards or write them as KUDo's: what the students will know, understand, and be able to do by the end of the lesson.

❷ Preassessment/Formative Assessment Notes

Next, record notes on the assessment data you have collected to guide the design of the lesson. Informal or formal preassessment information or formative assessment data influences modifications, adaptations, or extensions of learning goals as well as the design of application activities. Assessment notes in this area provide information on readiness, pacing, grouping, materials, and content most appropriate to the needs of learners.

❸ Hook

In a differentiated learning plan, the "hook" identifies the ways in which you actively engage your students' interests in and curiosities about the lesson's topic. Used at the beginning of a lesson, hooks increase motivation for learning as they engage students in an introduction to the day's work. You can present hooks using a variety of formats, including posing an open-ended question, presenting a problem to be solved, telling a story or anecdote, raising a moral dilemma, providing a quotation, or introducing survey or research results. Hooks may also include presenting a piece of artwork or a comic strip, playing a piece of music, or viewing a video clip. In recognition of the range of learning preferences in your classroom, hooks should represent a variety of ways to engage student interest in the work of the day. Additional ideas for hooks are included in **Figure 36** on page 60.

Describe the hook that will be used for your lesson in the box provided on the DLP template on page 60.

❹ Content Delivery

The content delivery phase of the learning plan identifies the content, skills, or processes to be addressed in the lesson. It describes *what* your students will learn. You may choose to use the same resources (e.g., materials, articles or textbook readings, Web sites) for all students or you may wish to differentiate initial instruction using different resources. Teachers may have a single goal for all students or differentiate the goals of the lesson based on the needs of the learners. For example, if some students have achieved the grade-level learning goal, you may determine a more advanced goal for them in order to provide new learning.

Differentiation of resources matches students with appropriate materials based on their specific learning needs. For example, teachers may match students with materials at appropriate reading readiness levels (e.g., Lexile scores). Other teachers may choose to match some students with bookmarked Web sites that include introductory information on a topic while matching other students with advanced knowledge or understandings with Web sites that present more complex, in-depth, or sophisticated content.

Differentiation of learning goals involves modifying goals for some students based on special education plans, a need for greater support, or a need for more advanced goals. During initial instruction, teachers may hold the same learning goal for all students in the classroom or they may establish different goals for different learners based on their needs. In addition, teachers may consider establishing a more advanced goal for those students whose differences demand higher levels of challenge or who already demonstrate advanced knowledge, skills, or processes.

On the DLP template, check the ways in which you will deliver content and write your specific plans in the box provided.

5 Instruction/Modeling

Phase 5 of the process addresses *how* your students will learn. Consider the ways in which you will actively engage students in the learning. Using deductive strategies, the teacher takes the primary role during this phase of the learning plan. Information is presented, skills and processes introduced, and modeling is provided for students. Using inductive strategies, the teacher guides students through processes of questioning, gathering information, and finding order or patterns to arrive at the concept or understanding, or master a skill or process. You may choose to use a single instructional strategy with all of your students, or you may decide to differentiate your instruction and modeling.

You can differentiate the instruction and modeling lesson component by presenting the content, skills, and processes in various ways that reflect the Multiple Intelligences–based learning preferences of your students. For example, you may do initial instruction through a mini-lecture (Verbal/linguistic learning preference) and then work with the students to complete a graphic organizer (Visual/spatial learning preference) to capture key ideas.

You may also choose to differentiate the instructional component by presenting the content, skills, or processes using multiple modalities. For example, you might present a science lab by providing oral directions (auditory modality) and by demonstrating the process while the students observe (visual modality).

On the DLP template, indicate the ways in which you will provide instruction and modeling and then describe your specific plans in the box provided.

FIGURE 36

Ideas to Hook Students into Learning

START YOUR LESSON WITH ONE OF THESE:	TELL YOUR STUDENTS A/AN:
Art activity	Riddle
Artifact or model	Anecdote
Artwork	Story
Photograph, illustration	Fable
Excerpt from a book or an article	Folktale
Excerpt from a biography or an autobiography	Myth
Case study	Metaphor or simile
Chart, graph, or diagram	Poem
Comic strip or cartoon	Quote
Computer software	Slogan
Discrepant event or puzzling situation	Related joke
Print or recorded advertisement or commercial	Humorous story
Web site	
Dance or creative movement	
Dramatic performance or reading	
Demonstration	
Display of related or unrelated items	
Editorial	
Editorial cartoon	
Letter to the editor	
Exhibit or collection of items	
Live or recorded interview	
Moral or ethical dilemma	
Video clip	
Song or piece of music	
Model	
Magazine or newspaper article	
Open-ended question	
Provocative question	
Picture book	
Problem statement	
Scenario	
Simulation	
Timeline	
Survey or research results	
Excerpt from a speech	

❻ Application Activities

Application activities are the second element addressing *how* your students will learn the concepts, skills, or processes presented in the lesson. These tasks engage students in applying or using what they have learned in the instruction/modeling phase of the lesson. Students are asked to make meaning of what they have learned. In addition, you have an opportunity to observe the students at work and determine whether they understood and can apply what was taught in the instructional phase of the lesson.

You may choose to have all students complete the same application activity, or you may decide to differentiate the activities the students will engage in. You may differentiate application activities by tiering them based on learning preference (based on Multiple Intelligences), readiness, or challenge/complexity.

Tiering is a critical strategy that specifically responds to learning differences. Tiered activities provide "just right, right now" learning experiences for students. Tiered application activities are designed with the intention of matching students to tasks that best represent their learning preference, readiness level, or need for more challenging or complex experiences. Tiered assignments also need to be modified or adapted based on the needs of special education students. See Chapter 6 for specific ideas on multiple ways to tier assignments.

Application activities may be completed individually, with a partner, or in a small group of learners. If your intent is to create better instructional matches through tiering, you should assign students a partner or place them in groups with like learning needs.

On the DLP template, check the kinds of application activities that students will engage in and describe the activities in the box provided.

❼ Independent Application

Independent application tasks are the ways in which students *demonstrate* their learning. These activities or assignments may be completed in class or may be assigned as homework.

Both the teacher and the student are able to assess learning through the completion of the task. Independent applications provide formative assessment data used to determine whether teachers need to reteach, move on, or differentiate learning in a subsequent lesson.

Depending on the assessment information you desire, independent applications can be completed as individual work, with a partner, or in a small group. Students should complete their own work if you want individual evidence of learning.

You may wish all students to complete the same task, particularly if the task evidences work on or accomplishment of a state or provincial academic standard or goal. However, you may differentiate independent application through tasks tiered based on learning preference, readiness, or the need for more challenge/complexity. You may also design multiple tasks, each assessing the same learning goal, and provide students an opportunity to *choose* which task they wish to complete based on their interests.

In this section of the DLP template, check appropriate descriptors related to independent application tasks, and then describe the specific activities in more detail in the box provided.

❽ Closure

The hook (phase 3) gets students engaged in learning; closure reinforces what they have learned. Though sometimes skipped because of lack of time at the end of a lesson, closure is your last chance to reteach what was taught. For many students who need more support to learn, this is a critical phase in a learning plan.

Closure might involve any of the following:

- A quick group activity reinforcing or demonstrating concepts
- The sharing of products created during class
- A large group or partner review of key ideas
- Carefully scripted questions posed by the teacher to elicit particular responses
- Opportunities for students to critically reflect on what they have learned

- The use of exit slips to do a quick check for understanding
- Students posing questions based on new curiosities

The DLP template provides space for you to jot down and commit to a closure activity.

9 What next?

The final component of the learning plan template asks you to critically reflect on the lesson after it is implemented with students. Using classroom observations and evidence from application and independent activities as formative assessment data, you make plans for subsequent lessons.

Ask yourself:

- Are there students who need more instruction, time, or practice the next day?
- Have the majority of students accomplished the learning goals?
- Is there a need the next class session for tiered assignments to reinforce or extend today's learning?
- Is there sufficient evidence to indicate that the concepts, skills, or processes should be retaught in a new way the following day?
- Is the class ready to move on to another curriculum goal?

The final box on the learning plan template allows you to note comments, reminders, and next steps in planning.

When and How to Differentiate Using a DLP

Although the learning needs of students are considered in each of the nine phases in the design of a differentiated learning plan, only four of the phases (4–7) address differentiation more specifically, as mentioned earlier. In the content delivery, instruction/modeling, application activities, and independent application phases, strategies are suggested for differentiating the plan. These differentiation strategies are noted with an asterisk (*).

Teachers integrate specific strategies for differentiation into *one or more of these four phases* of the lesson. For example, a teacher may choose to:

- Use the same resources for all students in content delivery
- Use a single strategy in direct instruction
- Differentiate the application activities through tiering tasks by readiness
- Have all students do the same independent activity with a partner

In this example, strategies for differentiation were utilized *only* at the application activities phase of the lesson.

Strategies for differentiation are offered on the planning template for each of these four phases. The strategy is noted by an asterisk. Again, commit to integrating strategies for differentiation into *at least one phase* of the learning plan. **Figures 37 to 40** provide examples of differentiated learning plans in several grade levels and subject areas.

Why Use a Differentiated Learning Plan?

- **It provides a more systematic approach to planning with the diverse needs of students in mind.**
- **It encourages flexibility in planning. Differentiation may occur at any phase of the plan, and there is no single way to differentiate a lesson.**
- **It enables differentiation to be deepened and moves it into more sophisticated applications.**

The purpose of the differentiated plan is to encourage you to consider the specific learning differences in your classroom as you decide how you might differentiate a lesson. Remember, it is sufficient to differentiate one element in a phase of the plan. As your skills continue to develop in differentiation, you may consider more than one element. As always: start small, but start somewhere.

FIGURE 37

Differentiated Learning Plan: Example #1

ENGLISH/LANGUAGE ARTS: READING
ELEMENTARY

* indicates a strategy for differentiation

1. Standards/KUDo's:
Identify the sequence of events in a story.

Understand the meaning of the order words: first, next, finally.

2. Preassessment/Formative Assessment Notes:
Based on Lexile score reading-readiness data, students represent three readiness groups:

- students with scores in the 100s
- students with scores in the 200s
- students with scores in the 400s

We have worked with story maps before, but most students need more time, instruction, and practice creating them independently.

3. Hook:
Show the students a cocoon and an eggshell and ask them to discuss what comes out of each. Discuss how each "container" is alike and different. Tell students that the book today is a story about a caterpillar's life and that the cocoon is one of the stages in its life.

4. Content Delivery (WHAT they will learn)

X same resources

___ different resources (e.g., leveled)*

___ same goal for all

___ advanced goal for some*

___ modified goal for some*

Notes:
- *Students read* The Hungry Caterpillar *(Lexile 460) from their textbook with teacher guidance using "thinking aloud" strategies.*
- *Tell them to listen for the beginning, middle, and end of the story and to watch for the cocoon.*
- *NOTE: Blake will identify only first and last event.*

5. Direct Instruction/Modeling
(HOW they will learn it)

X single strategy that engages all

___ more than one learning preference (based on Multiple Intelligences)*

___ more than one modality (e.g., auditory, visual, kinesthetic)*

Notes:
- *Ask questions related to the story using order words:* first, next, finally. *Prompt the students for the meaning of the order words. Show order words printed on cards.*
- *Draw a story map of* The Itsy Bitsy Spider *using order words and illustrating beginning, middle and end.*
- *Explain how story maps help us understand what we read.*

6. Application Activities
(HOW they will learn it)

X same for all

___ tier by learning preference (based on Multiple Intelligences)*

___ tier by readiness*

___ tier by challenge/complexity*

CONTINUED ➡

FIGURE 37 CONTINUED

Notes:
- *Ask students to assist in creating a story map for* The Hungry Caterpillar. *Prompt them to use order words.*
- *Ask for students to volunteer other stories to illustrate as a group.*

7. Independent Application (How they will DEMONSTRATE their learning)

_X_ individual work
_X_ with a partner
___ in a small group (based on Multiple Intelligences)*
_X_ tier by readiness*
___ tier by challenge/ complexity*
___ student choice based on interest*

Notes:
- *Assign partners to Eric Carle book clubs based on Lexile scores:* The Busy Spider *(Lexile 130),* The Very Clumsy Click Beetle *(Lexile 210),* The Mixed-Up Chameleon *(Lexile 450). Partners read the book, individually draw story maps showing beginning, middle, and end, and label the sections with the correct order word:* first, next, finally.
- *Partner Blake with his autism aide to work on modified goal.*
- *Sit* Busy Spider *group with me for coaching.*

8. Closure: Activity/Question and Answer/Sharing of Products/Exit Slip/Review/ Critical Reflection/Question Posing

Notes:
- *Buddy up students with someone who read a different book and share story maps.*
- *Ask students to repeat the order words as they show their work.*
- *Select some students to share with the whole class.*

9. What next?

Formative Assessment Notes:
Annie, Terrill, Blake, and Tasha continue to struggle with sequence. Have them use the cut-apart comic strips for practice in sequencing during workstations tomorrow.

FIGURE 38

Differentiated Learning Plan: Example #2

MATH: GEOMETRY
ELEMENTARY

* indicates a strategy for differentiation

1. Standards/KUDo's:
Sort and compare two-dimensional objects according to their geometric attributes.

Recognize and create patterns using concrete objects and pictures.

2. Preassessment/Formative Assessment Notes:
Students have done basic patterning with concrete objects. Based on observation as well as paper/pencil tasks, some students are still working on understanding attributes of two-dimensional objects.

3. Hook:
Present riddles related to 2-D shapes and have the students guess the "mystery shape." (e.g., "I have no corners. I have no sides. What shape am I?")

4. Content Delivery (WHAT they will learn)

_X_ same resources

___ different resources (e.g., leveled)*

_X_ same goal for all

___ advanced goal for some*

___ modified goal for some*

Notes:
- *Review the concept of patterning by recalling past experiences.*
- *Demonstrate repeating shape patterns through the use of 2-D shape blocks.*
- *Present simple patterns of shapes (e.g., ABC) by having groups of students hold large cards with pictures of 2-D objects.*
- *Students "read" the patterns along with me.*

5. Direct Instruction/Modeling
(HOW they will learn it)

_X_ single strategy that engages all

___ more than one learning preference (based on Multiple Intelligences)*

_X_ more than one modality (e.g., auditory, visual, kinesthetic)*

Notes:
- *Put students in small groups.*
- *Have groups create repeating patterns of 2-D shapes using shape cards.*
- *Student groups present their patterns to the class, and class "reads" the pattern.*

6. Application Activities
(HOW they will learn it)

___ same for all

___ tier by learning preference (based on Multiple Intelligences)*

_X_ tier by readiness*

_X_ tier by challenge/complexity*

CONTINUED ➡

FIGURE 38 CONTINUED

Notes:
Based on observation of the first activities and readiness related to shape attributes, divide students into two instructional groups:

Group 1: Using shape blocks, students create repeating patterns of 2-D shapes.

Group 2: I introduce and model repeating patterns of combinations of 2-D shapes (e.g., AABCC). Students create their own patterns using shape blocks.

7. Independent Application (How they will DEMONSTRATE their learning)

___ individual work	_X_ tier by readiness*
___ with a partner	___ tier by challenge/ complexity*
_X_ in a small group (based on Multiple Intelligences)*	___ student choice based on interest*

Notes:
Students create pattern sequences by drawing 2-D shapes using templates.

Group 1: Students create repeating patterns of 2-D shapes (e.g., ABC).

Group 2: Students create repeating patterns of combinations of 2-D shapes (e.g., AABCC).

8. Closure: Activity/Question and Answer/Sharing of Products/Exit Slip/Review/ Critical Reflection/Question Posing

Notes:
- *Students exchange patterns with a "buddy" from the same instructional group and continue the presented patterns using shape blocks.*
- *I review patterning by presenting a set of patterns on shape cards that students are to complete as a group.*
- *Students name each shape as they "read" the pattern.*

9. What next?

Formative Assessment Notes:
- *Set aside time to spend with Mai and Rayjaun to reinforce attributes of 2-D objects.*
- *Review of patterns developed with templates showed Erin, Will, Mai, and Jimmy need reinforcement of ABC patterns.*

FIGURE 39

Differentiated Learning Plan: Example #3

LIFE SCIENCE: DESERT ECOSYSTEM
MIDDLE SCHOOL

* indicates a strategy for differentiation

1. Standards/KUDo's:
Identify populations that live together in an ecosystem and the factors with which they interact.

2. Preassessment/Formative Assessment Notes:
Use an individual graphic organizer on the desert ecosystem's plants, animals, and climate/geography as a preassessment.

3. Hook:
Students assist me in constructing an interrelationship web. Tell them: "All organisms within an ecosystem interact with each other in either major or minor ways. Think back to our unit on the rainforest ecosystem and help me map out some of the connections you remember."

4. Content Delivery (WHAT they will learn)

___ same resources
_X_ different resources (e.g., leveled)*

_X_ same goal for all
___ advanced goal for some*
___ modified goal for some*

Notes:
Assign students bookmarked Web sites on deserts, based on their prior knowledge about the ecosystem evidenced in the preassessment graphic organizer. Some students are assigned to sites with introductory information, others to sites with more in-depth or sophisticated information.

5. Direct Instruction/Modeling
(HOW they will learn it)

___ single strategy that engages all
_X_ more than one learning preference (based on Multiple Intelligences)*
___ more than one modality (e.g., auditory, visual, kinesthetic)*

Notes:
Students may choose to take notes on the information from their Web site on interrelationships of desert plants and animals, using either a double-entry journal (Verbal/linguistic learning preference) or a graphic organizer (Visual/spatial).

6. Application Activities
(HOW they will learn it)

_X_ same for all
___ tier by learning preference (based on Multiple Intelligences)*
___ tier by readiness*
___ tier by challenge/complexity*

CONTINUED ➡

FIGURE 39 CONTINUED

Notes:
- *Create groups of students who are using different resources so they can "jigsaw" their information.*
- *Groups create an interrelationship web showing the connections between various desert plants and animals.*
- *Groups present the webs to the class.*

7. Independent Application (How they will DEMONSTRATE their learning)

_X_ individual work
___ with a partner
___ in a small group (based on Multiple Intelligences)*
___ tier by readiness*
___ tier by challenge/complexity*
_X_ student choice based on interest*

Notes:
- *Students choose an animal or plant from their interrelationship web and imagine that it disappears.*
- *Students illustrate the effects on the ecosystem by writing (Verbal/linguistic learning preference) an article or creating a chart or diagram (Logical/mathematical) with captions.*

8. Closure: Activity/Question and Answer/Sharing of Products/Exit Slip/Review/Critical Reflection/Question Posing

Notes:
Use exit slips that ask:
- *What are three new ideas or facts you learned about the desert ecosystem?*
- *What additional questions would you like us to explore about this ecosystem?*

9. What next?

Formative Assessment Notes:
Aiden and Daneesha are clearly fascinated with this topic! Discuss compacting and doing more in-depth "replacement" work with them.

FIGURE 40

Differentiated Learning Plan: Example #4

SOCIAL STUDIES: MEDIA LITERACY
HIGH SCHOOL

* indicates a strategy for differentiation

1. Standards/KUDo's:

Critically analyze information found in electronic and print media.

Make informed judgments about messages promoted in media such as those in film, television, radio, online, and print media.

2. Preassessment/Formative Assessment Notes:

- *Students have identified differences in how a single story is presented in three different media: local newspaper, national newspaper, and television newscast.*
- *Students vary in reading levels and in their ability to comprehend nonfiction articles.*

3. Hook:

Show a photograph of a presidential candidate from his/her campaign organization. Ask students for their impressions. Ask students to identify the message that the campaign has chosen to send through this photograph.

OR

Show an editorial cartoon featuring the same candidate. Ask: "What message has been chosen to send to the public with this cartoon?"

4. Content Delivery (WHAT they will learn)

___ same resources

_X_ different resources (e.g., leveled)*

___ same goal for all

_X_ advanced goal for some*

___ modified goal for some*

Notes:

- *Students read different news articles based on reading-readiness levels.*
- *All articles are on the same topic, but have different perspectives.*
- *Basic goal: Identify the message conveyed by the words and images.*
- *Advanced goal: Determine the target audience, and their experiences and prejudices.*

5. Direct Instruction/Modeling
(HOW they will learn it)

___ single strategy that engages all

_X_ more than one learning preference (based on Multiple Intelligences)*

_X_ more than one modality (e.g., auditory, visual, kinesthetic)*

Notes:

Present a media clip, a Web page, and a newspaper article on the same topic.

CONTINUED ➡

FIGURE 40 CONTINUED

6. Application Activities
(HOW they will learn it)

___ same for all

___ tier by learning preference (based on Multiple Intelligences)*

___ tier by readiness*

_X_ tier by challenge/complexity*

Notes:
- *Compare/contrast a commercial network, cable station, and public television report on the same topic. In what ways are the messages alike and different? Why?*
- *Basic tier: Focus on the facts presented.*
- *Advanced tier: Focus on the facts, the message's purpose, and what the message wants an audience to conclude.*

7. Independent Application (How they will DEMONSTRATE their learning)

___ individual work

___ with a partner

___ in a small group (based on Multiple Intelligences)*

_X_ tier by readiness*

_X_ tier by challenge/complexity*

_X_ student choice based on interest*

Notes:
- *Students choose to present their conclusions in an essay, poster, or diagram or chart, based on learning preference.*
- *Basic tier: Identify the intended message, purpose, and audience for the report.*
- *Advanced tier: Identify another point of view or perspective on the report.*

8. Closure: Activity/Question and Answer/Sharing of Products/Exit Slip/Review/Critical Reflection/Question Posing

Notes:
- *Students partner with someone who has completed a different task and discuss their results.*
- *Class discussion summary. Ask: "What techniques do media use to influence our viewpoints or perspectives on an issue?" "What 'do's' can we note that would help people critically analyze what they see or hear in the media?"*

9. What next?

Formative Assessment Notes:
Eva needs much more support in stepping through task. Consider a more guided approach for her when tasks become complex.

CHAPTER 5 Critical Element: MOTIVATING LEARNING THROUGH CHOICE OPPORTUNITIES

In many classrooms, the first step in differentiation is the use of student choice.

Indeed, choice opens up opportunities and provides students with varied experiences.[1] Curriculum expert Robert Marzano suggests that students' intrinsic motivation is linked to their interests. Students are simply more motivated to do the work if they are able to act on their interests through choice. But for choice to truly reflect differentiated instruction, teachers must be both analytical and planful in the design of choice experiences. Choice is not haphazard, random, or uncontrolled. In a differentiated classroom, choice is "controlled choice." You determine when student choice may occur, you design the activities students may choose from, and you control which choices students may make.

Choice provides students the opportunity and power to act on their interests; and the key to motivation is interest. Not only does choice motivate students to learn but also to actively engage in their learning. Choice "hooks" students into learning and doing the work. Whether your students are kindergartners or high school seniors, they want power. Choice is a way to enable students to gain a real measure of control over their learning.

Choice opportunities are also an easy and time-saving strategy for designing and facilitating multiple tasks in your classroom. Multiple activities are planned ahead, therefore, saving you some day-to-day planning time. Another time-saver is to develop "generic" choice opportunities, for example, a choice board presenting spelling activities that can be used repeatedly with each new list of words.

> Nothing should be offered as a choice unless *all* students have previously worked with the process or product.

Creating choice boards with broad themes such as historical events or genres of literature enable you to reuse choice boards, thus decreasing your planning time.

In designing choice opportunities, the most critical rule to follow is: Nothing should be offered as a choice unless *all* students have previously worked with the process or product. If a choice is offered to students to create a Web page, a tri-fold display board, or an artifact box to convey family history, and the students have not been introduced to these products previously, you have a management problem. Given their lack of experience with these products, you would need to teach each small group how to do the project of their choice. Why do that to yourself? Teach your whole class how to conduct a process or create a particular product *before* you use it as a choice option. This potentially

1 Robert J. Marzano, *The Art and Science of Teaching* (Alexandria, VA: Association for Supervision and Curriculum Development, 2007).

means that at the beginning of a school year you offer fewer choices than at the end of the year, when you have introduced your students to many processes and products.

> Choice boards are differentiated *only* if they are designed with learning differences in mind.

Offering Choices in Content, Process, and Products

Students may be offered choice in content, process, or products. Choice in content reflects opportunities for students to select *what* they might learn. While guided by learning goals or academic standards, you can offer students opportunities to act on their interests or go into greater depth on particular topics. At its simplest level, students might choose from a list of amphibians and engage in more in-depth research on the animal. At more sophisticated levels, you might assemble a collection of historical fiction books related to a social studies topic that represent a variety of reading-readiness levels (based on, for example, Lexile scores). Then, you organize the books into collections by readiness levels and ask students to choose any book of interest to them from specific collections of books based on their reading-readiness levels. In another example, students may be working on the same learning goal related to writing summaries, but the materials to summarize may be open to controlled student choice. You provide reading materials representing a variety of topics reflecting your students' interests. Choice in content enables students to act on their interests and motivates them to complete the assignment.

When you enable students to choose *how* they learn, you are using choice in process. This kind of choice can be implemented as easily as telling students that they may read their science textbook pages alone, with a buddy, by listening to an audio recording of the textbook reading, or in a small group with your guidance. Following the reading choices, all students complete a graphic organizer to record their facts. Another example of choice in process may involve students exploring their family's immigrant history. You could allow your students to choose to either do print or online research or to interview family "historians" to gather information. In each of these examples, the students have choice in how they will learn about something.

Students may also engage in choice of products. This kind of choice enables students to choose how they will *demonstrate* what they have learned. It is important with this kind of choice that you represent a variety of learning preferences based on Multiple Intelligences. For example, students creating an invention to solve a household problem may construct a working or nonworking model (Bodily/kinesthetic learning preference) or create a labeled diagram (Visual/spatial learning preference). Allowing students to choose the way they demonstrate their learning enables them to capitalize on their strengths.

Formats for Choice Opportunities

There are a variety of formats teachers use to offer choices to their students. Choice boards, tic-tac-toe boards, RAFTS, two-by-two's, and show-and-tell boards are examples of formats teachers use to present choices to their students in motivating and manageable ways. Each is described in the following sections.

CHOICE BOARDS

Choice boards are collections of curricular problems, questions, assignments, projects, or activities from which students may choose. However, choice boards are differentiated *only* if they are designed with learning differences in mind. A random collection of tasks tossed on a choice board does not represent differentiated learning experiences for students. Creating a differentiated choice board requires reflection and planning. Page 73 provides a checklist to consider when designing differentiated choice boards.

Checklist of Six Essential Features of Differentiated Choice Boards

1. ____ Presents activities clearly focused on learning goals or academic standards

2. ____ Presents activities involving a process or product that all students have previously experienced

3. ____ Presents activities reflecting multiple learning preferences

4. ____ Organizes tasks in ways that control choices to benefit students

5. ____ Offers engaging, interesting choices for all students

6. ____ Represents a variety of tasks purposefully differentiated by learning preference, readiness, and challenge and/or complexity (one board for all students)

or

____ Represents tasks specifically differentiated and prescribed to respond to the needs of a particular group of learners (several boards, each assigned to a group based on learning needs)

TIC-TAC-TOE BOARDS

A tic-tac-toe board is a form of choice board that provides students with nine choices of activities, assignments, projects, or questions arranged on a tic-tac-toe board, and requires them to choose three in a row to complete. Key considerations in creating differentiated tic-tac-toe boards are:

- to design tasks that are clearly focused on student learning goals
- to design tasks that represent different learning preferences, readiness needs, or levels of challenge or complexity
- to arrange the activities on the board so that you control the students' choices
- to provide criteria checklists or rubrics for each task that is being used as assessment rather than practice

The following tic-tac-toe board examples represent fiction and nonfiction book projects. As more and more teachers use leveled reading resources, the task of coming up with book projects for each possible book being read in your classroom can be overwhelming! These "generic" boards can be used regardless of the book being read by the student. Students do one project per book. Thus, each tic-tac-toe board represents projects for three different books and eliminates the need to plan activities for each possible book that students may read.

In **Figure 41**, projects are arranged so that any way the student completes the tic-tac-toe requires that they do at least one advanced activity. Projects labeled with an "A" are advanced or complex activities written at the analysis, evaluation, or synthesis levels of Bloom's Taxonomy. Those labeled "B" are more basic activities that are written at the application level of Bloom's Taxonomy. Plan to include a variety of activities so that more than one learning preference is represented. Remember, you want the choices to be interesting and engaging for the students to motivate them to do the work. *Important:* Be sure not to label the activities "A" or "B" on your students' boards. The advanced and basic labels on these examples are merely there so you can see the pattern of choices being offered.

In contrast, **Figure 42** establishes the rule that each student's tic-tac-toe route must cross through

FIGURE 41

Nonfiction Book Tic-Tac-Toe

ENGLISH/LANGUAGE ARTS
ELEMENTARY

Create a crossword puzzle of vocabulary words from the book. (B)	Write a newspaper article using facts from the book. (B)	Create a board game using the facts from the book. (A)
Create an informational brochure with the facts from the book. (A)	Create a topic web for the facts from the book. (B)	Create a PowerPoint presentation of at least four slides using facts from the book. (A)
Construct a diagram, model, or chart of facts from the book. (B)	Script and role-play a news report with the facts from the book. (A)	Create a rap, poem, or song with the facts from the book. (A)

Key: A = advanced or complex activities written at the analysis, evaluation, or synthesis levels of Bloom's Taxonomy; B = basic activities written at the application level

the center. Thus, all students complete the activity posted in the center square. There are times when you want all students to complete an assignment. Whenever that is the case, use this "center" rule. Notice also that the activities along each diagonal route are all advanced. If you have some students who would benefit from more encouragement to take on challenges, tell them individually that their best choices are along the diagonals and to select from those activities. This way you are steering your advanced learners toward making the best choices based on their needs. Keep in mind that any choice made by a student with an IEP, a 504 plan, or who is engaged in interventions related to RTI, would need modifications as appropriate to the needs of the student.

FIGURE 42

Fiction Book Tic-Tac-Toe

ENGLISH/LANGUAGE ARTS
ELEMENTARY, MIDDLE SCHOOL

Create a new ending, an epilogue, or sequel to the story. (A)	Compose a letter to a character, the author, or between two characters. (A)	Write and dramatize a commercial promoting the book. (A)
Illustrate a poster about the book. (B)	Construct a story map or story board of events. (ALL)	Create a journal or diary entry for one of the characters. (A)
Compare/contrast two characters in the book using a chart. (A)	Write a character sketch for one of the characters. (B)	Create a conversation between two characters in the book. (A)

Key: A = advanced or complex activities written at the analysis, evaluation, or synthesis levels of Bloom's Taxonomy; B = basic activities written at the application level; ALL = all students must complete activity

FIGURE 43

Math Review Tic-Tac-Toe

MATH
HIGH SCHOOL

Solve three problems using both analytical and graphing methods. (B)	Create a new way of demonstrating your understanding of the concepts and ideas in the chapter. (A)	Define the chapter's vocabulary words using sketches or diagrams. (B)
Solve two of the challenge problems in your textbook. (A)	Take the end-of-chapter test. (ALL)	Complete the fourth problem in each section of the chapter review. (A)
Create three word problems using the concepts in the chapter. (A)	Solve one even-numbered application problem from each section of the chapter. (B)	Describe four ways that the concepts or ideas in this chapter are used in the real world. (A)

Key: A = advanced or complex activities written at the analysis, evaluation, or synthesis levels of Bloom's Taxonomy; B = basic activities written at the application level; ALL = all students must complete activity

FIGURE 44

Spelling Tic-Tac-Toe

ENGLISH/LANGUAGE ARTS
ELEMENTARY

Directions: Choose the eight spelling words from this week's list that are the most difficult for you. Then, select three spelling activities in a row from the tic-tac-toe board.

Using the first letter of your words, create an alliterative sentence for each. (A)	Find a way to classify your words. Label each group. (B)	Write and illustrate a comic strip using all of your words. (A)
Write a synonym, an antonym, or a rhyming word for each of your words. (B)	Write four words related in some way to each of your words. (A)	Draw a clue for the meaning of each of your words. (B)
Write a dialogue between two or three fictional characters using all of your words. (A)	Create word pyramids for each of your words. For example: S Sn Sna Snak Snake (B)	Write a poem, rap, or rhyme using all of your words. (A)

Note: The diagonals on this tic-tac-toe board offer more challenging activities to students.

Key: A = advanced or complex activities written at the analysis, evaluation, or synthesis levels of Bloom's Taxonomy; B = basic activities written at the application level

FIGURE 45

Mythology Questions Tic-Tac-Toe

ENGLISH/LANGUAGE ARTS
MIDDLE SCHOOL

Who are the main characters in this myth? (K/C)	What are the problem and the solution presented in the myth? (AP)	What are the positive and negative characteristics of one of the characters? (AN)
How would the myth be different if it took place today? (AN/EV)	What life lesson can you learn from this myth? (ALL)	What elements of mythology are used in this story? Give specific examples. (AP)
Who do you think is the most important character? Why? (AN/EV)	How are two of the characters alike and different? (AN)	What might be a new way to solve the problem in the myth? (AN/EV/SY)

Bloom's Taxonomy Key: K = knowledge, C = comprehension, AP = application, AN = analysis, EV = evaluation, SY = synthesis

Figure 43 shows the use of activities from a student's math text utilized in a tic-tac-toe board. Student textbooks and teacher's guides frequently have resources that, while inappropriate for use with all students, could be used with some students. Choice boards give you an opportunity to use these activities appropriately with those students who can most benefit from them. The purpose of the activities on the tic-tac-toe board in Figure 43 is to provide a review of the key concepts in the chapter prior to the end-of-chapter test; it is test-preparation.

Figure 44 shows the use of tic-tac-toe boards with weekly spelling activities. Teachers report that once they changed from everyone doing the same spelling assignment each day to using choice, their students' motivation soared! Although the same or similar spelling assignments were used as those required previously of everyone, teachers report that their students enjoy the power of choice in what to do and when to do it. Some teachers put each spelling assignment on a card with a fabric fastener strip on the back and then create a tic-tac-toe on a bulletin board with fabric fastener strips in each box. The board can then be easily modified by replacing or rearranging assignment cards.

Tic-tac-toe boards can present questions to students as in **Figure 45**. The questions on the board are labeled here according to Bloom's Taxonomy levels and organized to ensure that all students are answering at least one high-level question. (Again, you would *not* write these labels on the actual board you present to students.) A question board could be used before a discussion, so all students come prepared to answer at least three questions. This example is also a "center" board, where all students respond to the question in the center box that the teacher has deemed important for all to answer.

FIGURE 46

Learning Preference Tic-Tac-Toe Template

LM Diagram Flow Chart Graphic Organizer	**VS** Cartoon Comic Strip Storyboard	**LM** Compare/ Contrast Chart Diagram
M Song Rap Jingle Slogan	**VL** Letter Article Essay	**BK** Script and Perform Skit Role Play
VS Poster	**N** Display Collection Diorama	**VS** Sketch Illustration

Multiple Intelligences Key:
LM = Logical/mathematical, VS = Visual/spatial, VL = Verbal/linguistic, BK = Bodily/kinesthetic, N = Naturalist, M = Musical

FIGURE 47

Basic Order of Operations Choice Board

MATH
ELEMENTARY/MIDDLE SCHOOL

9 – (9 – 8) =	(8 x 8) x 2 =	(4 x 8) + 10 =
4 x (1 – 4) =	9 x (2 – 2) =	8 – (4 – 3) =
(8 x 8) – 8 =	(4 x 5) + 4 =	(8 + 10) – 3 =

FIGURE 48

Advanced Order of Operations Choice Board

MATH
ELEMENTARY/MIDDLE SCHOOL

1 – (7 x 5) – 4 =	10 x (6 – 6) + 10 =	(4 + 4 – 1) – 7 =
(5 – 7) – (5 x 5) =	(4 + 5 + 6) =	(4 x 6) + (4 – 5) =
(5 x 9 + 2) x 4 =	(5 – 10) x (8 x 8) =	(1 + 2) x (3 – 2) =

Tic-tac-toe boards can also be organized around the learning preferences of Multiple Intelligences. **Figure 46** provides a template you can use to design and arrange activities to control the choices of your students. Simply fill in content using the products reflecting each learning preference. The arrangement of products on the board ensures that your students engage in more than one learning preference. For example, students in a health class who choose the LM-VL-VS diagonal path could complete a *graphic organizer* using material in their textbook, *write a letter* for the school newspaper regarding a teen health risk, and *illustrate a list* of tips for teen wellness. **Note:** The Intrapersonal and Interpersonal Multiple Intelligences are not involved in this activity.

USING MULTIPLE VERSIONS OF CHOICE BOARDS

You can further differentiate choice boards by creating more than one version of the board, enabling you to match students more specifically to the tasks. In this way, you can "prescribe" particular boards to particular students based on their current learning needs. Keep in mind that *all* students deserve challenging, engaging activities. If you use multiple-choice boards, take care to design the tasks so that students view all assignments as equally active, engaging, and interesting.

If your purpose is to respond to readiness differences, you may want to consider putting application, reteaching, or reinforcement tasks on one board, and more challenging or complex tasks on the other. Then, assign students to the board most appropriate for their immediate learning needs. **Figures 47 and 48** show examples of this type of choice board differentiation.

Alternately, you could create one board that reflects *both* basic and advanced/complex tasks, questions, and projects, and a second version of the board offering *only* advanced/complex tasks. Assign students who need more of a challenge to the board containing only challenging or complex tasks.

FIGURE 49

Solar System Tic-Tac-Toe: Basic Version

SCIENCE
ELEMENTARY

Draw and label a diagram of the solar system. LM, VS (B)	Use words and pictures to create a topic web of facts about the sun, moon, and planets. LM, VS (B)	Create a Venn diagram to compare two planets, or the sun and the moon. LM (A)
Create an illustrated timeline showing the phases of the moon. LM, VS (B)	Illustrate a new constellation and write an original myth that explains its origin. VL, VS (A)	Create a guide to the stars, including important constellations and their mythical stories. VL (B)
Create an illustrated flipbook that includes riddles about a particular planet or object in space, and a final page with the mystery planet or object revealed. VS, VL (A)	Create a picture dictionary for your solar system vocabulary words. VS, VL (B)	Plan a demonstration to show the characteristics of the seasons and day and night, explaining how and when they happen. BK, N (B)

Multiple Intelligences Key: LM = Logical/mathematical, VS = Visual/spatial, VL = Verbal/linguistic, BK = Bodily/kinesthetic, N = Naturalist, M = Musical

Assign all other students to the version that offers a variety of challenge and complexity levels.

Figures 49 and 50 show examples of two versions of tic-tac-toe boards on the solar system. Figure 49 is assigned to students who need reinforcement of the concepts of the unit. It includes both basic (B) and advanced (A) activities. Figure 50 is assigned to students who need more complex or challenging activities, as they already have a good understanding of the concepts. All activities on this board are designed at an advanced level (A). Tasks on both boards are also balanced by learning preference. When students choose three in a row, they automatically engage in more than one learning preference.

TWO-BY-TWO BOARDS

A two-by-two board is another variety of choice board that offers two rows with two activities each, for a grid of four choice opportunities. Although tic-tac-toe boards are fun to use with students, sometimes you just won't be able to come up with nine activities that are significant and focused enough to work on learning goals. Or perhaps you can't take the amount of time needed for students to do three activities each. When using a two-by-two board, you determine how many of the four possible assignments, problems, or activities students are required to complete. Two-by-two boards are differentiated in the same ways as other choice boards (by learning preference, readiness, challenge/complexity), and can also be used in a single version for all students or in multiple versions for different groups of learners.

Figure 51 shows examples of two versions of a two-by-two board. Students are assigned the version that provides the best instructional match for them. One box on each board is designated a "must do" for all, and then students choose one of the remaining

FIGURE 50

Solar System Tic-Tac-Toe: Advanced Version

SCIENCE
ELEMENTARY

Imagine that you are an astronaut in the International Space Station. Write three days of journal entries discussing what you see, do, think, and feel about your experience. Include facts about space in your entries. VL (A)	Develop at least two new ways to categorize the planets. Label your categories and diagram your results. LM (A)	What planet or space object do you most resemble? What characteristics do you share? Write a portrait of yourself beginning, "Just like (name of planet or object), I . . . " Use accurate characteristics of the planet or object in your portrait. VL (A)
In what ways might we use the moon and its resources to benefit Earth? Write a letter to NASA, using facts about the moon to support your ideas. VL (A)	Illustrate a new constellation and write an original myth that explains its origin. VS, VL (A)	Create a Venn diagram to compare two planets, or the sun and the moon. LM (A)
Create an illustrated flipbook that includes riddles about a planet or object in space and a final page with the mystery planet or object revealed. VS, VL (A))	Use our solar system vocabulary words to create a script for an ad promoting space exploration. VL (A)	Plan a demonstration that explains the effects on Earth if rotation and revolution ceased to exist. BK, N (A))

Multiple Intelligences Key: LM = Logical/mathematical, VS = Visual/spatial, VL = Verbal/linguistic, BK = Bodily/kinesthetic, N = Naturalist, M = Musical

three assignments to complete. Thus, each student completes a total of two assignments. Note that the advanced level board provides the most challenging or complex tasks. It should be assigned to students who need the greatest "stretch" in their learning.

Figure 52 shows a world language two-by-two board offering two activities for each concept the teacher wants to address. Students choose one task for sports and one for clothing. The design of each task pair offers one basic activity and one activity that is more advanced in its use of the world language. In the sports tasks, number two is the more advanced choice, while in the pair of clothing tasks, number one is the more advanced. You can offer all students a choice of all four tasks, or you can create one board with only the advanced tasks and

FIGURE 51

Informational Text Two-by-Two Board

ENGLISH/LANGUAGE ARTS
ELEMENTARY
Basic Level

1. Create a topic web with key facts from your textbook.	2. Construct a crossword puzzle that includes at least four key facts from your textbook.
3. Draw a sketch, diagram, or comic strip to present at least four key facts from your textbook.	4. Write a text message to a friend that tells about at least four key facts from your textbook.

Advanced Level

1. Create a topic web with key facts from your textbook.	2. Create a poem, jingle, or rhyme to help you remember at least four key facts from your textbook.
3. Sketch a design for the CNN Web page highlighting key ideas from your textbook. Include illustrations, charts, or graphs on the topic.	4. Consider what you know about this topic that was not included in your reading. Write at least two paragraphs sharing this information.

FIGURE 52

Sports and Clothing Two-by-Two Board

WORLD LANGUAGE
ELEMENTARY/ MIDDLE SCHOOL

Sports	1. Make a memory game of vocabulary words related to sports.	2. Use sports vocabulary words to create a sports news article or news broadcast.
Clothing	1. Script and role-play a scenario with a teenager and his or her mom disagreeing in a store about a clothing purchase.	2. Write a dress code for our school outlining what is and is not acceptable.

another with only the basic tasks, and then match the appropriate board with each student based on language development.

SHOW-AND-TELL BOARDS

A show-and-tell board[2] is a third type of choice board that provides students with opportunities to create their own tasks focused on a learning goal. All students work on the same goal; however, the tasks they engage in differ based on their choices of project elements. The top row of the board signifies *show:* how will the students show what they have learned? The bottom row signifies *tell:* how will the students tell what they have learned?

Figure 53 on technical writing engages all students in writing a set of directions for a household task or school activity. However, what each student will do is determined by the students' choices on the show-and-tell board. Each element in the top row should be able to match with an element in the bottom row to create the maximum number of project possibilities. If a student chose "how-to brochure" from the top row, it could be paired in the following ways with elements from the bottom row:

2 Carol Ann Tomlinson, *Fulfilling the Promise of the Differentiated Classroom: Strategies and Tools for Responsive Teaching* (Alexandria, VA: Association for Supervision and Curriculum Development, 2003).

FIGURE 53

Technical Writing Show-and-Tell Board

ENGLISH/LANGUAGE ARTS
MIDDLE SCHOOL

Task: Write a set of directions for a household task or school activity.

Show	Illustrations	Diagram or flow chart	How-to brochure
Tell	Use topic headings and paragraphs	Use detailed numbered or bulleted steps	Write detailed sentences

The student will create a how-to brochure and

- use topic headings and paragraphs to provide the directions.
- use detailed numbered or bulleted steps to provide the directions.
- write detailed sentences to provide the directions.

Figure 54 provides an example of a history show-and-tell board. Using the newspaper article as the show, the following tasks could be designed by the students:

The student will create a newspaper article and

- use charts and graphs to convey significant information about the event.
- present a timeline of incidents related to the event.
- use photographs to convey significant information concerning the event.

When you design a show-and-tell board, you do not need to have any specific number of items in each row. The key is creating the largest number of possibilities by enabling each element in the top row to work with each element in the bottom.

FIGURE 54

Civil Rights Movement Show-and-Tell Board

AMERICAN HISTORY
MIDDLE SCHOOL

Task: Write a set of directions for a household task or school activity.

Show	Newspaper article	Video news interview	Role play
Tell	Charts and graphs	Timeline or chronicle of incidents related to the event	Illustrations, photographs, graphics, or artifacts

Remember to review your choice boards!
Before employing any type of choice board with your students, be sure to use the "Checklist of Six Essential Features of Differentiated Choice Boards" (page 73) to ensure the design reflects critical characteristics of relevance, rigor, and variety. Refer to the checklist often as you design new boards or evaluate existing boards for use in your classroom.

RAFTS

RAFT charts were first developed by language arts teachers and used as writing prompts.

R = **R**ole
A = **A**udience
F = **F**ormat for a task
T = **T**opic of the activity

On a RAFT, students read across each row and choose one of the tasks to complete. **Figure 55** shows an example of a RAFT for fractions. **Figure 56** shows a RAFT for history.

Design Tips for a RAFT

1. Identify the KUDo's for the tasks. What will the students know, understand, and be able to do as a result of their choices?
2. Start with the topic column. What should the task be about? What content or topics should receive focus because of their importance in the curriculum unit?
3. Next, consider the role and the audience columns. Who would be engaged in some sort of communication about the topic?
4. Finally, consider possible formats for communication. Use the Multiple Intelligences to get ideas so the formats reflect a variety of learning preferences. Also consider what format might work best with the role and audience.
5. Read the completed task for clarity. Consider whether the task will be engaging and interesting to the students.
6. Provide a blank row on the table for students to design their own tasks once they are accustomed to the process. Have them check in with you before they begin their work on the task.

FIGURE 55

Fractions RAFT

MATH
ELEMENTARY

ROLE	AUDIENCE	FORMAT	TOPIC
Fraction	Whole number	Reunion invitation	How we're related
Mixed number	Improper fraction	Persuasive letter	Why it should convert to a mixed number
Equivalent fraction	Equivalent fraction	Song or rap	How we can become equal
Numerator	Denominator	Poster	How we're alike and different

The tasks read like this:

Basic template: "I am a [ROLE] talking to a [AUDIENCE]. I am creating a [FORMAT] to explain [TOPIC].

1. "I am a **fraction** talking to a **whole number**. I am creating a **reunion invitation** to explain **how we're related**."
2. "I am a **mixed number** talking to an **improper fraction**. I am creating a **persuasive letter** to explain **why it should convert to a mixed number**."
3. "I am an **equivalent fraction** talking to another **equivalent fraction**. I am creating a **song or rap** to explain **how we can become equal**."
4. "I am a **numerator** talking to a **denominator**. I am creating a **poster** to explain **how we're alike and different**."

FIGURE 56

American History RAFT

SOCIAL STUDIES ELEMENTARY

ROLE	AUDIENCE	FORMAT	TOPIC
King George	Redcoats	Wanted poster	Capture of Washington, Jefferson, and Franklin
The Colonists	King George	Advice column	How to make us happy
Benedict Arnold	Future Americans	Letter from exile	Why I did what I did
Write Your Own Idea Here!			

Using Choice Opportunities with Primary Students

Primary students may not be able to read choices on their own, but they can identify choices accompanied with picture icons. **Figure 57** offers a choice to primary students regarding how they want to work (alone or with a partner) and how they want to share what they have learned. The choices are: making an audio recording, writing a report, doing a puppet show, making a booklet, painting a picture, or doing a presentation in front of the class. **Figure 58** offers primary students a choice of book projects reflecting a variety of learning preferences and challenge levels.

FIGURE 57

Primary Choice Board

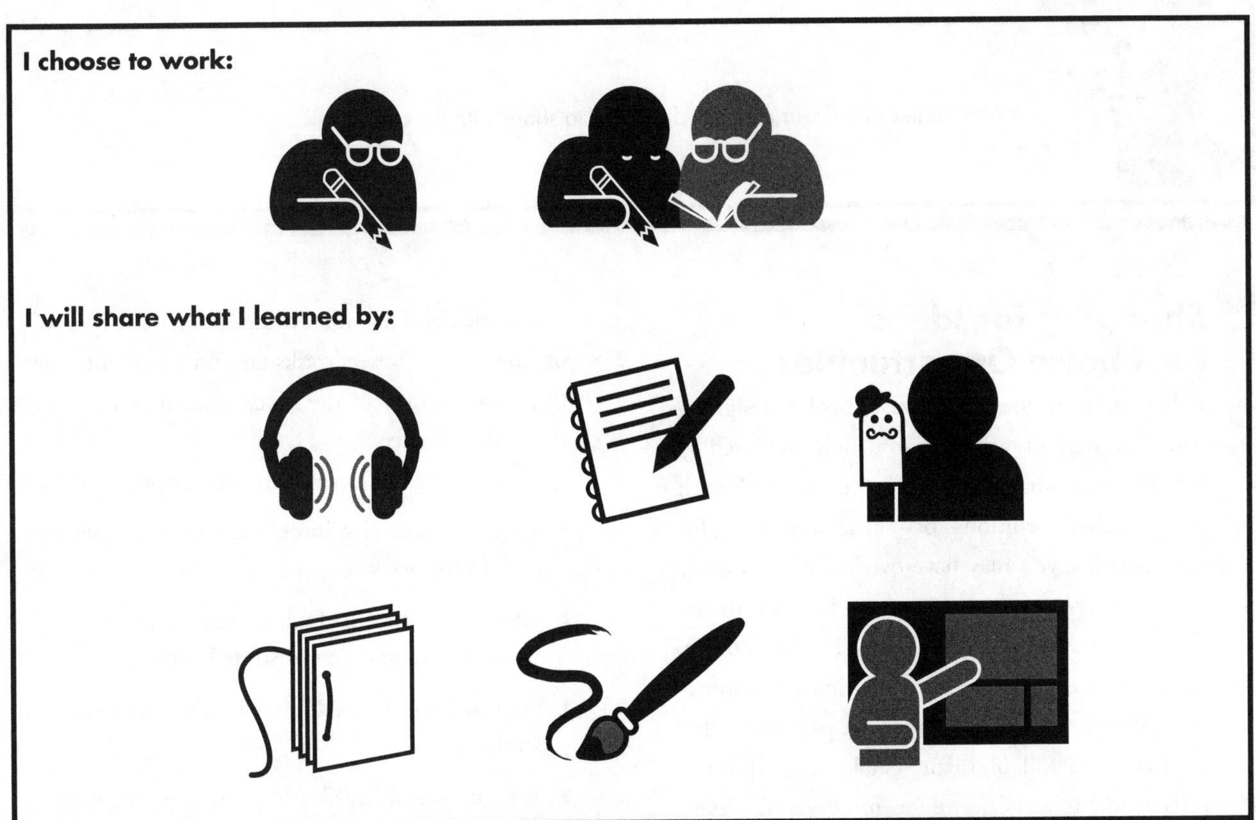

FIGURE 58

Choice of Primary Book Projects

Read *Danny and the Dinosaur* and then choose from the projects below.

	Listen to a recording about dinosaurs provided by your teacher. List 3 new facts about dinosaurs. List 2 things you already knew. Write one new question you have about dinosaurs.
	Write a story about dinosaurs including facts. Make a booklet with pictures and sentences.
	Sort a stack of dinosaur pictures provided by your teacher in as many ways as possible. Create bar graphs with labels to show your results.
	Create a flannel board story about dinosaurs and present it to the class.
	Write riddles about four different dinosaurs to share with the class.

Shopping for Ideas for Choice Opportunities

Differentiation does not always involve designing your own student tasks. It is sometimes achieved by simply using what you have in new ways. Search your teacher's editions or curriculum files for activities that you may have overlooked previously because they were not appropriate for all learners. Consider activities you deemed too hard or too easy for use with all of your students. Think about something you used with students in the past that didn't work well for all of them. Choice opportunities offer students activities representing various levels of complexity. Therefore, those "too hard for some" or "too easy for others" tasks take on a new purpose: to provide variety in the kinds of activities offered for student choice.

Well-designed, controlled choice opportunities:

- increase the motivation of students to engage in and do the work
- reach more students by presenting a variety of ways to learn and demonstrate learning
- offer multiple levels and types of challenge to students
- engage students by clearly identifying the tasks and determining how the students make choices

CHAPTER 6

Critical Element: Prescribing Tiered Assignments and Using Flexible Grouping

What happens in your classroom when you are working with certain content, skills, or processes, and you know you have two distinct groups of learners—those who "get it" and those who appear clueless? What happens when what you have planned for tomorrow will clearly be too difficult for some of your students or too easy for others? What do you typically do in these situations? For many teachers, the most appropriate response is to use tiered assignments managed in flexible instructional groups to address differing learning needs. However, it's easy to feel overwhelmed with planning and facilitating multiple tasks and groups in your classroom. This chapter will provide some ready-to-implement ideas for these strategies and tips for making them more doable.

Tiered Assignments

Tiered assignments are teacher-prescribed learning activities that are specifically designed to respond to differences in readiness, interests, or learning preferences. They are the most prescriptive, learner-responsive, and sophisticated strategy for differentiation. First, you *diagnose* the needs of your students based on preassessment, formative assessment, or such informal methods as observation and reflection on your students' learning. Then you *find* or *design* an activity, task, or project that responds specifically to those needs. Finally, you *prescribe* specific tasks to particular students, creating a match between the learner and the learning experience. Tiered assignments are managed in practice through the use of flexible instructional groups, which will be discussed in detail later in this chapter.

Tiered assignments are purposeful. They are designed by the teacher to respond to specific learning needs of students and are used for specific purposes. As such, there are many ways to design tiered assignments. Although Bloom's Taxonomy is commonly used in designing student tasks, the practice of tiering involves far more than merely assigning a high task to some students and a low task to others, in "bluebird and buzzard" fashion.

The practice of tiering involves far more than merely assigning a high task to some students and a low task to others.

At some point, *all* students will need differentiated instruction based on their particular learning needs. Tiered assignments and flexible instructional groups both address and manage learning tasks responding to differences. Since tiered assignments are typically not necessary on a daily basis, how do you know when you may need to offer them in your classroom?

Use a tiered assignment when:

- students represent different developmental stages
- readiness for learning differs among your students
- learning preferences differ among your students
- some students need more support or structure for their learning, while others are able to work with greater independence and openness
- differences arise while teaching content, concepts, processes, or skills, indicating some students need more time, instruction, and practice, and others are ready for a new challenge
- students need to use different curricular resources due to reading-readiness levels or differences in prior knowledge about a curricular topic
- instruction or a task is not necessary or appropriate for *all* students, only *some* students
- based on knowledge of your students, you know something you have planned will be either *too hard* or *too easy* for some students
- some students are best suited to work with more basic applications and others need greater complexity to be challenged and engaged

What characterizes a tiered assignment that is well designed to serve differing learning needs, yet also is viewed by students as fair? Page 87 provides a checklist to guide your planning and use of tiered assignments in your classroom.

You do not need to use tiered assignments as a daily practice; you use them as necessary and appropriate. There are days when everyone in your class needs an introduction to content, or everyone needs to learn a skill or process because it's new for all students. And there are other days when learning differences make using a tiered assignment the logical approach to instruction.

When you decide to use a tiered assignment in your classroom, you are doing so because there are significant learning differences that need to be addressed. Each task is clearly focused on particular learning goals. No one is simply being "kept busy."

As you design or find the activities that will make up the tiered assignment, you are structuring the tasks to clearly represent "just right, right now" learning experiences for all students. You are also careful that issues around work, fun, and homework are addressed. If students look across the room and sense that those working on the other "tier" are doing less work or having more fun; then you have not designed the tasks appropriately. Design tasks so each are equally active, engaging, and interesting so one is not perceived as more work than the other (the work should be *different*—not more or less). Also, carefully calculate the workload so the amount of time required to complete each tier is relatively the same. For example, if one tier can be completed in a day, another tier should not require homework.

You will need to decide how the students will do their work. You may want students to work alone.

The total learning experience for all students comes from bringing the tiers together.

In other circumstances, you may let them choose to do their work with a partner with like needs, or in a small group of like learners. The total learning experience for all students comes from bringing the tiers together. Students need to see the results of all tiered assignments. These may be shared with the whole class through a classroom presentation. Or, for purposes of saving time, you can "buddy up" groups or individuals, so they can each share what has been accomplished. In this way, students learn from each other and everyone's work is honored.

Remember that tiered assignments are for practice only; they are not for summative assessment. You are tiering the assignments because you are still working on the learning goals. Although the results of tiered assignments will inform your plans for instruction, they are not meant to be a source of grades. They are *practice* with content, skills, or processes.

Criteria for Well-Designed Tiered Assignments

- ☐ Are used as necessary and appropriate to address the learning differences in a classroom.
- ☐ Are clearly focused on learning goals.
- ☐ Reflect work on critical content, processes, or skills.
- ☐ Are designed to respond to the immediate and specific learning needs of different groups of students (tiered by readiness, challenge and complexity, degree of structure, level of abstraction, learning preference, or need for support).
- ☐ Are equally active, engaging, and interesting.
- ☐ Reflect differences in purpose and are not simply more or less or redundant work.
- ☐ Require similar time commitments. Either all can be completed during the class period or all require homework.
- ☐ May be assigned to be completed individually, with a partner with like needs, or collaboratively in a small group of like learners.
- ☐ Offer an opportunity for students to learn from each other. Tiers should offer different but related experiences. Students should share their work.
- ☐ Are used as practice or daily work, not as an assessment task to be graded.

A GUIDE TO TIERING ASSIGNMENTS TO ADDRESS LEARNING NEEDS

Based on the needs of your learners and the purposes for the tiered assignments, you may choose to design your tasks using one of six ways.

1. Tiering by Readiness

You may design or find tasks that respond to readiness differences in your classroom. Examples of this would include using leveled reading resources to respond to reading-readiness differences or designing tasks responding to learning readiness.

Teachers may match students with appropriate resources in two different ways. You can collect materials at a variety of reading levels (e.g., Lexile scores) and assign students to choose from a particular collection of books. Or students may be assigned resources based on their prior knowledge about a topic. In this case, you collect print resources or Web sites that reflect introductory information on a topic as well as other resources or Web sites that reflect more in-depth, complex, sophisticated, or technical information. Then you assign students to resources based on their prior knowledge revealed through preassessment strategies. Following the assignment of resources, students may be assigned to the same task or differentiated tasks based on their learning needs. **Figure 59** shows tiered assignments that use differentiated reading resources *and* differentiated tasks based on reading readiness.

Tiering by learning readiness offers an opportunity to reinforce or reteach a lesson to one group of learners, and to extend or enrich learning for other learners.

Debriefing this tier . . .

Task one is designed for students who are competent readers. They are reading an article at a higher reading level (e.g., Lexile score) and are asked to independently complete an analysis task utilizing the content of the article. Task two uses a text at a lower reading-readiness level and provides more support for pulling facts from the text. The chart guides the students toward the facts to look for. A teacher-led discussion with the students doing task two can initiate comparisons between the life of children in ancient Greece and today.

FIGURE 59

Tiering by Readiness: Example #1

SOCIAL STUDIES
ELEMENTARY

Ancient Civilizations: Task One

1. Read the article about home life in ancient Greece.
2. Think about the roles and responsibilities of women in ancient Greece.
3. Imagine yourself living in ancient Greece.
4. In what ways are the lives of women in ancient Greece different from the lives of women today?
5. Make a Venn diagram to show how women's lives in ancient Greece are like and unlike women's lives in the 21st century.

Ancient Civilizations: Task Two

1. Read the article about life as a child in ancient Greece.
2. Complete this chart with facts about children's life in ancient Greece and your life.

	Ancient Greek Life	My Life
School		
Home		
Clothing		
Games		
Social life		

Tiering by learning readiness offers an opportunity to reinforce or reteach a lesson to one group of learners, and to extend or enrich learning for other learners. **Figure 60** shows a readiness-based pair of assignments for a unit about fantasy genre literature.

Debriefing this tier . . .

Task one is the extension of learning about problems and solutions presented in a story. These students do not need any more time on comprehending the story. Task two provides an opportunity for students to spend more time on the problems and solutions presented in a story. The teacher may lead the discussion with students doing task two. If students from both task groups were put together (as in mixed-readiness cooperative groups), the students from task one would likely dominate the task since they readily comprehend the content. Thus, if you want students to work on particular goals based on their needs, you should group them for instruction based on likenesses, not differences. In addition, the products for both groups—a poster with symbols and sketches—makes the task more accessible for English language learners.

FIGURE 60

Tiering by Readiness: Example #2

ENGLISH/LANGUAGE ARTS
ELEMENTARY

Cinderella: Task One

1. As a group, think about the problems in *Cinderella* and their solutions.
2. Divide up the problems among the members of your group.
3. Each member determines at least one new way your problem could be solved if Cinderella (or "Cindy") lived today.
4. Draw the problem on one sheet of paper. Draw your new solution on a second sheet of paper. Use only sketches or symbols to share your ideas.
5. As a group, create a poster with two columns of pictures. One column should represent the problems and next to each its solution.

Cinderella: Task Two

1. As a group, think about the problems in *Cinderella.*
2. Divide up the problems so that each member of your group gets at least one.
3. Think about how the problem was solved in the story. Draw the problem on one sheet of paper and the solution on a second sheet of paper. Use only sketches or symbols to share your ideas.
4. As a group, create a poster by making two columns of pictures. One column should represent the problems and next to each its solution.

2. Tiering by Level of Challenge and Complexity

Based on the needs of the students in your classroom, are basic applications of content, skills, or processes more appropriate for some learners? Could other students benefit from more complex applications,

FIGURE 61

Tiering by Level of Challenge/Complexity: Example #1

SOCIAL STUDIES: POLITICAL SCIENCE
HIGH SCHOOL

Art of Persuasion: Task One

How is the art of persuasion evidenced in politics?

1. Brainstorm ideas with your group.
2. Analyze the strategies of persuasion on your brainstormed list.
3. Create two continuums:
   - Continuum One: From least to most effective strategies of political persuasion
   - Continuum Two: From most deceptive to most ethical strategies of political persuasion
4. Write each strategy where it would be placed on each continuum.
5. Be ready to present and explain the strategies, and defend their placement on the two continuums.

Art of Persuasion: Task Two

How is the art of persuasion evidenced in politics?

1. Brainstorm ideas with your group.
2. Consider the ways the strategies might be classified.
3. Create a poster with pictures, symbols, and/or words to represent your ideas.
4. Be ready to share your work with the class.

given their prior knowledge or experience or their need for greater learning challenges? **Figure 61** shows an example of a high school assignment tiered by challenge and complexity.

Debriefing this tier . . .

Students assigned to task one need to go further in analyzing the strategies of persuasion in politics. They need a more complex task to keep them engaged and stretch their thinking. They are asked to analyze and evaluate the strategies using two lenses: effectiveness and ethics. Task two also engages the students in generating strategies of persuasion but asks them to analyze the resulting list to determine possible ways to classify the strategies. The results of both tiers are shared with the class, which allows for discussion of perspectives among all students.

Tiering by level of challenge and complexity provides basic applications of content, skills, or processes for some students, as well as more complex applications to benefit those students who need greater challenges in learning.

Figure 62 shows an example of an assignment tiered by challenge and complexity based on an informational chart received by all students.

Debriefing this tier . . .

Students assigned to task one are easily able to read and analyze the data presented in the chart. They are also capable of interrelating the data. They are challenged to create food webs connecting plants and animals in the river and detailing their interrelationships. Students in task two will find interpreting the data in the chart more challenging. They are asked to make linear connections. An appropriate task for these students would be creating food chains representing what eats what in the river. Tiering by level of challenge and complexity provides basic applications of content, skills, or processes for some students, as well as more complex applications to benefit those students who, given their prior knowledge or experience, need greater challenges in learning.

3. Tiering by Degree of Structure

Some students benefit from greater degrees of structure in their tasks. Others need opportunities to take a task further or approach it in more unique ways. These students seek more open-ended tasks so they can determine their own direction. **Figure 63** shows an example of tiering tasks in this way.

Debriefing this tier . . .

In task one, the students are guided to look for characteristics of teen males and females and then draw conclusions about the images presented in the magazine. Finally, they are asked to consider similarities and differences in the representation

FIGURE 62

Tiering by Level of Challenge/Complexity: Example #2

SCIENCE
MIDDLE SCHOOL

Living Things in a River: Task One

1. Review the information in the chart showing the homes, food, and characteristics of living things in a river.
2. Construct a *food web* to show the relationship of the animals and plants in the river. Keep in mind that an animal or plant may be used for food for more than one animal.

Living Things in a River: Task Two

1. Review the information in the chart showing the homes, food, and characteristics of living things in a river.
2. Choose an animal and look for what it eats and what eats it.
3. Draw at least three *food chains* to show how animals and plants depend on each other in the river.

of males and females. Task one provides greater structure and guidance for the students' thinking about the images in the magazine. Task two uses the same teen magazine format but asks the students to independently investigate the images and then consider the messages they send. The students are free to explore a variety of possible themes derived from the pages of the magazine. They are left to determine the messages to teens, and must support their assertions with evidence from the magazine pages. Tiering by degree of structure provides some students with more support or direction for their work, as other students engage in a more open-ended task in which they are able to determine their own direction.

Tiering by degree of structure provides some students with more support or direction for their work while other students engage in a more open-ended task.

FIGURE 63

Tiering by Degree of Structure Example

MEDIA LITERACY
MIDDLE SCHOOL

Propaganda Devices: Task One

1. Review teen magazine pages examining the ways in which boys and girls are represented.
2. Create a poster that suggests the "ideal male" and the "ideal female" using photographs from the magazine and its ads, as well as adding adjectives of your choosing.
3. Next, compare and contrast the images of males and females and present your conclusions to our class. You may present your conclusions using charts or graphs with your poster.

Propaganda Devices: Task Two

1. Review the teen magazine pages and examine the ways in which teens are represented.
2. Create a poster illustrating the messages that you think the magazine's editors and advertisers are attempting to send to teens.
3. Use photographs from the magazine and its ads to support your assertions.
4. Present a convincing argument for your assertions to our class.

4. Tiering by Degree of Abstraction

You may design tasks that differ in the degree of abstraction required. For example, some students need concrete applications to understand and apply their learning. Others are ready for more abstract applications. **Figure 64** shows an example of tiering tasks in this way.

Debriefing this tier . . .

Task one suggests more concrete representations of the novel's character. For example, the character likes the sea, so the student places a shell in the box. Or the character is a musician, so a piece of sheet music is included. Task two asks students to select items to symbolize the character and also encourages thematic references. This is a more abstract approach to an artifacts collection. The student

FIGURE 64

Tiering by Degree of Abstraction Example

ENGLISH/LANGUAGE ARTS
HIGH SCHOOL

Characters in a Novel: Task One

1. Collect at least 10 items to create an artifacts box representing a character in the novel.
2. Provide informational cards to explain your selections and their connections to the character and novel.

Characters in a Novel: Task Two

1. Collect at least 10 artifacts box items to *symbolize* a character in the novel.
2. You may also include *thematic references* to the novel.
3. Provide information cards to explain your selections and their connections to the character and the novel.

may include pieces of a jigsaw puzzle to represent the complexity of the character's personality.

Tiering by degree of abstraction allows some students to engage in more concrete applications of skills, processes, or content, and others in more abstract applications.

A piece of yarn may be included to convey the character's desire to connect to others in his life. Tiering by degree of abstraction allows some students to engage in more concrete applications of skills, processes, or content, and others in more abstract, theoretical, or conceptual applications.

5. Tiering by Level of Support

Some students require more scaffolding, or support, for their learning. They may need tasks broken down into smaller steps or more strategies for organizing their thinking and work. **Figure 65** is used as a word bank for three tiered assignments reflecting different levels of support for students.

Debriefing this tier . . .

These tiered assignments represent three different degrees of support or scaffolding. Students are assigned the task that best matches their need for support. Tiering by degree of support better enables students to be successful in a task by providing higher levels of scaffolding, greater structure, or more direction. Other students who require less support in their learning are asked to engage in a task with less structure provided by the teacher.

Tiering by degree of support better enables students to be successful in a task by providing higher levels of scaffolding, greater structure, or more direction.

Task one has the least amount of scaffolding. Students need to review the words in the word bank and determine how they might go together. They need to identify both major topics (forests, water, deserts, grasslands) and determine the subtopics or characteristics of each. They are given the challenge of creating their own visual to share the facts about ecosystems.

Task two provides additional support and guidance for students. They are given a four-square organizer with the titles of each of the four ecosystems. Students select characteristics from the word bank and write them in the appropriate square.

FIGURE 65

Tiering by Level of Support Example

SCIENCE
ELEMENTARY

Ecosystems: Task One

1. Review the words in the word bank (Figure 66).
2. Identify the four ecosystems.
3. Determine which words are characteristics that describe each ecosystem.
4. Create your own chart, diagram, or graphic organizer to present each of the four different ecosystems and their characteristics.

Ecosystems: Task Two

1. Review the words in the word bank (Figure 66).
2. Find the characteristics in the word bank that go with each ecosystem.
3. Notice that the chart (Figure 67) is divided into four sections, one for each ecosystem. Copy the characteristic into the box of the ecosystem it describes.

Ecosystems: Task Three

1. Review the words in the word bank (Figure 66).
2. Select the words from the word bank that match each ecosystem.
3. You have one graphic organizer for each ecosystem: forests, water, deserts, grasslands (Figure 68). The boxes on each graphic organizer tell you how many facts you need to find for each ecosystem. Copy the words from the word bank onto the correct graphic organizer.

Task three provides the greatest level of scaffolding. Students are provided with a graphic organizer for each ecosystem (Figure 68 shows only the forest graphic organizer). The boxes reflect the exact number of characteristics they need to find in the word bank. This tier provides the greatest level of support for students as they search for and organize characteristics of the four ecosystems.

6. Tiering by Learning Preference

Students can learn and represent what they have learned more effectively when they are working in their learning preference. If you are aware of your students' learning preferences, you can use preference as a way to tier assignments. Students are assigned to the specific task that best reflects their preferences. **Figure 69** shows an example of tiering in this way.

Debriefing this tier . . .

Students assigned to task one are those perceived to be Bodily/kinesthetic learners. These students prefer hands-on, build-it kind of learning experiences. Task two would appeal to learners who represent Logical/mathematical and Visual/spatial preferences. These students have the ability to picture the resulting product in their heads and best represent their ideas through drawings, sketches, or diagrams. Both groups of students need to write an explanation of their design process and describe the ways in which the product was refined. This Verbal/linguistic product is required of all learners.

> Tiering by learning preference enables students to demonstrate what they know or understand by being "matched" with tasks by learning preference.

Tiering by learning preference enables students to demonstrate what they know or understand by being "matched" with tasks by learning preference.

FIGURE 66

Ecosystems Word Bank[1]

Forest	Deserts	Coniferous trees
Less than 10 inches of rain	Ocean	Moose, bears, wolves
Large flat areas covered with grass	Lakes and streams	Cold winters, hot summers
Cactus plants	Coastal forests	Water
Covers 70% of Earth's surface	Deciduous trees	Grasslands
Tropical rainforest	Tall grass, few trees	Tide pools
Very dry	Snakes and lizards	Two kinds: hot and cold
Ponds and rivers	Antelopes, rabbits, prairie dogs	Prairies, pampas, steppes

FIGURE 67

Ecosystems Chart

Forests	Water
Deserts	Grasslands

FIGURE 68

Ecosystems Graphic Organizer

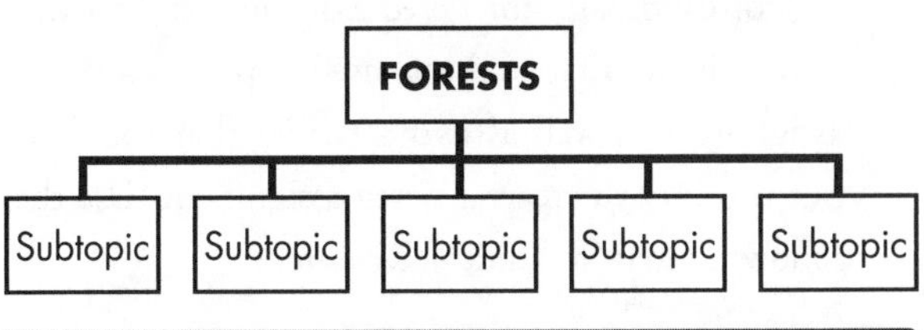

1 Adapted from a collaborative work by Diane Heacox and Catherine Thorne, 2007.

FIGURE 69

Tiering by Learning Preference Example

SCIENCE, TECHNOLOGY, ENGINEERING, MATH (STEM)
HIGH SCHOOL

Engineering Design: Task One

1. Identify an engineering design problem. Refine the design to ensure quality, efficiency, and productivity of the final product.
2. Create a prototype, construction paper model, clay sculpture, or simulated model of your product.
3. Write an explanation of your design process, and describe the ways in which the product was refined.

Engineering Design: Task Two

1. Identify an engineering design problem. Refine the design to ensure quality, efficiency, and productivity of the final product.
2. Create a mechanical drawing of your product.
3. Write an explanation of your design process, and describe the ways in which the product was refined.

FINDING TIERED ASSIGNMENTS

Most of the time when you need a tiered assignment, you do not have to create two new tasks but rather utilize activities you may already have on hand. The following scavenger hunt can be used with your teacher's editions or your curriculum unit's resource file.

Scavenger Hunt for Tiered Assignments

Review the activities suggested in your teacher's edition, collected in a curriculum file, or published in curriculum resource books when you are looking for candidates for tiered assignments. You will find activities that could be used as part of a tiered assignment as well as two activities that could be put together to create a tiered assignment. Use the following steps to guide your search:

1. Find an activity that is just right for certain students but not right for all students. Could it be used as a tiered assignment for just some students?

2. Reconsider activities that you used in the past for all students that may have been too hard for some students. They could be advanced, more abstract or complex tiers.

3. Reconsider activities that you used in the past for all students that may have been too easy for some students. They could be basic, more concrete or less complex tiers.

4. Find activities that represent different Multiple Intelligences that could be matched to students with like learning preferences.

5. Find activities or questions that represent various levels of Bloom's Taxonomy (in particular look for high level tasks or questions) that could be used as tiers.

6. Find an activity noted as "reteach" or "reinforce." Then question: Is this activity presenting content or a skill in a new way? Is it at least at the application level of Bloom's Taxonomy? Does it provide greater scaffolding or support in learning? Does it provide more practice? Should it be used as part of a tiered assignment?

7. Find an activity noted as "extension" or "challenge." Then question: Is this activity at a higher level of Bloom's (analysis, synthesis, evaluation)? Is it a more complex application? Does it contain new content? Or is it simply more work or redundant practice? Should it be part of a tiered assignment?

8. Find two activities or versions of activities that could be paired to create a tiered assignment representing different levels of complexity, difficulty, abstractness, or structure.

Once you have found some ideas using the scavenger hunt, double-check your "found" tiered assignments by reviewing the "Criteria for Well-Designed Tiered Assignments" checklist on page 87. Rephrase, rewrite, or modify what you have found as necessary to meet the goals of the tasks and the needs of your particular students.

DESIGNING TIERED ASSIGNMENTS

If do not find the material for your tiered assignment, it's time to design it yourself. There are particular elements that need to be thought through as you design a tiered assignment. Not everything is tiered. It is important to clearly focus on significant learning goals, design tasks that respond specifically to the learning needs of your students, and create learning experiences that meet the students' demands for fairness. The following seven-step process walks you through the process of designing an effective tiered assignment.

Steps in Streamlining the Design of Tiered Assignments

1. Determine whether a tiered assignment is necessary. Does the content, skill, or process reflect a significant learning goal? Is this critical learning based on a state standard or provincial goal? Use tiering as necessary and appropriate and only when the learning is critical in nature. You don't tier "fluff," i.e., less essential or less significant content, skills, or processes.

2. Determine the most appropriate way to tier the assignment based on the needs of the students. Do you need to tier by readiness, by level of complexity, through varying degrees of structure, by level of abstractness, or through more or less scaffolding?

3. Shop for ideas in your teacher's guide or resource materials (see Scavenger Hunt for Tiered Assignments, page 94) then design, modify, or redesign tasks that will provide "just right, right now" learning experiences for your students.

4. Do a "fairness" check.
   - Do the tasks reflect different work, not just more or less work?
   - Are the tasks equally active, engaging, and interesting?
   - Do the tasks reflect equal demands on time? Can each task be completed during a class period? Or does each task need to be completed as homework?
   - Is each task clearly focused on a significant and critical learning goal?

5. Determine which students need to be assigned to each tier. Who *needs* to do what?

6. Determine whether students will complete the task alone, with a partner with like learning needs, or with a small group of like learners.

7. Create work cards to present directions for each task. Be sure that the directions can stand on their own. Can a student proceed with a degree of independence based on the clarity and precision of your directions? Do you need to provide models or examples to clarify the task? Do you need to present the directions in sequential steps?

THE THREE-TIER TASK PLANNING FRAMEWORK

In most cases, you will be able to accomplish your goals with three tiers: the first an on-target tier, the second an advanced tier, and the third a modification or adaptation of most frequently the first tier. This modification or adaptation may be directed by an individual learning plan, a 504 plan, or as part of an intervention strategy in RTI. Page 96 provides a framework for planning three-tier tasks in this way.

Five Steps in Creating Three-Tier Tasks

1. Record your learning goals (KUDo's) in the box at the top. This serves as a reminder as you plan the tasks to focus on the goals.

2. Based on your students' learning needs, determine the way in which the tiers will be created. Do you need to tier by readiness, by levels of challenge and complexity, through varying degrees of structure, by degree of abstraction through more or less scaffolding, or by learning preference?

3. Create tier one, the on-target task that will be appropriate for most of your students.

THREE-TIER TASK PLANNING FRAMEWORK

KUDo's (learning goals)

Tier by:

- ☐ Readiness
- ☐ Level of Challenge/Complexity
- ☐ Degree of Structure
- ☐ Degree of Abstraction
- ☐ Level of Support
- ☐ Learning Preference

Tier Three: For Some	**Tier One: For Most**	**Tier Two: For Some**

4 Working from tier one, create tier two that reflects a more complex, open-ended, or abstract task. It may also be designed to have less direct support and demand more independence on the part of the students. Tier two is appropriate for some of your students who may need more challenge to engage them in learning.

5 Finally, again working from tier one, consider special learning issues in your classroom. Modify or adapt tier one to create a third tiered assignment appropriate for some of your students who are following an individual educational plan, a 504 plan, or who have other specific learning differences, including those who are engaged in RTI interventions. However, keep in mind that some students, depending on their learning issues, might be able to do the more advanced tier two with greater support or scaffolding. Special educators warn teachers not to assume that tier three is always a modification or adaptation of the on-target tier one task.

Figure 70 is an example of a three-tier task on heroes and villains in a novel. Note that *all* students are working on the same KUDo's. They are just working on them in different ways based on their learning needs. The tiers were created using differing degrees of structure and through varying levels of challenge/complexity.

There is not one correct way to differentiate a tiered assignment; there are multiple ways, each directed at the particular and specific learning differences that are present in your classroom.

Figure 71 shows how these tiers would look on the planning framework.

DESIGNING TIERED ASSIGNMENTS

Once you have created your tiers, you begin designing the individual tasks and engage in a series of decisions related to how to differentiate a task. There is not one correct way to differentiate a tiered assignment; there are multiple ways, each directed at the particular and specific learning differences that are present in your classroom. The "Tiered Assignment Design Template" (page 100) enables you to examine the many ways a task may be differentiated. The template walks you through the design process encompassing the four elements of a tiered assignment—goals, materials/tasks, products, and work arrangements. To differentiate a task, you need to differentiate at least one of the first three elements; asterisk (*) notations on the template signify a differentiation strategy in each. The final element, work arrangements, does not offer a specific differentiation opportunity.

FIGURE 70

Three-Tier Task Example

ENGLISH/LANGUAGE ARTS
MIDDLE SCHOOL

Heroes and Villains

KUDo's

Students will *understand* that stories present characters with both positive qualities (heroes) and negative qualities (villains).

Students will *be able to identify* characteristics of heroes and villains in books or stories.

Task One

Identify the characteristics of heroes and villains and provide examples from your book on a chart. Summarize in a paragraph what makes the character a hero or a villain.

Task Two

What redeeming characteristics does the villain of the book exhibit? What is the "shadow side" of the hero character in the book? Write and present a convincing argument for the villain's positive qualities and the hero's negative qualities.

Task Three

Chart characteristics of the hero and villain from the book using a graphic organizer.

Steps in Using the Tiered Assignment Design Template

General guidelines: It should not be your intent to differentiate each of the first three elements in the design process. Instead, your goal should be to include *at least one* element of differentiation in your design plan.

❶ **Determine who will work on which learning goals.** All students may be engaged in working on the same goal, or there may be different learning goals for different students based on their learning needs. Differentiation occurs when different goals are established for different learners. On the design template, check off which strategy you will use: *same goal for all* or *different goals for different students.* If you choose the latter, note the goals on lines A and B.

❷ **Decide who will engage with which materials/resources and tasks.** This is a second element in the design that could be differentiated. Students might be using the same materials and resources, or different materials and resources. They can also be engaged in the same task or in different tasks. If you choose *same materials/resources* and *same task,* you are not differentiating this element. In the notes section, describe the materials/resources and the task(s) that the students will engage in.

FIGURE 71

Sample Three-Tier Task Planning Framework

ENGLISH/LANGUAGE ARTS
MIDDLE SCHOOL
HEROES AND VILLAINS

KUDo's (learning goals)

Students will *understand* that stories present characters with both positive qualities (heroes) and negative qualities (villains).

Students will *be able to identify* characteristics of heroes and villains in books or stories.

Tier by:

- ☐ Readiness
- ☑ Level of Challenge/Complexity
- ☑ Degree of Structure
- ☐ Degree of Abstraction
- ☐ Level of Support
- ☐ Learning Preference

Tier Three: For Some	Tier One: For Most	Tier Two: For Some
Chart characteristics of the hero and villain from the book using a graphic organizer.	Identify the characteristics of heroes and villains and provide examples from your book on a chart. Summarize in a paragraph what makes the character a hero or a villain.	What redeeming characteristics does the villain of the book exhibit? What is the "shadow side" of the hero character in the book? Write and present a convincing argument for the villain's positive qualities and the hero's negative qualities.

3 **Determine who will complete which products.** The third element that may be differentiated in a tiered assignment is the product. You may want all students to complete the same product, or give them a choice in products. Neither of these methods would result in differentiation of this element. Differentiation only occurs if you match products to students based on their needs or learning preferences. If you are differentiating this element, describe the products in the notes section.

As your skills in designing tiered assignments become more sophisticated, you may decide to differentiate more than one element to create more dynamic tasks.

4 **Settle on a student work arrangement.** The final element in the design process is to determine how the students will do their work. Decide whether your students will work alone, with a partner with like learning needs, or in a small group of students with like learning needs. While important, this element does not provide an opportunity for differentiation.

Figure 72 provides an example of how the tiered literature assignment in Figure 70 would appear if written on the design template. **Figure 73** shows an elementary mathematics tiered assignment.

This template makes the design work of tiering easy to do. *Remember:* You may choose to differentiate only one element. As your skills in designing tiered assignments become more sophisticated, you may decide to differentiate more than one element to create more dynamic tasks. The four sections of the template guide your thinking and your decisions about what and how you might differentiate a task. The template opens up possibilities and broadens the ways in which you can design tiered assignments to meet your students' specific needs.

Grouping in a Variety of Ways for a Variety of Purposes

As a teacher, you likely use grouping methods in your classroom for many different purposes. You might group students in collaborative or cooperative groups and in groups for instructional purposes. You may assign students to these groups, or allow your students to randomly form their own groups.

In collaborative groups, you may often form groups of students representing mixed readiness. In this manner, students with particular skills or content knowledge work together with students who lack such skills or content knowledge. The hope is that those who "have it" can help those who don't.

You may also assign students to groups for purposes other than readiness. Spreading student behavior problems over several groups or assigning highly motivated students to groups with less motivated members are examples of some other uses of groups. With these grouping strategies, the focus is placing students with differences together in a group.

Another process for grouping is to have students form their own groups based on particular interests. For example, you might list different topics on the whiteboard and let students form their own collaborative groups based on which topic they want to learn more about. Or you might post sign-up sheets for sections of the classroom newspaper. Students form their groups based on their interest in working on particular sections of the paper. In this process, the formation of the groups is random.

USING FLEXIBLE INSTRUCTIONAL GROUPS

Flexible instructional groups are the types of groups used to manage tiered assignments. These groups are purposeful, not random, groupings of students based on likenesses rather than differences. Students are assigned to particular groups based on common instructional needs to complete tiered assignments. Within each group, the students may be doing their assignment alone, with a partner with like learning needs, or with a small group of like learners.

TIERED ASSIGNMENT DESIGN TEMPLATE

* indicates a differentiation strategy

1. GOALS

___ Same goal for all: ____________________

___ Different goals for different students *

A. ____________________

B. ____________________

2. MATERIALS/RESOURCES — TASKS

____ Same materials/resources . . . . same task

____ Same materials/resources . . . . different tasks*

____ Different materials/resources . . . . same task*

____ Different materials/resources . . . . different tasks*

Notes:

3. PRODUCTS

____ Same product for all students

____ Different products matched by needs or learning preferences*

____ Choice of products representing different interests, learning preferences

Notes:

4. WORK ARRANGEMENT

____ Individual work

____ Partner work by likeness

____ Small group work by likeness

FIGURE 72

Tiered Assignment Design Template: Example #1

ENGLISH/LANGUAGE ARTS
MIDDLE SCHOOL
HEROES AND VILLAINS

* indicates a differentiation strategy

1. GOALS

_X_ Same goal for all: *Identify the characteristics of heroes and villains in literature.*

___ Different goals for different students *

A. ________________

B. ________________

2. MATERIALS/RESOURCES — TASKS

____ Same materials/resources .... same task

_X_ Same materials/resources .... different tasks*

____ Different materials/resources .... same task*

____ Different materials/resources .... different tasks*

Notes:

On-Target: Identify the characteristics of heroes and villains and provide examples from the book/story. Explain what makes the character a hero or a villain.

Adapted, Modified: Chart characteristics of a villain and a hero from a story/book using a graphic organizer. Be prepared to share your ideas.

Advanced: What redeeming qualities does the villain of the story/book exhibit? What is the "shadow side" of the hero character in the story/book? Write and prepare a convincing argument for each to share with the class.

3. PRODUCTS

____ Same product for all students

_X_ Different products matched by needs or learning preferences*

____ Choice of products representing different interests, learning preferences

Notes:

On-Target: Written summary

Adapted, Modified: Chart

Advanced: Written argument

4. WORK ARRANGEMENT

_X_ Individual work

____ Partner work by likeness

____ Small group work by likeness

FIGURE 73

Tiered Assignment Design Template: Example #2

MATHEMATICS
ELEMENTARY
PATTERNS

* indicates a differentiation strategy

1. GOALS

___ Same goal for all: ____________________

_X_ Different goals for different students *

A. *Identify and extend a presented pattern.*

B. *Construct complex, multiple patterns using at least three elements.*

2. MATERIALS/RESOURCES — TASKS

___ Same materials/resources .... same task

_X_ Same materials/resources .... different tasks*

___ Different materials/resources .... same task*

___ Different materials/resources .... different tasks*

Notes:
All students will use the animal shape cards but will engage in different tasks with them:

A. Students will identify and extend patterns presented on a math task sheet.

B. Students will independently construct complex, multiple patterns using at least three elements. Students will record their patterns on construction paper.

3. PRODUCTS

_X_ Same product for all students

___ Different products matched by needs or learning preferences*

___ Choice of products representing different interests, learning preferences

Notes:
All students will construct patterns using animal shape cards.

4. WORK ARRANGEMENT

_X_ Individual work

___ Partner work by likeness

___ Small group work by likeness

The more strategies you use for creating groups in the classroom, the less noticeable it is when you group for instruction. Different purposes for grouping students mix them around so that they are not consistently working with the same group of students. If your purpose is to match students to tasks that respond to their learning needs, you must group students for instruction by likeness, not by differences. Then, prescribe the appropriate tiered assignment to the appropriate group.

The more strategies you use for creating groups in the classroom, the less noticeable it is when you group for instruction.

EIGHT WAYS TO MAKE FLEXIBLE INSTRUCTIONAL GROUPS DOABLE

1. Send Students to Groups Efficiently

Use your prep time for preparation, not for writing lists of students' names for instructional groups. Create a system where the students can check and confirm what group they are in without needing to ask you to repeat the lists.

Tips for Primary Groups

- Write each student's name on a craft stick. Glue a magnet on the backside of each stick. Use the craft sticks on your white board, moving the sticks around to create your groups.
- Put each tiered assignment into a clear plastic, stand-up picture frame. Write each student's name on a clip clothespin. Clip the student's clothespin onto the frame of the tiered assignment they are assigned to complete.

Tips for All Groups

- Run a copy of your class list or put it on an overhead transparency. Use colored markers to circle the names of students in each group. For example, if you have red, blue, and green groups, circle the students' names with the appropriate colored marker to inform them what group they are in. Show the group assignments using the overhead projector or document camera. This strategy eliminates the need to create new group lists each time you use flexible groups.

2. Provide Clear, Specific Directions for Each Task

Try using work cards with the directions for each tiered assignment on them. Giving students directions aloud for more than one task can be confusing to everyone.

Run each work card on different colored paper. That way you can distribute them more easily (who needs the peach one, who needs the blue) and you can spot who is working on what task by looking for the colors.

If students are working together on a tiered assignment, they can share the card. Try laminating the cards or sliding them into page protectors so they last through multiple uses. If students are working alone, you need to run as many work cards as group members.

Tips for Writing Work Cards

- Make sure the directions are clearly stated in kid-friendly language.
- Include specific details (e.g., "Give a minimum of three examples").
- Include criteria for quality or a rubric so students clearly know your expectations for their work.
- As appropriate, sequence the steps students need to follow.
- Include examples or samples of work as necessary.
- Explain how students will share their work.
- Double-check that the directions can be followed by students independently.

If some groups need more specific direction from you, meet with each group separately. You may also wish to make an audio recording of directions for clarification for some students.

3. Use Teacher Assistants

Designate one student from each tier as the group's teacher assistant or TA. This student can assist you in getting the work cards out to the appropriate students. The TA is also the first person others go to if they need clarification of the assignment or additional materials or resources to complete their task. TAs are also responsible for monitoring clean up and submission of student tasks at the end of the work time.

In addition to using TAs, if you have parent volunteers, special education aides, or paraprofessionals, it is only smart to plan your tiered assignments for when they are in the room to help you facilitate the students' work.

4. Use Differentiated Workstations

Many teachers use workstations as a method for managing multiple tasks in the classroom. Although work cards can be used to provide directions for tiered assignments for intermediate and secondary students, in primary classrooms such independence is not always possible. Workstations may be particularly helpful in managing differentiated tasks with primary students. Students are taught routines and practices for using workstations early in the year. It is an easy transition from traditional workstations to differentiated ones.

Step 1: Examine the kinds of activities offered in your stations. Differentiated activities include:

- Materials reflecting different stages of development
- Content ranging from introductory-level to more in-depth
- A sequence of skill progressions
- Activities ranging from simple to complex applications
- Readiness-based reading resources
- A variety of ways for students to learn and demonstrate their learning that reflect Multiple Intelligences learning preferences

Step 2: Assign students to the workstations and activities that address their specific learning needs. A single activity at a station that everyone must complete—whether they need it or not—is *not* differentiation.

This is the twist that makes a workstation differentiated: teachers prescribe particular activities to particular students to create a match between the learner's needs and the learning tasks. Using differentiated workstations, students may be assigned to particular stations offering activities that best address their needs, *or* all students may go to the same station (e.g., a writing station) but be assigned to do different activities there.

Different Workstations, Different Activities

In this process, students are assigned to particular stations based on their learning needs. You create different activities representing the needs of your students and place each activity in a separate station. Then you assign students to the appropriate stations. For example, not all students in a class need to continue to work on patterning, but some students may need more practice. Only those students who can benefit from more practice are assigned to the patterning workstation.

Workstations may be color-coded, so you can direct students to the appropriate stations by using a color code by their names on a bulletin board chart. Students can also be given color-coded "tickets" to their assigned stations.

Same Workstation, Different Activities

In this process, all students visit every workstation but are assigned to do different activities once there. Provide a range of activities within each station to address the needs of all students. At a writing station, for example, a purple activity might engage students in completing a thank-you note to a school helper by filling in their own words on a letter template. The red activity might ask students to select a school helper and write their own thank-you note on stationary provided. Students are assigned to the appropriate task based on their current writing skills, as well as on their need for greater support or more independence.

Materials for the different activities can be placed in color-coded bins or folders at each station. Activity sheets can be coded with stickers. Students need to know how to identify their assignments once they reach the workstation. Again, students may be assigned a color code using a bulletin board chart. Or they can be given a "passport" with an appropriate color sticker next to icons symbolizing each station.

Tips for Designing Workstations

As you reconsider previously used activities and find or design new ones, keep these tips in mind:

- All workstation activities must be focused on significant learning goals (KUDo's).
- Activities should represent a range of entry-level to more advanced skills and processes.
- Activities should reflect a variety of ways to learn and demonstrate learning.
- Activities should represent differing levels of complexity yet engage all students in challenging learning.
- Reading resources should match your students' readiness needs.
- An activity should be included in a workstation only after is has been modeled as a whole class activity. For example, if students have never made a booklet before, don't put a booklet into a station until your class has completed a booklet project.
- Activities can be completed alone, with a partner, or with a small group at the workstation. Inform students how they are to do the work.
- Tasks should be demonstrated as needed for the appropriate group of students.
- Explicit directions for how to complete tasks should be provided at each workstation. For multiple-step tasks, supply students with step-by-step procedures using icons to guide their work. Provide models and samples as necessary.
- Assign a TA for each workstation or set of activities. Students go to this person with questions if you are meeting with another group of students.

5. Organize and Distribute Materials and Resources Efficiently

It is important that materials and resources for tiered assignments are organized and readily available to the students. You may place materials and resources in bins or tubs labeled by the group's color. Or you may use resealable plastic bags or clear plastic 8½ " x 11" envelopes to package together work cards and task materials (such as articles to read, graph paper, or charts and tables) for quick distribution. Consider clustering desks together to create workstations for each flexible group. Organize and label your closets or shelves so that students can locate and return materials easily.

6. Manage Movement and Interruptions

Develop guidelines for when students may be out of their desks. Set parameters for students around disrupting you when you are working with a group of students. Determine how, when, and under what circumstances students may ask for your help.

Offer a procedure such as "Always ask a TA for assistance before asking me," so that students learn to become less dependent on you for clarification. You might provide "Help wanted" signs for students to place on a desk to signal you. Or you might have students write their name on a sticky note and post it on the whiteboard when they need help from you. Subsequent students place their notes beneath the first student, creating an order for assistance. If you are using TAs, it would be their job to post the student's name if they cannot help a student resolve an issue.

7. Develop and Post Cleanup Routines

Some cleanup routines can be ritualized. Recycling paper, submitting work, and returning resources to their appropriate storage areas commonly apply for most tasks. Describe, discuss, practice, and post these routines. Make sure all students know what to do, where things go, and when they clean up. Do they operate on their own timetables or do they wait until they are told it is cleanup time?

8. Provide Direction for What Comes Next

It is critical that students know what to do if they finish their task early. Anchor activities are thoughtful assignments that can be worked on independently and are connected to important curriculum, topics, or themes that extend students' learning.[1] It is important that anchor activities are discussed with students and posted in the classroom to answer the question "What next?" More specific information about identifying appropriate anchor activities is provided in Chapter 10.

Tiered assignments managed in flexible instructional groups are critical features of an academically diverse classroom. Teachers engage in a process of diagnosing their students' learning needs, finding or designing activities specifically addressing these needs, prescribing "just right, right now" activities matching the learner to the learning task. Tasks are facilitated using flexible instructional groups. Tiered assignments personalize the learning process by giving all students what they need. Matched with appropriate yet challenging learning, students more readily experience success. This success increases your students' sense of confidence and competence in learning.

1 Carol Ann Tomlinson, *How to Differentiate Instruction in Mixed Ability Classrooms,* 2nd ed. (Alexandria, VA: Association for Supervision and Curriculum Development, 2001).

CHAPTER 7

Critical Element: Maintaining Flexibility in Planning and Teaching

Flexibility is a critical element in a differentiated classroom. As a teacher, you need to be flexible in the ways in which you provide instruction, the kinds of tasks that your students engage in, and the ways in which you assess their learning.

Think about how you use your classroom space, your materials and resources, and your time to best respond to the needs of your students. Consider the best ways for your students to work, sometimes asking for individual work and other times encouraging partners or small group collaboration on tasks. Goals for grouping might involve learning needs or interests; other times grouping may simply be intended to develop your students' ability to work as a diverse team.

Use of preassessment and formative assessment causes you to adjust your curricular plans, your pace of instruction, and the kinds of tasks your students may engage in. Flexible instructional grouping based on changing data on student learning results in students being grouped and regrouped in a variety of ways. In a differentiated classroom, you are always ready to act on new information about your students' learning progress, actively seeking to better understand what they know, what they need to know, and what they need to know next.

> In a differentiated classroom, you are always ready to act on new information about your students' learning progress.

This chapter seeks to provide some insights into lesson routines and the ways in which they can support your work in differentiation. It also offers 25 formats for differentiation that clearly show there is not just one way to differentiate. Better yet, many of the formats require little or no preparation!

Flexibility in Lesson Routines

In the facilitator's guide to the video series, *The Common Sense of Differentiation,*[1] Carol Tomlinson introduces the concept of lesson routines as a way to critically examine where and how a teacher may choose to differentiate a lesson. Lesson routines are typical instructional processes or procedures that a teacher uses repeatedly. For example, the way in which a math teacher typically provides instruction in a math skill or process may look like **Figure 74**. **Figure 75** follows with a sample lesson routine for fraction and decimal equivalents. If we examine the lesson routine, we can identify many different points at which differentiation may be necessary and appropriate.

1 Carol Ann Tomlinson, *Common Sense of Differentiation: Meeting Specific Learner Needs in the Regular Classroom,* DVD and book. (Alexandria, VA: Association for Supervision and Curriculum Development, 2005).

FOUR STEPS IN THE MATH LESSON ROUTINE

Here are the four steps you would follow in the math lesson routine on fraction and decimal equivalents.

Step 1: Introduce the Skill

Not all children learn in the same way, therefore, how you introduce the math skill needs to reflect the ways in which your students learn best. When you consider modalities alone, you'll recognize that some students will understand the skill when you simply talk or lecture about it, others need you to sketch it out on the board so they can see it visually represented, and others need to work with manipulatives to be able to construct the concept.

Also consider whether all students need an introduction to fraction and decimal equivalents. Preassessment data may suggest that the lesson is inappropriate and unnecessary for some of the math students. What if some students already know or have "tested out" of fraction and decimal equivalents?

Step 2: Model the Skill

The number of problems needing to be modeled in order for the process to be understood will differ from student to student. Some students need many examples; others have it from the very first example provided. How do you monitor how many problems students need? How do you provide more for some, less for others?

Step 3: Have Students Practice the Skill

Some students need very few practice problems to demonstrate their understanding of the concept. Other students need reteaching and additional

FIGURE 74

Math Lesson Routine

MATH ELEMENTARY

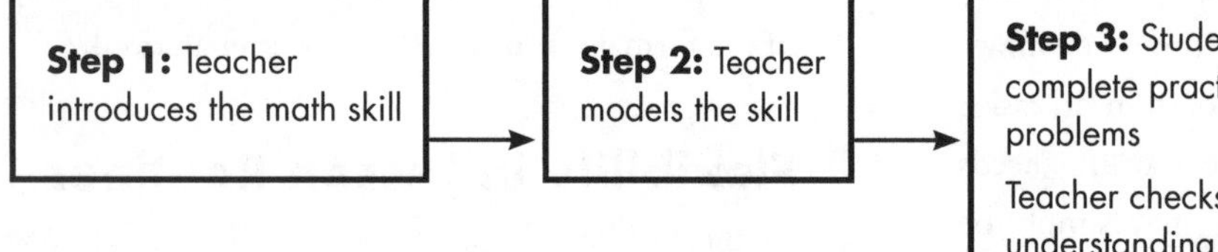

FIGURE 75

Sample Math Lesson Routine: Fraction and Decimal Equivalents

MATH ELEMENTARY

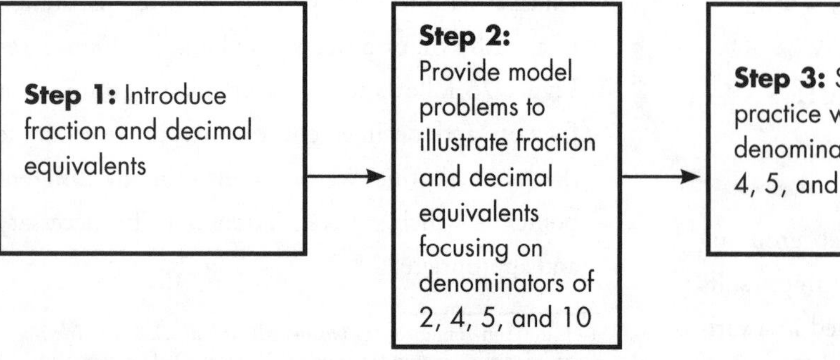

coaching. Some students need considerably more practice problems before they are ready to work independently. Others are waiting to get to work.

Pace differs also. Some students will quickly complete the required practice problems; others won't be done by the time you want to move on. What do you do with those who have a quick understanding of the skill and finish the problems early? What about those who need to continue practicing to master the skill when others have finished and are ready to move on?

Step 4: Give an Assignment

When you give any assignment, some students will be done quickly and others will need significantly more time. Do all students need to do the same number of problems? Do some students require modifications of the assignment? Do all students need to do the same kinds of problems? Would some students benefit from more complex applications of the skill? Does everyone get the same homework or is the homework differentiated?

FIGURE 76

Differentiated Math Lesson Routine: Fraction and Decimal Equivalents[2]

MATH ELEMENTARY

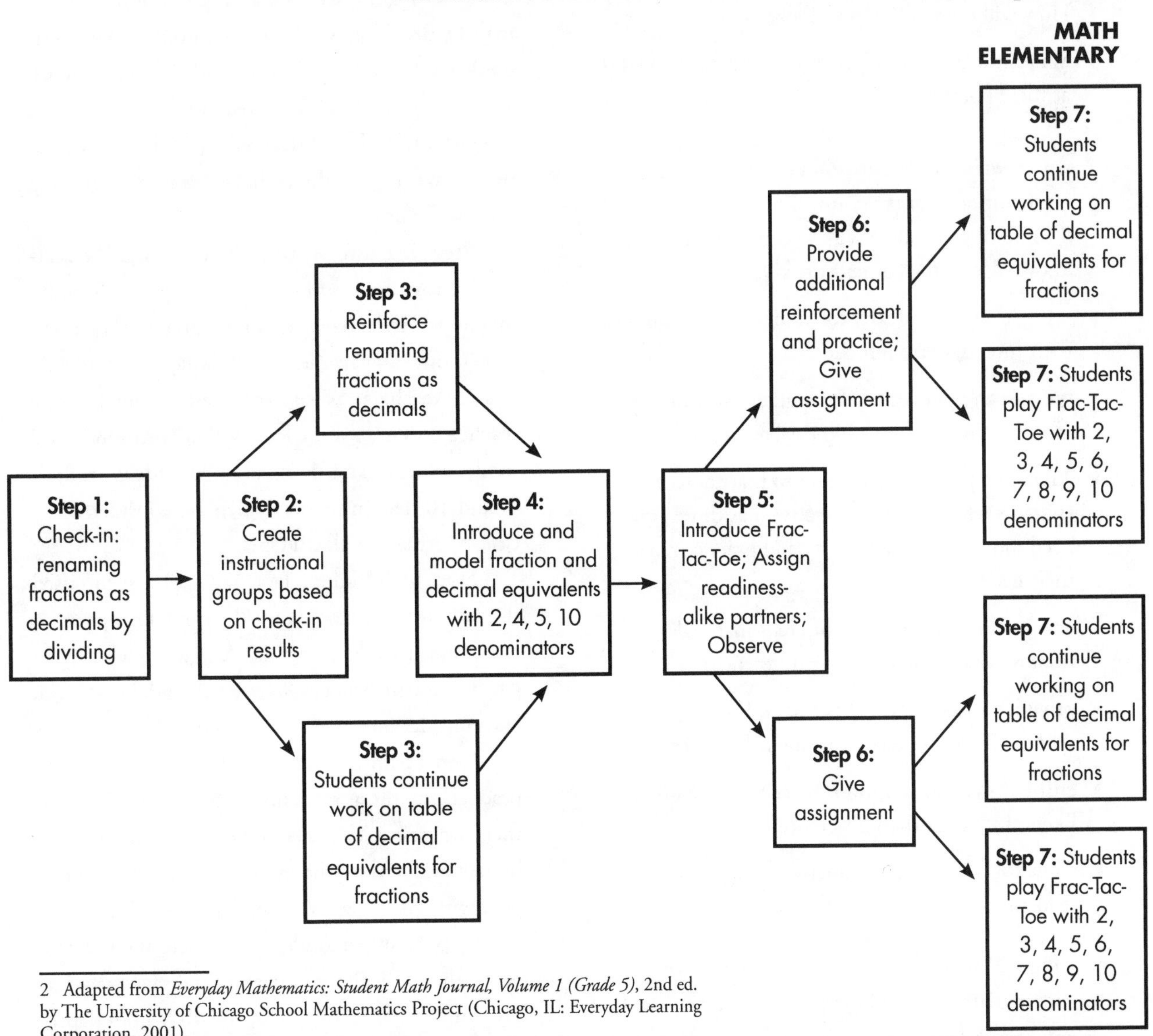

2 Adapted from *Everyday Mathematics: Student Math Journal, Volume 1 (Grade 5)*, 2nd ed. by The University of Chicago School Mathematics Project (Chicago, IL: Everyday Learning Corporation, 2001).

By discussing the four steps in the math routine, you can see that at any point in the lesson, the routine could be differentiated. It's not necessary for you to dive that deeply into differentiating lesson routines initially. Just consider the points in which a routine might benefit from differentiation, and commit to differentiating *one* component.

Differentiating a lesson routine can come through using multiple instructional strategies, opening up a component to student choice, or using a tiered task to prescribe particular activities to particular students. In considering where and how you might differentiate a lesson routine, ask yourself:

- Where are learning differences likely to emerge?
- How will these differences look?
- What strategies of differentiation might be used at these points?

Lesson routine differentiation strategies may

- create different entry points into the lesson if some students already have considerable knowledge of the content or skill.
- provide an opportunity for students to act on their interests through choice.
- provide an opportunity for students to work according to their learning preferences.
- adjust the pace of instruction so that those students who learn quickly as well as those who need more time, instruction, and practice have their needs met.
- engage students in using different materials or resources based on readiness differences.
- provide tiered assignments responding specifically to students' learning differences.
- create instructional groups based on students' likenesses rather than differences.
- allow for different assignments based on students' interests or learning needs.

Figure 76 on page 109 shows one possible way to differentiate the math routine on fraction and decimal equivalents.

SEVEN STEPS IN THE DIFFERENTIATED MATH LESSON ROUTINE

Here are the steps you would follow to differentiate the math lesson routine on fraction and decimal equivalents.

Step 1: Use the check-in strategy (see Chapter 3) to gather information about your students' understanding of what was taught the previous day: renaming fractions as decimals by dividing.

Step 2: Next, create two instructional groups based on your observations as the students work, as well as a quick scan and sort of collected check-in papers.

Step 3: Work with the group of students that is still struggling with renaming fractions as decimals by dividing. Model and reinforce the process; guide students through some additional problems. The group that has mastered this skill continues to work on a table of decimal equivalents for fractions that the students have been constructing during the unit.

Step 4: However, your responses may be scattered across the continuum and yet you still might maintain a well-managed, differentiated classroom. Classroom management techniques vary greatly among teachers. What works effectively for one teacher may not work for another. Introduce and model fraction and decimal equivalents with 2, 4, 5, and 10 denominators, which are considered the easiest format for all students.

Step 5: Introduce Frac-Tac-Toe, a game used throughout the school year. The game focuses on 2, 4, 5, and 10 denominators. Assign readiness-alike partners for the game. Observe the students at work and consider members for instructional groups.

Step 6: Provide additional reinforcement and practice for those students who need it. Monitor their progress as they begin the day's assignment or homework. Those who are ready to move on independently may begin to complete the assignment.

Step 7: When students complete their assignment, they may choose a partner and play Frac-Tac-Toe with 2, 3, 4, 5, 6, 7, 8, 9, and 10 denominators, an extension of the first game.

However, students who met with you at the beginning of the class period (Step 3) work on their table of decimal equivalents for fractions.

In this way all students work on the table, but some do so at the beginning of the class period and others at the end. This allows you to meet with the small group for reinforcement without needing to come up with an alternative task for them. During this unit, all students have been working on the table so they all know what to do without teacher assistance. (See Warm-ups and Cool-downs in *Differentiating Instruction in the Regular Classroom*[3] for more information about this strategy.)

3 Heacox, 2002, p. 98.

Be sure that the remediation or reteach group is not the only group you work with during lesson routines. Those who have quick mastery also need to have some instructional time with you to extend their practices. Advanced learners should not be expected to consistently go it alone. Think through and monitor your attention so that, over time, all learners have opportunities to interact with you.

LESSON ROUTINE SCENARIOS

There are many possible ways to differentiate a lesson routine. The decision about where and how you offer differentiation is based on the curriculum you are working with, the learning goals for the

FIGURE 77

Lesson Routine Scenario A

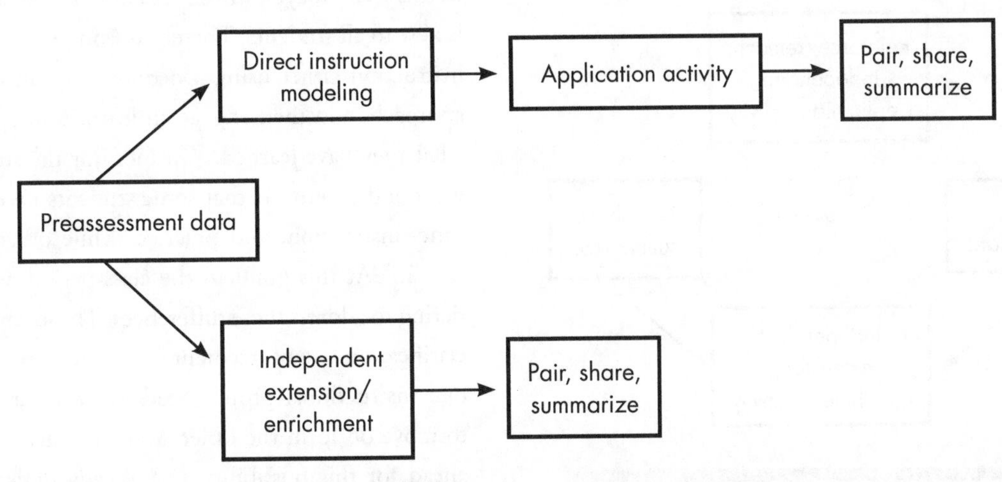

FIGURE 78

Lesson Routine Scenario B

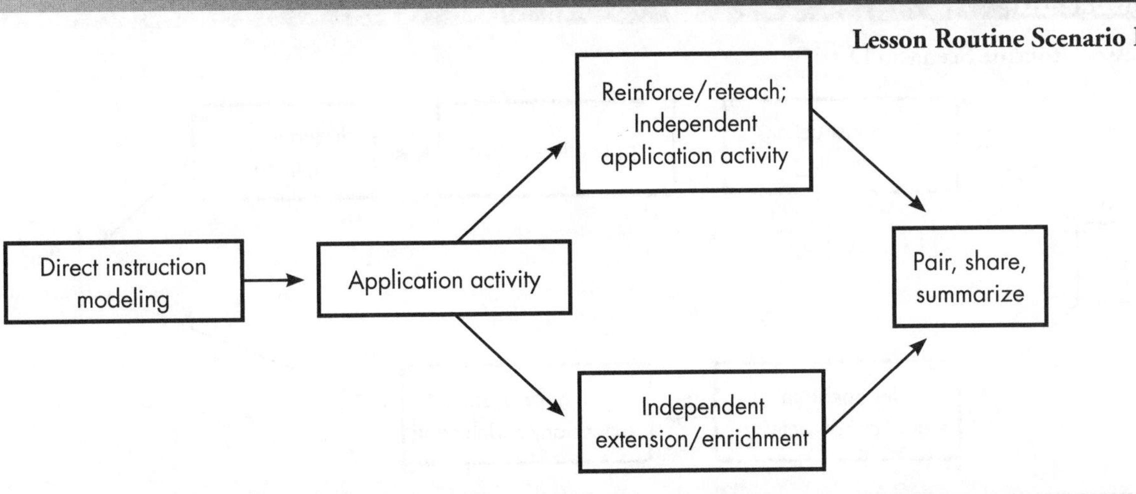

lesson, and the diversity and needs of your students. Opportunities to tier an activity or assignment may occur at many different points in your routine. **Figures 77 to 80** show scenarios presenting four ways in which a lesson routine may be differentiated.

Scenario A

In scenario A, you have reviewed preassessment data prior to the lesson. You have made a decision that the lesson routine must utilize tiered assignments from the very beginning of the lesson. You form instructional groups for the day's work. Students who have mastery of the content or skill are immediately engaged in an independent extension/enrichment activity providing more complex applications of the skills or more in-depth information related to the content. These students are not necessarily accelerated on to the next learning goal, but are not expected to engage in a reteaching of something they already know.

Students who need direct instruction and modeling remain with you and then proceed to an application activity to practice the new skill, or continue to work with the new content. At this point, you may check in with the group doing the extension/enrichment activity. At the end of the class period, each student pairs with another from the *same* instructional group and summarizes what he or she has learned.

FIGURE 79

Lesson Routine Scenario C

Formative assessment data → Reinforce/reteach; Independent application activity → Pair, share, summarize

Formative assessment data → Independent extension/ enrichment activity → Pair, share, summarize

Scenario B

In this scenario, you introduce content or a skill that is new to all students. Therefore, you provide direct instruction either using a deductive or an inquiry approach, and then engage all learners in applying what they have learned. You monitor the students' work and determine that some students need more time, instruction, and practice, while others have "got it." At this point in the class period, you use tiering to address these differences. Those who need clarification, reinforcement, or reteaching form one instructional group. Students who are ready to move on form the other. You will have planned ahead for this possibility and already designed or

FIGURE 80

Lesson Routine Scenario D

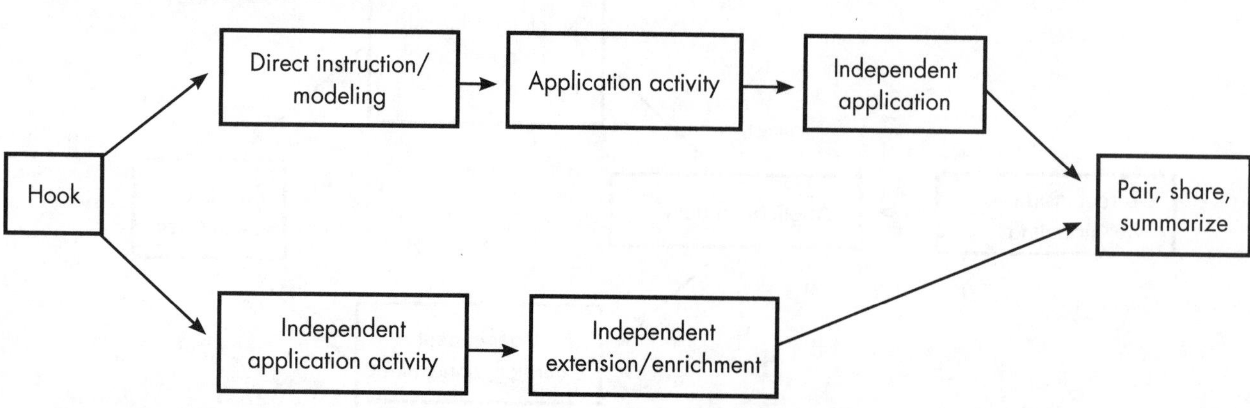

located an enrichment task in your teacher's guide that is ready to go. You may also have found some ideas for another way to approach the content or skill for those students who need more time and instruction. At the end of the class period, students choose their own partner and summarize what they have learned.

Scenario C

In scenario C, you have work from the previous class period that provides formative assessment data you can use to plan. Based on the student work, you form two instructional groups. Students who have mastery of the skill are immediately engaged in an independent extension/enrichment activity providing more complex applications of the skills. Those who need additional instruction and modeling remain with you and then proceed to an application activity. At this point, you may work with the students engaged in the extension/enrichment activity, either reviewing the work with them or providing instruction and practice in a more complex application of the skill or process. Both the application and the extension activities address the same learning goal and engage all students in creating similar products at different levels of complexity. At the end of the class period, students meet with a member of the other instructional group to share their work.

Scenario D

You engage all students in the "hook" or exploratory part of the lesson (see Chapter 4). Then you immediately utilize tiered tasks to respond to differences in your classroom. For example, the students are to work on a rocks and minerals lab. Students who need more scaffolding of the task have the lab experience broken down into more accessible steps. With this group, you specifically model and demonstrate the procedures. You actively assist them as they apply the lab processes. At the end of this guided practice, these students are expected to complete a lab sequence on their own. The more independent group is quite skilled at lab processes as evidenced earlier in the grading term. Following a procedure checklist, they work through the rocks and mineral application lab independently. Then, you join them to explain a more sophisticated lab that you have determined is good for some, but not all, of your students. This group goes on to the new lab experience following your introduction. At the end of the class period, all students engage in a large group discussion, each sharing the results of their lab work.

FIGURE 81

Reading Readiness: Story Maps

ENGLISH/LANGUAGE ARTS ELEMENTARY

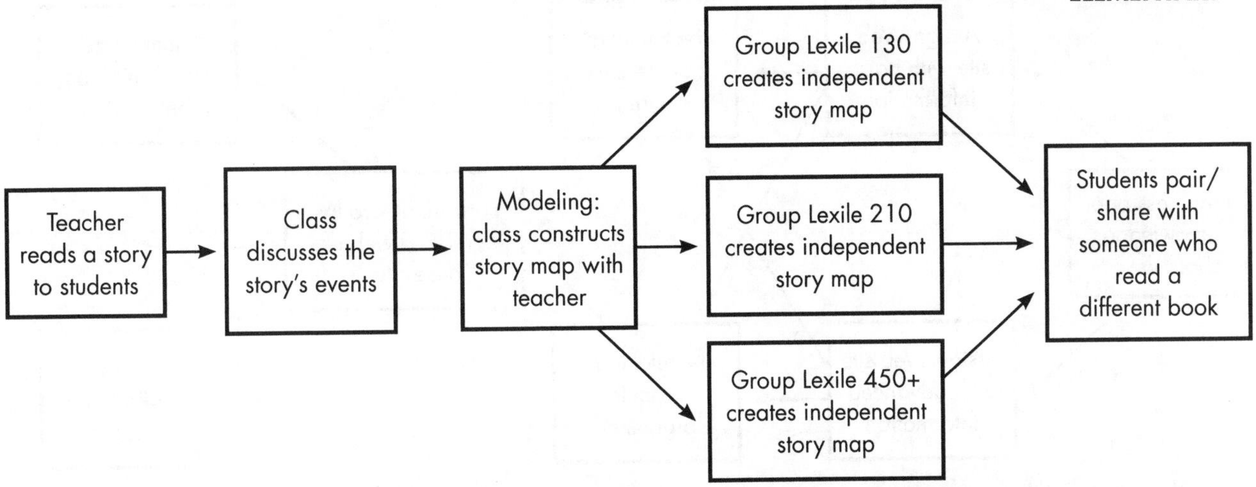

Teacher reads a story to students → Class discusses the story's events → Modeling: class constructs story map with teacher → Group Lexile 130 creates independent story map / Group Lexile 210 creates independent story map / Group Lexile 450+ creates independent story map → Students pair/share with someone who read a different book

The key to effective lesson routines is flexibility. For any lesson, there may be several ways to differentiate it. The previous four scenarios used tiering as the primary strategy for differentiation. **Figure 81** uses leveled reading resources as a differentiation strategy in a lesson on sequence of events. Students work as a class until they are grouped by reading-readiness level to independently create a story map.

Figure 82 adds choice to the lesson routine. You preassess students to identify what prior knowledge each has about deserts. You plan to take students to the computer lab and match them to the appropriate Web sites. Students who already know foundational information about deserts are assigned to a site with more advanced content. The students who are new to the topic are assigned to a site with introductory information. Students are given a choice on how they wish to capture facts about the desert: they may choose to use either a double-entry journal or a graphic organizer template. When the students return to the classroom, you assign them to cooperative groups representing both Web sites to share what they learned. Each small group creates a web of facts to share and post in the classroom. Finally, students individually choose to either summarize what they learned about deserts in an essay (Verbal/linguistic learning preference) or a labeled poster (Visual/spatial learning preference).

Critical examination of your typical lesson routines enables you to determine where and how you may need to differentiate. Reflecting on your lesson routines in light of your students' readiness needs, learning preferences, and interests results in better instructional matches for all learners. There is more than one right way to differentiate a lesson routine.

Lesson routines that best support differentiation:[4]

- are clearly focused on your learning goals.
- anticipate and specifically respond to the learning differences of your students.
- reflect your students' learning preferences, interests, and readiness needs.
- are open to change and modifications (even on your feet!) as necessary to the changing needs of your students.
- adjust timelines based on your students' needs.

4 Adapted from Tomlinson, 2005.

FIGURE 82

Student Choice: Deserts

SCIENCE
MIDDLE SCHOOL

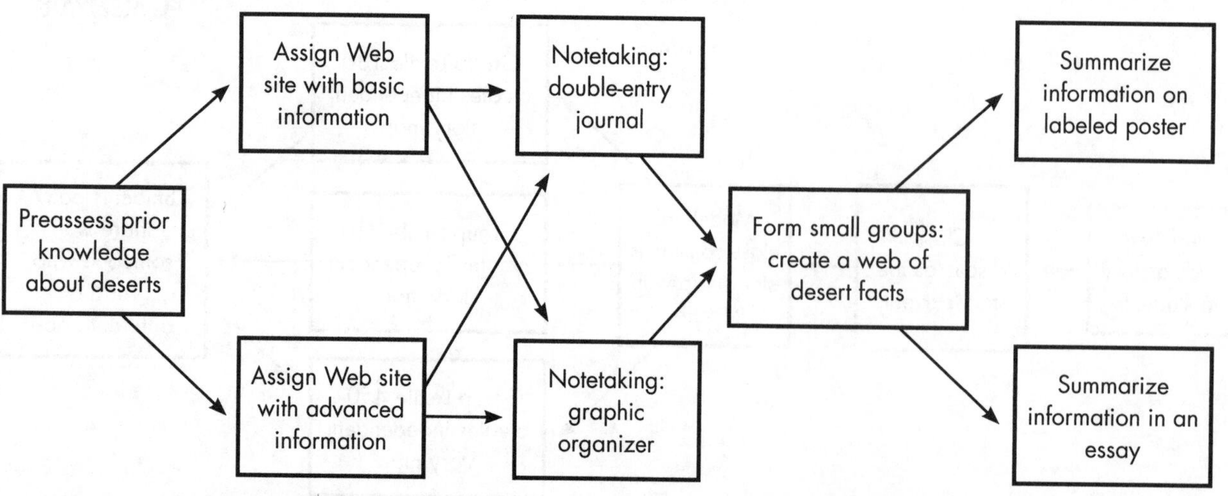

Flexibility in Delivering Differentiated Activities

There are a variety of ways that differentiated activities can be offered in the classroom. Formats for differentiated activities include those that engage students in making choices, as well as those that are prescribed by the teacher. As you know, prescribing particular tasks to particular students is the most specific and targeted kind of differentiation.

You make decisions about the ways in which you differentiate based both on your own teaching style and on the students in the classroom. Some formats you are simply more comfortable using with your students. Pages 116–117 offer a collection of 25 formats for presenting differentiated activities in the classroom, categorized by those that engage students in choice and those that you prescribe to meet specific needs of students. Following each format is a more specific example of how the format might look when used in the classroom. Formats noted with an asterisk (*) require little or no prep.

Use this list as a menu of ways to differentiate. You may also wish to use it as a self-assessment. Check off the formats you already use with students in differentiation, then review the formats you have not tried and make a commitment to try one new format during the next grading term. Remember, the key is to *start small, but start somewhere.* Differentiation is a collection of strategies that you continue to add to over years in the classroom.

Differentiation is a collection of strategies that you continue to add to over years in the classroom.

Flexibility is essential in academically diverse classrooms. You need to be flexible in your approaches to instruction, the learning tasks in which you engage your students, and the ways in which you use assessment data to inform your classroom practice. Each day in the classroom demands a reflective and critical look at what your students know, what they need to know, and what they need to know next. A planful teacher with a responsive classroom clearly examines the needs of his or her students and then purposefully and flexibly responds to them.

25 Formats for Differentiation

Formats Offering Student Choice

1. Choice of assignments designed by learning preference (Multiple Intelligences)
   Example: Students choose from a list of activities relating to a topic that reflect a variety of learning preferences: sing it, write it, diagram it, draw it, act it out, etc.

2. Choice of assignments skillfully designed by challenge and complexity level
   Example: Teacher uses a tic-tac-toe, show-and-tell, two-by-two, or other such choice board presenting differentiated tasks with teacher-planned choices.

3. Journal prompts provided by the teacher and selected by the students based on interest *
   Example: Students select from a list of writing assignments related to a theme, concept, or topic of study.

4. Choice of work style: individual, with a partner, in a small group *
   Example: Students do the same task but have a choice of ways to complete it.

5. Availability of study guides like notetaking templates or graphic organizers
   Example: Teacher-developed graphic organizers that capture key ideas from the text or lecture are used for preparation for assessments/exams.

6. Choice of topic by interest, same task *
   Example: All students complete the same task (e.g., construct an informational brochure), however, they choose the topic for their product (e.g., choose from a list of key topics related to the rain forest).

7. Choice of activity by interest *
   Example: All students choose to do particular parts of a group project (e.g., a newspaper project in which students choose the role of columnist, editorial cartoonist, editorial page editor, etc.).

8. Choice of topic, same task, leveled reading sources assigned by teacher
   Example: A compilation of articles related to the selected topics are placed in colored folders classified by reading level. Students select a topic and are directed to the folder containing the resources matched to their reading readiness.

9. Choice of ways to share information *
   Example: Students may write, present, draw, or diagram information.

Teacher-Prescribed Formats

10. Tasks based on readiness demonstrated in preassessment
    Example: Students are assigned to science labs involving different topics and different tasks based on their prior knowledge; all groups share their results with the class.

11. Tasks with similar content, different levels of difficulty or complexity
    Example: Students work with the same content, but are assigned to different activities based on their learning needs.

12. Tasks assigned based on learning preference
    Example: Bodily/kinesthetic students perform a skit, while Visual/spatial students create a poster.

13. Readings or research in small groups assigned by prior content knowledge *
    Example: One group explores introductory or foundational information; another explores more complex, in-depth, technical information. All groups share.

* indicates formats that require little or no prep

CONTINUED ➡

14 Tasks supported by greater scaffolding
Example: Students who need more support in their learning, or who need a complex task broken down into more accessible steps, are provided necessary templates, formats, or procedure checklists to increase their likelihood of success.

15 Tasks supported with technology resources
Example: Students who have extensive knowledge and interest in a particular topic are matched to online resources to extend their learning beyond the core curriculum. Other students use online sources to supplement or support text content.

16 Tasks demanding different levels of abstraction
Example: Some students are assigned more concrete applications to assist them in understanding; other students engage in tasks that demand more abstract thinking.

17 Tiered graphic organizers
Example: Students using the same content are assigned to particular graphic organizers differing in their degree of structure and level of complexity or abstraction.

18 Essay questions or journal prompts tiered by level of difficulty
Example: Essay questions reflecting varying levels of complexity or abstractness are assigned to particular students.

19 Tasks tiered by demonstrated readiness
Example: Students are assigned to particular activities based on their readiness levels (e.g., additional practice with vocabulary/skills, application of vocabulary/skills, extension of vocabulary/skills).

20 Same project, student roles assigned by teacher *
Example: Teacher assigns particular students in each group to take leadership roles based on their particular talents or learning preferences (e.g., the lead writer, the lead researcher, etc.).

21 Paired reading and question responses with partner of similar ability, struggling readers with teacher *
Example: Struggling readers can be better coached through reading and response by a teacher than by an age peer; other students may select to join the teacher's group if they wish.

22 Mini-lessons on skills or content by invitation and self-selection *
Example: Students who lack particular skills or content based on formative data are invited by the teacher to join the mini-lesson; other students may select to attend based on their own perceived needs.

23 Work partners assigned based on same content knowledge *
Example: Students work with partners who are at the same knowledge level related to the content being studied.

24 Same topic, different reading sources based on reading readiness
Example: All students read about the same topic but their resources vary by reading readiness.

25 Same topic, primary or paraphrased readings
Example: All students read about the same topic but some are assigned primary resources while others are given paraphrased readings (e.g., either Martin Luther King Jr.'s original speech, or a summary of his key points, ideas, and themes).

* indicates formats that require little or no prep

CHAPTER 8

Critical Element: Developing Student Responsibility and Independence

Your Management Profile

When we think about classroom management, we consider time, instruction, materials and resources, and student behavior. All four are clearly linked together, as in a jigsaw puzzle. If you are unable to effectively manage instructional time, behavior issues arise. If you are ill prepared to teach and facilitate a lesson, both time and behavior issues arise. If materials and resources are not organized and readily available to students, both time and behavior issues arise.

Therefore, in thinking about management, you must carefully consider effective use of time, thorough instructional planning, efficient organization of materials and resources, and ways to engage your students that are respectful and safe yet buzz with the excitement of learning. Throughout this book, ideas for better managing a differentiated classroom have been presented as they apply to each strategy. This chapter will take a closer look at ways in which you can develop greater student responsibility and independence in your differentiated classroom.

The classroom management continuum on page 119 enables you to explore your current management practices in light of differentiation.

Interpretation of Your Results

Descriptors on the far right of the continuum typify characteristics of a well-managed differentiated classroom. However, your responses may be scattered across the continuum and yet you still might maintain such a classroom.

> Well-managed classrooms are well-managed differentiated classrooms.

FIGURE 83

Classroom Management Jigsaw

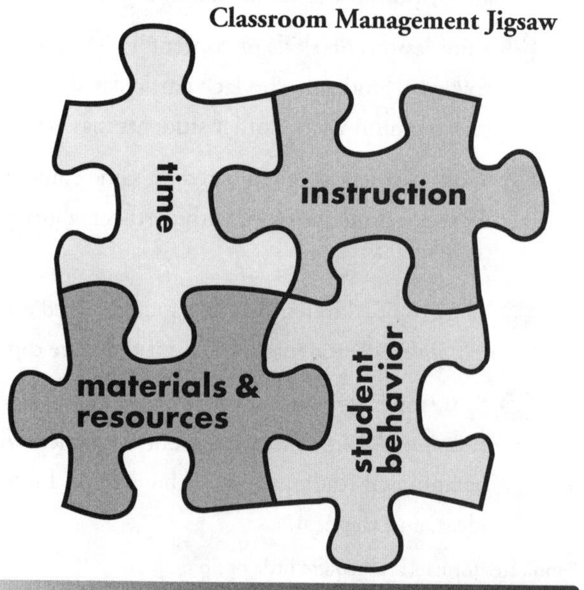

Classroom Management Continuum

Note with an "X" where you would place yourself on the continuum between the various descriptors listed.

1. TEACHER'S FOCUS

Focuses on what is taught	Takes student needs into consideration	Student-focused teaching and learning

2. TEACHER'S ROLE

Directs learning	Monitors student progress and facilitates learning	Diagnoses student learning needs, then prescribes and facilitates learning experiences

3. STUDENT INDEPENDENCE

Little student independence in thought or action	Some independence with teacher guidance	Self-reliant, independent learners

4. STUDENT RESPONSIBILITY

Teacher assumes major responsibility	Individual student responsibility is assumed	Teacher creates a community that values collaboration, support, assistance

5. TASK MANAGEMENT

Preference is one task for all	Comfortable with multi-tasks	Confident with multi-tasks

6. ORGANIZATION OF TIME AND TASKS

Few prompts for what, when, how, what next	Sufficient prompts that lead to limited or irregular self-direction	Organized and explicit system for what, when, how, what next

7. ORGANIZATION OF STUDENT WORK

Few explicit systems for organizing and managing student work	Some systems provided but limited or irregular student follow-through	Purposeful, effective systems organizing and managing work

8. PROVIDING STUDENT FEEDBACK

Teacher feedback only	Teacher feedback, student self-evaluation	Teacher feedback, student self-evaluation, peer feedback

Classroom management techniques vary greatly among teachers. What works effectively for one teacher may not work for another.

However, if you are in the middle of the continuum or at the far right, you will find moving to more sophisticated levels of differentiation easier. If the majority of your responses are on the far left, you may find that moving to higher levels of differentiation can be stressful, until you become more comfortable with the practices on the right side of the continuum. Well-managed classrooms are well-managed differentiated classrooms. As you set up classroom routines and procedures that support higher levels of student independence and responsibility, you will notice a decrease in the chaos level in your classroom.

Routines to Make Everyday Events Go Smoothly

Routines establish the ways in which your students respond to recurring events and conduct their work in the classroom. The absence of classroom routines can reduce learning time and result in behavior issues. Established and practiced routines enable students to operate more independently. The following student questions regarding recurring events in a differentiated classroom can be addressed with routines that encourage student independence and responsibility:

- How do I prepare for a new activity?
- What if I finish my work early?
- How do I know what task to do when not everyone is doing the same thing?
- How and when can I leave my desk or workspace?
- What should I do when I'm stuck and don't know what to do?
- When can I ask the teacher for help?
- Who should I ask for help if the teacher is not available?
- When can I use the restroom or get a drink of water?
- What should I do when the teacher gives the signal to be quiet?
- How should I behave in different areas of the room?
- When and how loud can I talk during work time?
- How do I work best with a partner?
- What is the best way to work in a group?
- When can I sharpen my pencil?
- What should I do if I'm late to class and activities have already started?
- How do I clean up at the end of an activity?
- How and where do I hand in my completed work?
- What do we do if technology fails?
- Where and when do I get supplies and materials?
- When and how do we rearrange classroom furniture?

Routines to address these questions need to be discussed, modeled, and consistently practiced to be effective. Post routines in appropriate areas of your classroom to serve as reminders for students. With younger children, directly instruct them on how the routine works, model it, allow the students to practice it, and observe the students as they try it independently.

MANAGEMENT STRUCTURES

There are many ways you can facilitate differentiation through various structures in your classroom and school. Stations, including cybercenters, and within-grade-level and across-grade-level collaborations can make meeting diverse needs more doable.

Workstations

Workstations (or work centers) are discussed in Chapter 6 as a way to facilitate tiered assignments for young learners. They can also be used with students in higher grade levels. You can assign students to rotate through a specific set of activities designed to respond to their needs. These tiered assignments are completed one step at a time as students rotate to a new station for each sequential step. For example, you might design a series of science lab activities to walk students through the scientific method one step at a time. Different levels of support in the process would be provided at stations designed to meet the needs of particular students.

Stations could also present single tasks assigned to particular students. For example, in a science class you may use a number of experiments with rocks and minerals ranging in level of complexity. You would decide which students should do which experiments and assign them to the appropriate lab station. Refer to Chapter 6 on pages 104–105 for additional ideas for designing and managing workstations.

Cyberstations

You can also use your classroom computers as cyberstations. Cyberstations offer students appropriate learning opportunities through Web sites or software. Cyberstations can also engage individual students in WebQuests. WebQuests are inquiry-based lessons that link students to Web-based resources and materials. Bernie Dodge at the University of San Diego maintains a highly regarded WebQuest site (www.webquest.org). This site provides hundreds of WebQuests that teachers can search for by grade and subject area. Since teachers from across the country provide WebQuests for this site, make sure you compare their learning goals to your state standards or provincial goals before you use them with your students. Also, consider whether a particular WebQuest is appropriate for some or all of your students. You may also decide to assign particular tasks within a WebQuest to certain students based on their learning needs.

Partnerships

In order to reduce the preparation time for tiered assignments and eliminate some of the management issues, some grade levels and departments create partnerships. For example, two fourth-grade teachers may move students between their classrooms when tiered assignments are appropriate. One teacher takes the group of students who need more work with topic sentences; the other takes the students who have mastered topic sentences. In this way, the teachers have only a single preparation to complete and a single group of learners to manage. One teacher prepares to work with the students who need more time, instruction, and practice with topic sentences; the other designs a writer's workshop activity for those students ready to move on in their writing. Teachers may informally chat with one another to identify what skills or content each is working on, and then establish a date and time for exchanging students. *Note of caution:* Make sure there is not a pattern established related to a particular teacher always having a particular group of students. You want to keep the teacher and student group pairings fluid so they appear random to the students.

Across-Grade Grouping

Across-grade grouping is sometimes necessary when students are considerably out of alignment with the grade-level curriculum. When it is too difficult for you to differentiate experiences to the degree necessary to meet a student's needs, it may make more sense to move the student into another grade level's classroom. In this example, you are not grade-skipping the child, because the majority of the school day is spent with age peers. You are simply looping the student to the next grade level for subject-specific instruction.

Clock Buddies

Clock Buddies is a way that you can quickly group students in a variety of ways for different purposes. Students are paired with a partner for the clock hours: 12:00, 3:00, 6:00, and 9:00. (*Note:* these clock hours do *not* correspond with the actual time in your classroom.) The following grouping strategies are used in Clock Buddies:

12:00 Buddies are readiness-alike
3:00 Buddies are learning preference-alike
6:00 Buddies are readiness-different
9:00 Buddies are random and selected by students

FIGURE 84

Clock Buddies

You can create clock buddies for your students by assigning partners for all hours except 9:00. Or you can have your students involved in choosing their clock buddies, giving them a greater sense of independence. To reduce the time needed to prepare these clocks for your students, have them work with you in making their own clocks. Use the following process:

1. Create two lists of students: the blue group and the green group. Blue group students represent those who are working at or above grade level. Green group members represent students who are working at or below grade level.

2. Students choose their **12:00** buddy from the students in their color group. For example, green group members approach other green group members and exchange names for the 12:00 spot on their clocks. These are *readiness-alike buddies.*

3. Students pick a **3:00** buddy from those students with similar learning preferences. If students have completed inventories on Multiple Intelligences, you can create posters or lists of students organized by learning preference. Students choose buddies from the list of students with like learning preferences. These are *learning preference-similar buddies.*

4. Students find a **6:00** buddy from the opposite color group as theirs. For example, green group members choose members from the blue group. This creates *readiness-different buddies.*

5. For **9:00** buddies, students have free choice. However, they need to pick someone who is not already on their clock. These are *random buddies.*

Depending on the purpose for grouping (readiness-alike or different, similar learning preference, or random pairings), tell the students who they should buddy with for activities (e.g., "Find your 12:00 buddy.") In this way, students are independently able to organize themselves as partners. If a clock buddy is absent, you create a group of three by matching the single student with another pair using the same grouping strategy. For example, if students are assigned to readiness-alike (12:00) buddies, the single student must be matched with two other students of like readiness. You can also create larger groups by combining partners, such as combining two 6:00 buddy groups to make a group of four.

RESOURCES AT THE READY

There are certain duplicated materials that students refer to consistently over a grading period or school year. Examples may include a particular process that needs to be used for peer editing, critical elements required in all lab reports, troubleshooting tips for ailing computers, or a writing rubric that is used consistently at your grade level throughout the school year. Following are ideas for how to effectively manage these resources and create more student independence.

Script Books

Have students collect these duplicated items in three-ring notebooks called *script books.* Script books enable students to seek answers for their own dilemmas, find out what to do and how to do it, and evaluate their work independently. Direct students to use dividers to separate items by subject area or purpose to speed retrieval, and to use page protectors for each item to increase its durability.

Conduct script book checks periodically to make sure the content is current.

Hanging File for Rubrics

When we engage students in choice and want quality work, rubrics or checklists need to be provided for each choice. Making these self-evaluation tools available to students enables them to be more independent and responsible for checking the quality of their work. The challenge becomes how to keep track of and distribute the rubrics. One solution is to place a hanging file in an accessible spot in your classroom so students can independently select the rubric appropriate for their project. Make separate file folders for each rubric, and slide rubrics into page protectors. Creating generic rubrics saves preparation time as they can be used repeatedly. For example, the criteria for a poster will remain constant; only the content of the poster will change with curriculum topics.

Student Office Area

Create a student office area where students pick up work that has been reviewed or graded, store work in progress, submit completed work, and access materials for assignments or projects.

Returning Work and Distributing Notices

Cardboard mailbox units can be purchased from an office supply store and work well for elementary teachers. Some elementary teachers use the pockets in a hanging plastic shoe storage unit for mailboxes. Secondary teachers usually use workfiles: hanging file folders with different colored files for each section or hour of a course.

Collecting Completed Work

Establish a system for students to use when turning in completed work. Elementary teachers may station a basket in the student office area to collect submissions. Secondary teachers may use different colored letter bins by hour or section of the day to collect papers from different sections of courses. If you are also using color-coded workfiles, use the same color code for submission bins to avoid confusion.

Also, create and post a check-in sheet with the students' names or, for confidentiality, student numbers and the assignment (see page 124). Make it a routine for students to check off their names as they submit work. Thus, with a quick glance you can see the status of work completion.

Workfiles

In place of or in addition to mailboxes and submission bins, workfiles are efficient for submission and return of work, for storing work in progress, and for distributing notices and letters. Workfiles are personal file folders that students retrieve from a hanging file at the beginning of the day or class period. Any work that needs to be submitted goes into this file, as well as any work that you are returning to students or other communications you have for them. Students can also put "work in progress" into these files. Folders are labeled with the student's name, and are numbered and organized in alphabetical order. Secondary teachers should use different color file folders for each section of a course.

Review or grade work directly from the workfiles. Do not empty the contents of all files at once to review or grade, as then you'd need to refile the work again later. Workfiles get student work distributed quickly, confidentially, and independently. If a student is absent, the workfile remains in the hanging file and you insert any makeup work that needs to be completed. Secondary teachers can assign a student the responsibility of distributing materials to absent classmates' files. However, workfiles are not portfolios; once work has been reviewed or graded, the students remove it from the file.

Storage Area

Storage room for larger projects can also be located in the student office area. Plastic crates can be used if shelves or cupboard space is not available. You can also use tall plastic wastebaskets to store work that can be rolled up (supply rubber bands). Hangers with clips can be used to hang work in a closet, on a coat rack, or on a rope strung along a wall.

Assignment Check-In Sheet

	Assignment titles									
STUDENT NAME/ STUDENT NUMBER										
1										
2										
3										
4										
5										
6										
7										
8										
9										
10										
11										
12										
13										
14										
15										
16										
17										
18										
19										
20										
21										
22										
23										
24										
25										

The student office area can also store materials and resources students may need for class assignments. Construction paper, writing paper, extra pencils, scissors, masking tape, staplers, and markers can be organized into bins or labeled cupboards to enable students to access what they need independently. This also enables students to return materials to their designated spot without your assistance. Remember to set up procedures for when and who might access these materials.

EIGHT TIPS FOR FLEXIBLE CLASSROOM SPACE

To maintain classroom flexibility as you form instructional groups and engage students in different kinds of work, keep these tips in mind:

1. Arrange furniture so that there is some open community space where students can gather. You may use this space to pull all students together for class activities or discussions. Chairs can be arranged into partner or small group configurations. And students can use the open space to work on activities that require more work room. Consider locating community space where blackboard or whiteboards are available.

2. Designate an area of your room for "messy" work. This should be out of the way of student traffic.

3. Designate one area for quiet work and another area for work noise. Some activities require more chatting and you want to separate those groups from students who need quiet to concentrate on the work at hand.

4. Consider traffic paths in your classroom. Arrange classroom furniture so that students can take the shortest route between areas of activity. Having students near high-interest areas such as materials or resources storage means more distractions during work time.

5. Post routines or procedures in areas where they can be easily referenced. For example, a routine for solving computer "glitches" can be posted on the wall by your computer station. Any routine that students may need can be written on a poster to enable them to operate as independently as possible.

6. Organize and store materials where they are likely to be needed. For example, storing paper and ink cartridges by the computer station enables students to get what they need without your help.

7. Create display areas where students can post their work. This is especially important for tiered assignments, since students need to see each other's work to share their learning.

8. Consider how and where you place student desks or tables in the room. You want to enable the students to move furniture into different configurations reflecting the needs of an activity. Give your students practice, under your direction, in moving furniture quickly and quietly. No bumper cars, please!

THE SIGNAL

The *Responsive Classroom*[1] approach to management encourages teachers to determine a signal that is used to prompt student attention. Signals are effective, quiet, and calm ways to gain the attention of students.

A signal can be a raised hand, the formation of an "L" with forefinger and thumb (standing for "Look" and "Listen"), a peace sign with two fingers raised, or anything you or your students come up with. When you give the signal, students give the signal back to you to spread it across the classroom. The signal means that all students are to stop whatever they are doing, become quiet, and wait for you to speak. Do not speak until all students are paying full attention to you.

The signal is never negotiated; it is absolute. Once established, the signal can be used anywhere in the school. If students are with you in the hallway or media center, the agreed-upon signal continues to be used. Some schools establish a school-wide signal. In these schools, it does not matter where in the building the students are or who is currently in charge of the group; the signal is honored.

1 Northeast Foundation for Children, *Responsive Classroom* (Turners Falls, MA: Northeast Foundation for Children, 2003).

In differentiated classrooms, when students are not always working on the same thing at the same time, it is essential to have a method such as this for getting the attention of your students when you need it.

ANCHOR ACTIVITIES

One management issue we all face is what students should do if they finish work before their classmates. What to do next and what will keep them learning are important considerations. Anchor activities are thoughtful assignments that can be worked on independently and are connected to important curriculum, topics, or themes that extend students' learning.

There are three kinds of activities that can be considered anchor activities:

❶ First are those activities that are *consistently offered* throughout the year. For example, you could consistently offer independent reading, "sketchbooks" in which students sketch the meanings of their vocabulary words, or notetaking from textbooks onto graphic organizers. You may extend the reading choices to include books, articles, or subject-specific magazines or journals related to a current curriculum topic or theme.

❷ A second kind of anchor activity is one that is *curriculum-based.* These are activities that offer additional applications of the skills or processes of a curriculum unit, as well as activities that extend or enrich a current curriculum topic. Cybercenters, for example, could serve either purpose.

❸ Finally, there are *student-based* anchor activities. These activities are developed around your students' interests discovered through interest inventories, discussions, or observations. These activities go beyond the required grade-level curriculum.

You might begin a discussion of anchor activities by having your students brainstorm "things we could do if we finish early," and then build on this list with additional ideas and resources that you have available. Consider activities and suggestions from your teacher's guide or your unit file that you have not had time to use in the past.

Post a list of acceptable anchor activities in your classroom. You may want to use a pocket chart, white board, or bulletin board to list the "all the time" activities, and then post additional curriculum-based or student-based activities as curriculum topics or interests change. You can divide anchor activities into "must do first" and "then do next" categories, if you wish to prioritize particular activities. There are times when students need a reminder of an assignment coming due soon, which would be listed in the "must do first" group. Page 128 provides some guidelines for selecting or designing anchor activities.

Managing Anchor Activities

There are some management decisions you will need to make concerning anchor activities in your classroom. Ask yourself the following questions before you implement this strategy.

1. When will the students work on these?
2. Are the activities worth points?
3. Should a certain number be required to be completed?
4. What about the students who need all the class time provided to complete their assignments?
5. Should some activities be "bigger" and others "done in a day or class period"?
6. Will activities be due? If so, when and how frequently?
7. Will activities only be worked on in school or can they become homework?
8. Will there be check-in points along the way?
9. How will students keep track of what they have done?
10. How can I easily check on their progress?
11. How will I organize task cards or directions for the activities?

12. How will I organize the necessary materials?

13. How will I collect the completed work?

14. How will I provide feedback?

15. Will activities be done individually or can a student work with a partner?

Activities from a tic-tac-toe board, a two-by-two board, a show-and-tell, a RAFT, or a project menu can also be used as anchor activities. **Figure 85** shows a writing project menu for primary students.

In this example, some activities are designed for shorter periods of time, like the recipe. Others require a longer time commitment, such as the daily news bulletin. Student choices are controlled through the arrangement of the activities. Even-numbered activities are more challenging writing activities; odd-numbered activities are more basic writing tasks. Do not announce the pattern of basic and advanced activities to your students. However, if particular students need more direction in making good choices, you can direct a student to particular activities. For example, you can nudge a capable writer to choose from the even-numbered activities. The student still has choice, but you are steering him to the best activities for his capabilities.

If you wish to further differentiate anchor activities, you could code them with stickers or place them in colored file folders. For example, red stickers/folders are "stretch" (challenging) activities; yellow stickers/folders are "take a leap" (most challenging) activities. Students could choose which activity they wish to do or you could prescribe stretch or leap activities.

Providing Feedback on Anchor Activities

The purpose of anchor activities is not to increase your paper load or add more items to your grade book. Their intent is to keep students learning. However, in some instances, a feedback loop may be helpful. Feedback on anchor activities can be provided through self-checking rubrics or checklists. As appropriate, scoring sheets or keys may be used by the student or a peer evaluator. Any of the self-reflection forms offered in Chapter 4 can also engage the students in evaluating their activities.

FIGURE 85

Sample Writing Project Menu

ELEMENTARY

1. Write a shopping list	2. Write clues to mystery animals	3. Complete a morning message	4. Write an original recipe
5. Write a story with sentence strips	6. Write a note to your teacher	7. Copy a family recipe	8. Review a book, game, movie, or TV show
9. Write a paragraph for a magazine picture	10. Write directions for how to make or do something	11. Make a list of facts about something	12. Write a daily news bulletin about our classroom
13. Create a birthday card with a message	14. Write an "I'm sorry" note	15. Make a list of characteristics for being a good friend	16. Write a message to a character in a book or story

Criteria for Well-Designed Anchor Activities

- ☐ Represent significant learning, not busywork
- ☐ Offer differentiated tasks that vary in challenge and complexity
- ☐ Are engaging and interesting
- ☐ Capitalize on student learning preferences and interests
- ☐ Are written with sufficient specificity so that students can engage in them independently
- ☐ Use processes similar to past tasks so that students are able to work independently on them
- ☐ Are self-monitoring
- ☐ Provide a feedback loop such as a self-checking rubric or scoring sheet as appropriate to the task
- ☐ May include a requirement as to how many must be completed over a specific period of time

Tips for Using Anchor Activities with Primary Students

- Anchor activities can be communicated through icons or pictures. Create a collection of picture cards with magnets attached to the back that note what students are to do if they finish early. Post selected picture cards on the white board in the order in which the students are to do the activities. (First do this . . . , then do this . . .) This strategy will also work in supporting English language learners.
- If you use workstations in your classroom, students may go visit one to do an anchor activity. Since students will be familiar with your process for using stations, the activities can be more self-managed. Match an icon or picture card posted on the board to icons at stations indicating where anchor activities are located.
- Employ a monitoring strategy to ensure that students' classwork is not being compromised or rushed through in a desire to move on to an anchor activity. Make sure your students know that their primary work is their classwork, *not* the anchor activities.

GET HELP TO MANAGE MULTIPLE TASKS

As a classroom teacher, your key to managing multiple tasks is planning ahead and looking for opportunities when you can partner with someone. Many educators have special education teachers or paraprofessionals who work in their classrooms. Others have parent volunteers or upper-grade students who come to help. Try to schedule your tiered assignments and flexible groups for times when you are not the only adult in the room. Collaborating with others makes managing multiple tasks more doable.

Think ahead and select a time for tiered assignments when you have help available. Have your tasks designed and your materials ready. Make sure you discuss student expectations and classroom procedures with your partner ahead of time. Determine when and how you will explain the activity that needs to be facilitated to your partner. Think about the group of students who most need your attention that day but also consider when you can rotate groups with your partner so that, over time, all students have opportunities to work with both of you.

If parent volunteers are your partners, you may want to consider setting up a consistent day and time for their help. Schools report that if parent volunteers know that they are depended upon to work with a group of students on a regular basis, they are more likely to show up in your classroom. When they are standing at our door and we are scrambling to figure out what we can have them do, they conclude their participation may be optional.

Smooth-running differentiated classrooms have responsible and independent students. This chapter has offered routines, structures, and strategies that enable you to set up and organize your classroom, establish routines, and form partnerships that encourage your students to work with greater independence and develop higher levels of responsibility for their work.

CHAPTER 9

Critical Element: Using Ethical Grading Practices

The way in which teachers use and calculate grades reflects a personal philosophy. Because of this, it is difficult to get even two teachers to agree on the purposes and practices of grading. However, we *can* discuss ethical grading practices. The purpose of this chapter is to open up the discussion about grading and to provide some perspectives about the conversations that are occurring internationally about grading in a differentiated classroom.

The way in which teachers use and calculate grades reflects a personal philosophy.

What Is Fair?

As teachers begin their work in differentiation, the issue that consistently arises and causes much consternation is how to fairly grade students. Common questions include:

- Is it fair that students who are doing different work are graded using the same range of possible grades from F to A?
- Should each level of a tiered assignment be eligible for the same number of points?
- If I grade differentiated activities using the same grade and point range, doesn't that send the wrong message to parents concerning the student's "actual" performance?
- If I grade differentiated activities fairly, doesn't that affect the final grade on the report card and provide false impressions about student progress and performance?
- If I don't grade everything, how will I get students to do the work?
- Won't some students get upset if they see that someone else can do a less rigorous activity and still get a good grade?

The Purposes and Problems of Grading

To address these questions, we first need to consider the purposes of grading. The primary goal of grading should be to accurately report to parents and students information about the student's achievement of learning goals, learning progress, and the work habits, attitudes, and behavior exhibited in the classroom. However, a single grade cannot report with specificity all three of these performance elements.[1] Thus, the grading process must be separated into three distinct and separate reports that address the following questions:

THE THREE PERFORMANCE ELEMENTS OF GRADING

1. Did the student achieve the learning goals established for this grading term?
2. Did the student make progress in his/her learning this grading term?

1 Carol Ann Tomlinson and Jay McTighe, *Integrating Differentiated Instruction & Understanding by Design: Connecting Content and Kids* (Alexandria, VA: Association for Supervision and Curriculum Development, 2006).

3. Did the student exhibit positive work habits, attitudes, and classroom behavior this grading term?

The problem is that many teachers are required to calculate a single grade. To do so they create a formula for calculating an end-of-term grade that may differ significantly from their colleagues' formulas. In other words, two students could have the same set of scores in a record book, but two teachers using different calculation formulas will end up with two different end-of-term grades.

Most teachers, in fact, can tell you what percentage of an end-of-term grade accounts for each of the three elements. One teacher may state 80 percent of her end-of-term grades relates to learning goals and 20 percent to work habits, attitudes, and behavior, with learning progress not being part of the calculation. Another teacher may say that 80 percent of his end-of-term grades relates to achievement of goals, and 10 percent each to learning progress and work habits, attitudes, and behavior. Mix in zeroes for missing work and decreasing points for late work, and you have end-of-term grades that do not accurately report information about student learning or progress over a term.

Grading in the Differentiated Classroom

Much has already been written about grading paradigms and their effects on academically diverse classrooms. Refer to the outstanding work of Rick Wormeli, Ken O'Connor, Carol Tomlinson, Jay McTighe, and Richard Stiggins listed in the References and Resources on pages 170–173. Each author contributes to our understanding of grading and assessment in differentiated classrooms and enables you to explore your opinions, attitudes, and beliefs about the purpose and practice of grading. The following are responses to some of the most pressing questions related to grading in the differentiated classroom.

1. How do I grade tiered assignments fairly?
Tiered assignments are used when learning differences need to be addressed in the classroom. Students are working on the same goal but in different ways. Tiered assignments are practice and daily work; they are what you are doing in class today to work on a learning goal. Their purpose is not summative assessment. You tier the tasks because you recognize learning differences in your classroom. You match students to tasks that are "just right, right now" for them as it relates to working on the goal.

Tiered assignments should not be graded. If you are compelled to grade them, then each tier should be eligible for the same number of points and same grade range. It would be unethical to assign different grade scales or point values to different tasks when you are designating a particular task to a particular student based on his or her needs. All tiers of the assignment must be equal in value to be fair.

2. Do I ever tier grades?
The only time to consider different grades or points for different tasks is if the student has a choice in the matter. It's an issue of fairness. If you design a tiered assignment based on student learning needs, you must match the student with the appropriate task. Some teachers argue that the more complex or advanced task should be eligible for more points or a higher grade because it is more difficult. However, I don't believe it's ethical to provide a higher point advantage or the possibility of a higher grade to only those students assigned a more complex, advanced task, and deny students who need more scaffolding or support an equal opportunity for higher points or grades. In practice, both tiers, regardless of their degree of complexity or level of scaffolding, should be eligible for the same range of points (e.g., 0–20 points) or the same grades (e.g., F to A).

Differentiating Instruction in the Regular Classroom suggests a strategy for linking grades to rigor.[2] This is a variation of the contract system that some teachers use to allow students to pick

2 Heacox, 2002, pp. 120–124.

their grade based on selection of particular tasks. Often the only difference between being eligible for an A and eligible for a C is the amount of work piled up rather than the level of rigor. Thus, if you are going to use this contract strategy, use the following procedure:

- To earn from an F to an A, the student must select from assignments that have been designed at the analysis, evaluation, and synthesis levels of Bloom's Taxonomy.
- To earn from an F to a B, the student must select from assignments that have been designed at the application and analysis levels of Bloom's.
- To earn from an F to a C, the student must select from assignments that have been designed at the application level of Bloom's.

Using this strategy, greater rigor—equated with tasks at the top levels of Bloom's Taxonomy—is eligible for higher grades. However, students must meet the criteria established by a rubric or checklist in order to earn the designated grade. Designing the tasks in this way clearly communicates to students a value for taking on a challenge. Your message is, "In this classroom, if you want to earn a higher grade for this assignment, you need to choose a more rigorous task." Keep in mind that you may need to do some individual counseling to help some students make good choices.

3. If I fairly grade differentiated tasks, what kind of message does that send to parents about student performance?

The grades you assign to daily work or assignments should be based on attainment of learning goals, and clear and specific criteria for quality. If the students meet the criteria, they earn the grade. It is assumed that if tiered tasks are assigned, then the criteria may differ based on the task. Parents should be aware that students may be assigned different tasks based on their learning needs and, as such, criteria may differ. However, all students are evaluated based on the quality of their work.

4. Are recovery points fair?

Recovery points are the opportunity to revise work in order to regain points that may have been lost on required elements presented on a rubric. In the reality of the classroom, some students need more time and practice to attain learning goals, and others need more specific feedback to identify the ways they may improve their work. If students are willing to keep working on and improving the quality of their work to achieve goals, you should be willing to accept it. After all, it's all about getting them to the goals!

Recovery points can be successfully used to encourage students to do quality work. For each task that is going to be graded, provide clear and highly specific criteria that describe "A" work. These criteria describe the qualities of a task that exhibit the attainment of a learning goal. If student work does not meet the criteria, encourage her or him to revise it, based on your descriptive feedback as well as the detail provided by the rubric. Determine a deadline for resubmission. All revised work must be in by that date to qualify for recovery points. You will need to decide whether students can attempt recovery points just once per assignment or whether they will be able to re-submit multiple times.

When students submit the revised work, they must also include the original work and the grading rubric. The points or grade on the original and revised work are not averaged; the revised work's score/grade replaces the previous score/grade. In your record book, write the revised score/grade next to the first submission, although only the revised score will be considered. At the end of the term, you can see who sought recovery points and who did not choose to do a revision. Rick Wormeli suggests that parents be involved in this process.[3] His students request an opportunity to seek recovery points, and their parents need to sign the original work and their student's request.

3 Wormeli, 2006.

What is eligible for recovery points is up to you. You may choose not to allow students to do oral presentations a second time. The real issue is class time. It is difficult to commit more class time to second presentations. However, perhaps students could film their presentation for recovery points. Whatever works for you!

5. How will I motivate students to do the work if I don't grade it all?

Remember the key to motivation is interest. You motivate students to do the work by either capitalizing on their interests, or by creating tasks that are interesting to them. Ask yourself, "Are the activities I ask students to engage in and the tasks I ask them to complete interesting, engaging, and meaningful?"

Unfortunately, teachers are responsible for "hooking" students on grades by over-grading student work. Although there is a general assumption that students will work for grades, there has been considerable research to suggest that this is not true.[4] In fact for some students, grades *discourage* performance. When the message of grades is always that they are not good enough, the result is diminished motivation.

Keep in mind that grades and assessment are not the same. You need assessment to help you determine learning progress and to shape your instruction, but every task that a student engages in does not need to be graded.

6. How will fair grading of differentiated tasks affect end-of-term grades?

During a term you gather considerable information about learning progress. Students have daily work and homework. You observe them as they engage in science labs or book discussion groups. Not everything should be graded, but students need descriptive feedback that tells them how they are doing and how they can improve.

4 Brookhart, 1994; Susan M. Brookhart, *Grading* (Upper Saddle River, NJ: Pearson, 2004); Thomas R. Guskey and Jane M. Bailey, *Developing Grading and Reporting Systems for Student Learning* (Thousand Oaks, CA: Corwin Press, 2001); Alfie Kohn, *What to Look for in a Classroom: and Other Essays* (San Francisco: Jossey-Bass, 2000); Richard J. Stiggins, "Assessment, Student Confidence, and School Success," *Phi Delta Kappan* 81, no. 3 (November, 1999): 191–198; Stiggins, 2004.

Summative assessment should be the *primary basis* of your end-of-term grades and should be carefully designed to allow students to demonstrate their proficiencies related to goals for the term.[5] Differentiation is what students are doing to work on the goal and gain proficiency. This practice does not need to be graded. Ongoing collection of data related to the students' learning progress is to inform instruction (assessment) not to make judgments about students' achievement of a goal (grades).

7. Won't students be upset if some classmates can do less rigorous work and still get a good grade on it?

In differentiated classrooms, you need to address differences. This does not mean sorting students into "the bright ones" and "the struggling ones," but rather pointing out how each student's strengths, interests, and learning preferences make each of them unique in the classroom.

In Chapter 3, the knowledge bar graph on page 33 provided an avenue for discussing differences in what students know about a new curriculum topic. Other teachers use student inventories on Multiple Intelligences to explore everyone's personal strengths. Explain to your students that the differences represented in your classroom will result in everyone not doing the same thing at the same time in the same way. Also tell them that each task will be held to high standards of quality, but that different tasks will, in fact, be evaluated in different ways.

Remind students about your desire to provide them with the best task for where they are right now in their learning. They should be asked to do work they can successfully complete with effort. They should not be given work that is too easy and bores them, or too difficult and frustrates them.

8. Is it fair that some students can turn in late work and still have it evaluated in the same manner as those who turned it in on time?

Keep reminding yourself that it is all about the learning goals. Late work is an issue related to work habits, attitudes, and behaviors. What you should

5 Tomlinson and McTighe, 2006.

really be concerned about is getting the work, so that you can evaluate the student's progress toward or achievement of a learning goal. Remember that a clear message about work habits goes to the parent when it is reported on separately, rather than hidden within the calculation of a single grade.

Rick Wormeli suggests that reducing points for late work distorts the meaning of the grade or point entry in your record book[6]. He suggests that you record two points/grades: one that represents the level of mastery indicated by the work, which is used to inform instruction; and one that reflects any late penalties.

9. How do I calculate grades if students have missing work and grades are supposed to reflect achievement of learning goals?

Some elementary and secondary schools have begun to enter "incompletes" on report cards to indicate to parents and students that work is missing. Teachers may require that the student meet with them immediately and write a contract that determines how the work will be completed and a timeline for its submission. It is advisable that the parent/guardian is also involved in this process. Schools using the "incomplete with a contract" process report that students don't want incompletes, because it means working on last term's work in addition to the next term's work; they are not left off the hook for missing work just because a term ends.

Schools may need to develop a policy on how long an incomplete may remain on a report card, and what grade will be assigned if the work is not completed. Implications for grade advancement for students with incompletes must also be determined.

6 Wormeli, 2006.

10. What if our reporting system does not allow us to separate achievement of learning goals, learning progress, and work habits, attitudes, and behavior?

The most effective reporting systems provide both accurate and specific information to students and parents and include all three of these performance elements. The need to summarize this critical information into a single grade, or use of a formula for calculating a single grade reflecting these elements, inhibits teachers' ability to fairly and ethically report on student learning.

Many teachers are perplexed by our current grading process. Here are just some examples of the conundrums:

- When you are required to condense the spectrum of student learning into a single grade, you are not able to recognize students, for example, who made outstanding progress but still earned a C because they didn't achieve the learning goals set for all students at their grade level, regardless of disabilities and disadvantages.
- When you report a single grade, you are not able to tell the parent of the bright child that although an A was earned, the student achieved it with little or no effort and made insignificant learning progress.
- When you give students a B instead of an A because of late work, you aren't talking straight with their parents about issues related to work habits.
- When you reduce a student's grade because of her attitude or behavioral problems, you are not clearly telling the student or the parent that her behavior needs improvement.

The only way to avoid these conundrums and specifically and clearly communicate feedback on student learning is to separate the elements and report on each.

Many teachers believe a change in grading needs to be a broad systemic change in their school or school district; they cannot change the paradigms on grading on their own. Although a community agreement would be helpful and significant, there are ways that you *can* change your approach to reporting without needing a system-wide change.

First of all, don't include reports on learning progress and work habits, attitudes, and behavior in the calculation of an end-of-term grade. End-of-term grades should report on achievement of learning goals *only*. There should be other elements in the reporting system for providing parents and students with specific information about learning progress and work habits, attitudes, and behavior.

Secondly, some secondary teachers will state that because their reporting system has comment lines where teachers can enter specific remarks related to the student's grade, the parents are alerted of any problems their student may be having. However, work habits, attitudes, and behavior are sometimes still used in the calculation of the grade *and* again in the "comments" line of the report card. The parents and students are typically unaware of the degree to which the end-of-term grade was impacted by these issues. Simply using a comment line to note issues to the parent and student does not clearly and separately report on all three elements: achievement of learning goals, learning progress, and work habits, attitudes, and behavior.

Consider adding a supplement to your current report card. If you must provide a summary grade, ask if you can supplement it with a page that provides more specific feedback on achievement of learning goals, learning progress, and work habits, attitudes, and behaviors. Let parents know that you will be using two reporting systems and explain to them the meaning of the summary grade on the report card. Consider electronic delivery of your reporting supplement to parent/guardian email accounts, send them by regular mail, or give them to students to take home with an expectation of a return signature from the parent/guardian.

Grading Is Personal

Because grading is such a personal matter that reflects our educational philosophies, values, and beliefs, it is difficult to reach agreement on the ways it is practiced in our schools. But what teachers need to do is thoughtfully and ethically evaluate student accomplishments, and provide students and parents with accurate and specific information related to the student's individual growth and progress toward learning goals.

CHAPTER 10 Critical Element: DIFFERENTIATING FOR GIFTED AND TALENTED LEARNERS

There is a misconception in some schools that if classroom teachers differentiate in general, the needs of gifted and academically talented students are automatically taken care of. It is true that gifted and talented students are being better served in differentiated classrooms because of the focus on responding to the learning needs of all students. However, there are significant differences between how we differentiate for all and how we need to differentiate for gifted learners. Gifted and talented students have a unique learning profile that varies significantly from average learners. Research-based best practices presented in this chapter specifically address their personal, academic, and learning differences. The chapter presents the conceptual foundations that define differentiation for the gifted, and offers classroom strategies that best address their learning needs.

How Is Differentiation Different for the Gifted?

The Council for Exceptional Children and the National Association for Gifted Children have produced national standards for gifted education.[1] The table on page 137 represents a synthesis of these standards and creates distinctions between differentiation for all students and differentiation for gifted and talented learners.

The column titled "For All Students" presents qualities of authentic differentiation. These qualities distinguish substantive differentiation from "tips and tricks" approaches. Differentiation in *all* classrooms for *all* students should reflect the qualities on the left.

> Gifted and talented students have a unique learning profile that varies significantly from average learners.

The qualities in the right-hand column "For Gifted Learners" should guide the work of gifted educators as well as classroom teachers in addressing the specific cognitive and affective differences of gifted and talented learners. Note the distinctions between the two columns.

Strategies for Differentiating for Gifted and Talented Learners

STRATEGY 1: DIFFERENTIATE CONTENT, PROCESS, AND PRODUCT

What you teach (content), how the students learn it (process), and how they demonstrate their learning (product) are the longstanding elements of differentiation. However, there are distinctions between how you differentiate these elements for all students and how you differentiate them for gifted learners. A review of the work in gifted education of Carol Tomlinson and Karen Rogers, and the classic

1 CEC–NAGC *Initial Knowledge and Skill Standards for Gifted and Talented Education* can be found at www.cectag.org

DIFFERENTIATION FOR ALL STUDENTS VS. DIFFERENTIATION FOR GIFTED LEARNERS

For All Students	For Gifted Learners
Applies state academic standards or provincial goals	Extends academic standards or goals into "next levels" of the curriculum area
Provides activities that reflect rigor and variety	Incorporates advanced, in-depth, and complex content and processes
Provides modeling, guided practice, and scaffolding as appropriate	Provides cognitively complex learning
Engages students in choices based on interest in topic, process, or product	Provides students opportunities to pursue interests that may be outside the school curriculum
Uses appropriate pacing; may remediate or accelerate	Accelerates learning as appropriate to the student's talents
Provides opportunities for collaboration with like readiness, interest, or learning preference peers	Plans for associations with expert-level mentors to extend learning
Adjusts instruction in response to ongoing learning progress	Individualizes learning plans and experiences based on interests, need, and readiness
Selects, adapts, and plans for differences in readiness, interests, and learning preference	Selects, adapts, and/or creates materials and activities that respond to exceptional gifts and talents
Incorporates appropriate technologies to lead to mastery or enrichment	Uses technology to extend content, process, or product differentiation
Provides descriptive feedback on learning progress	Provides "expert" feedback on authentic tasks
Increases independence, responsibility, and self-management	Increases skills for autonomous learning to reach high levels of independence
Uses assessment tools to identify and plan for learning preferences, readiness, and interests	Uses assessment tools to identify mastery and then eliminates, replaces, or extends learning tasks
Uses multiple assessment methods to monitor learning progress	Uses assessment data to identify exceptional learning needs and prescribe appropriate academic interventions

curriculum work of C. June Maker, provides insights into content, process, and product differentiation focused exclusively on gifted and talented learners. As you review or design learning tasks for use with gifted and talented students, these principles should guide your work.

Gifted and Talented Differentiation Principles

Content Differentiation[2]

- Consider using the "next level" curriculum goals if the students have accomplished current grade-level goals.
- Engage the students in more abstract concepts.
- Replace content that the students have already mastered with more complex, advanced, in-depth content.
- Engage the students in content that bridges into multiple curriculum areas (interdisciplinary content).
- Introduce the students to more advanced research skills so that they can develop greater independence in finding the answers to their questions and follow their curiosities.

Process Differentiation[3]

- Accelerate the pace of instruction to allow time for students to engage in investigations or advanced work beyond the grade-level curriculum. Eliminate and replace grade-level work; do not merely "pile on" more work.
- Be flexible about timelines. Under your guidance, allow students more independence to go beyond or deeper into their work.
- Provide more open-ended tasks. Scaffolding needed by average learners is less often needed by gifted learners.
- Consider the students' interests, which may be beyond grade-level curriculum, in developing learning tasks.
- Present tasks with high levels of rigor that demand the use of critical and creative thinking.

Product Differentiation[4]

- Engage students in solving "real problems" in contexts that show application of their learning in the world.
- Move students to reach beyond what is familiar to new ways of showing what they have learned.
- Provide authentic feedback on students' products, from subject-area experts as appropriate.
- Teach students to use their imaginations and create original products, not just "reproduce" other people's thoughts and ideas.

Apply the principles for differentiating content, process, or product as you design learning tasks for gifted students. Use these principles as you consider tiering assignments, or if you are teaching honors, accelerated, or enriched sections, or Advanced Placement or International Baccalaureate courses. If the latter is the case, you need to be particularly attuned to these principles since they are what distinguish a "regular" section or course from a section or course for the gifted.

Even as you tier assignments, make sure you are providing enough of a stretch to gifted learners. The principles will help you in doing this work. **Figure 86** shows an example of using them to tier an assignment for gifted learners.

Task two reflects the following Gifted and Talented Differentiation Principles:

Content Differentiation

Introduce the students to more advanced research skills so that they can develop greater independence in finding the answers to their questions and follow their curiosities.

2 Carol Ann Tomlinson, *The Differentiated Classroom: Responding to the Needs of All Learners* (Alexandria, VA: Association for Supervision and Curriculum Development, 1999); Karen B. Rogers, *Re-forming Gifted Education: Matching the Program to the Child* (Scottsdale, AZ: Great Potential Press, 2002).

3 Tomlinson, 1999; Rogers, 2002; C. June Maker, *Curriculum Development for the Gifted* (Rockville, MD: Aspen Systems Corporation, 1982).

4 Rogers, 2002.

Process Differentiation

- Provide more open-ended tasks. Scaffolding needed by average learners is less often needed by gifted learners.
- Present tasks with high levels of rigor that demand the use of critical and creative thinking.

Product Differentiation

- Engage students in solving "real problems" in contexts that show application of their learning in the world.
- Move students beyond what is familiar to new ways of showing what they have learned.
- Provide authentic feedback on students' products, from subject-area experts as appropriate.
- Teach students to use their imaginations and create original products, not just "reproduce" other people's thoughts and ideas.

STRATEGY 2: GO BEYOND YOUR GRADE-LEVEL STANDARDS

Regarding expectations for student learning, remember that your grade-level curriculum standards are the floor, not the ceiling. Although you must teach to these standards, you can also go beyond them. This may be particularly appropriate for your most talented students. You may not wish to accelerate your students to the next grade level's standards or goals, but you can consider the following:

- What would be an extension of this grade-level standard?
- What do you envision as the next step in learning for those most talented in this curricular area?
- What would be more cognitively complex learning related to this grade-level standard or goal?

FIGURE 86

Tiered Assignment for Gifted Learners

SCIENCE
ELEMENTARY

Academic Standard

Identify possible solutions to an environmental problem.

Task One (for most students)

1. Select a problem from a list provided by your teacher.
2. Work through the problem-solving process guided by your teacher.
3. Determine your best solution and create an action plan.
4. Present your action plan to the class using one of the following:
   - *60 Minutes* Exposé (skit or video)
   - Poster or Billboard
   - Public Service Video or Audio
   - Talk Radio Conversation
   - Informational Brochure
   - Web Page
   - Museum Display
   - Position Paper

Task Two (for gifted and talented learners)

1. Interview a member of the Department of Natural Resources (DNR) to identify a current environmental problem in your community.
2. Critically examine the current community responses to this issue.
3. Using the problem-solving process, identify an alternative solution to the problem.
4. Present your action plan to the class and the DNR representative using one of the following:
   - *60 Minutes* Exposé (skit or video)
   - Poster or Billboard
   - Public Service Video or Audio
   - Talk Radio Conversation
   - Informational Brochure
   - Web Page
   - Museum Display
   - Position Paper

***Note:* If you are unsure what a deeper extension of a grade-level concept might be, it's often helpful to tap the knowledge of subject-area experts at the secondary level. Many times they can offer multiple pathways for investigating a concept more deeply.**

Figure 87 shows an example of how advanced standards may be developed within a social studies unit.

STRATEGY 3: POSE QUESTIONS

In developing curriculum units for gifted students, it is important that the topics and activities meet what Joseph Renzulli from the National Research Center for Gifted and Talented at the University of Connecticut/Storrs calls the "could/would/should test"[5]:

- Could all students do this?
- Would all students benefit from this activity?
- Should all students do this?

If any of your responses are "yes," then the activity is not differentiated for the gifted and should be part of the regular instruction in the classroom.

Think about it:

If all students *could* do an activity, it does not represent the rigor and complexity level essential for gifted learners.

If all students *would* benefit from doing an activity, why is it only being offered to gifted students?

If all students *should* do an activity, then it is an integral part of grade- or course-level goals. All students not only should do it, but *must* do it in order to work on the required goals.

5 A. Harry Passow, *The Gifted and the Talented: Their Education and Development* (Chicago, IL: University of Chicago Press, 1979).

Educators of the gifted are fairly criticized for curriculum units and instructional activities offered exclusively to gifted students that don't meet the could/would/should test. So, how can you develop a differentiated gifted curriculum that passes the test?

Sandra Kaplan from the University of Southern California suggests 11 guidelines to ensure differentiated curriculum for the gifted reflects greater depth and complexity.[6] Based on her guidelines, you can ask questions to reveal topics, ideas, and explorations that will take curriculum topics into greater depth and complexity. In doing so, you create a solid curriculum for gifted learners.

On page 141 are questions to pose based on each guideline that develop greater depth and complexity in curriculum topics. Following, **Figure 88** shows how these questions would be formed to explore topics in a differentiated unit on weather and meteorology for gifted students.

6 Sandra Kaplan, *Differentiating Core Curriculum and Instruction to Provide Advanced Learning Opportunities* (Sacramento, CA: California Association for the Gifted, 1994); Sandra Kaplan, "Layering Differentiated Curriculum for the Gifted and Talented," *Methods and Materials for Teaching the Gifted* (Waco, TX: Prufrock Press, 2005), 107–132.

FIGURE 87

Developing Advanced Standards for Gifted Learners

SOCIAL STUDIES MIDDLE SCHOOL

Grade-Level Standard

Demonstrate knowledge of the causes and consequences of immigration.

Beyond the Standard

- Reconstruct a conflict situation. Evaluate beliefs, values, and points of view. Determine a way to resolve or reduce the conflict.
- Develop a method to communicate about a social problem to raise awareness and encourage action.
- Identify a global problem or concern. Construct a model to illustrate interrelated areas.

Guidelines to Develop Curriculum Depth and Complexity

1. Use the language of the discipline.

Ask:

- What is the specialized vocabulary of ____________?
- What specific skills and processes are used by professionals in ____________?
- What typical tasks do these professionals engage in?

2. Explore specific details.

Ask:

- What are the essential attributes of ____________?
- What are the factors or variables that affect it?
- What are its basic elements?

3. Identify patterns.

Ask:

- What recurring events, activities, or actions characterize ____________?
- Is there a particular order or sequence to these patterns?
- What are we able to depend on or predict will occur?
- What can we hypothesize, prove, or defend about ____________?

4. Identify trends.

Ask:

- Are there particular courses of action or trends related to ____________?
- What factors influence these trends?
- What might be the social, political, or ethical affects of these trends?

5. Consider unanswered questions.

Ask:

- What is still not known or understood about ____________?
- What factors influence our understandings of ____________?

6. Identify rules.

Ask:

- What structures exist in ____________?
- What orders or hierarchies are represented in it?
- What stated or unstated assumptions relate to ____________?

7. Explore ethics.

Ask:

- What dilemmas or controversies are involved in ____________?
- How does ____________ impact people?
- How might elements such as bias, prejudice, and discrimination affect ____________?

8. Identify the "big ideas."

Ask:

- What are the theories or principles represented in ____________?
- What connections or interrelationships are evident in ________?

9. Examine concepts over time.

Ask:

- How has the past, the present, and the future affected ____________?
- How has it changed over the past ___ years?

10. Identify different points of view.

Ask:

- What are the different perspectives on ____________?
- What are the opposing viewpoints related to it?

11. Make interdisciplinary connections.

Ask:

- What connections are there between ______ and other disciplines or subjects?

FIGURE 88

Sample Guidelines to Develop Curriculum Depth and Complexity

SCIENCE: WEATHER AND METEOROLOGY
MIDDLE SCHOOL

1. Use the language of the discipline.

Ask:

- What is the specialized vocabulary of a meteorologist?
- What specific skills and processes do meteorologists use?
- What typical tasks do meteorologists engage in?

2. Explore specific details.

Ask:

- What are the attributes of weather?
- What factors affect weather?
- What are the basic elements of weather?

3. Identify patterns.

Ask:

- What recurring events or activities characterize weather?
- What hypotheses do you have about weather?

4. Identify trends.

Ask:

- How do recent events in the United States affect the public's interest in meteorology?
- What are the social, political, or ethical effects of weather?

5. Consider unanswered questions.

Ask:

- What are some unanswered questions related to weather? To meteorology?
- What factors influence our understandings of weather?

6. Identify rules.

Ask:

- What structures exist in weather?
- What hierarchies are represented in meteorology?

7. Explore ethics.

Ask:

- What dilemmas or controversies are involved in meteorology?
- How does weather impact people?
- Do biases, prejudice, or discrimination affect meteorology? In what ways?

8. Identify the "big ideas."

Ask:

- What are the theories of weather?
- What interrelationships are evident in meteorology?

9. Examine concepts over time.

Ask:

- Has meteorology always been valued? Why or why not?
- How has meteorology changed over the past 20 years?

10. Identify different points of view.

Ask:

- How are different perspectives presented in meteorology?
- What opposing viewpoints are present in meteorology?

11. Make interdisciplinary connections.

Ask:

- How does meteorology use skills, concepts, or knowledge from other disciplines?

STRATEGY 4: INCREASE COMPLEXITY AND RIGOR IN TIERED ASSIGNMENTS

One of the concerns about the use of tiered assignments in inclusive classrooms is whether the "top" tier reflects the level of rigor and complexity necessary to meet the needs of gifted students.

Rigor

Rigor is defined as intellectual engagement that requires a learner to stretch beyond their comfort zone. Using the ideas of Lev Vygotsky, being in the zone of proximal development (ZPD) means that students are matched with tasks in which they can be successful *with effort*.[7] When students are "in the zone," they need to think, exert effort, and persist to be successful. They feel the challenge. If tasks are too easy, students can attain success with little or no effort. They may complain about being bored. Tasks below the zone can result in learning laziness. When students are beyond their zone, tasks become too difficult, they don't know where to start, or the task doesn't make any sense to them. This often results in frustration, anger, and resignation.

Rigor is defined as intellectual engagement that requires learners to stretch beyond their comfort zone.

Gifted learners need both rigor and complexity in their learning.

Bloom's Taxonomy is a familiar tool educators use to consider rigor when developing discussion questions or designing learning tasks. Page 144 presents the most current presentation of Bloom's ideas. Lorin Anderson's and David Krathwohl's change to the original Taxonomy was to reverse the order of evaluation and synthesis. In Bloom's original work, evaluation appeared at the top of the Taxonomy. Anderson and Krathwohl contend that true creative thinking requires the learner to reflect on prior learning and "what is," and from there decide how to innovate and create unique thoughts, ideas, or products.

Complexity

Complexity is a cognitive process that requires:

- metacognitive skills
- sophisticated forms of inductive and deductive critical reasoning
- creative thinking in the form of idea generation
- problem-solving skills

Metacognition describes an awareness of your own thinking, an ability to be reflective, to analyze and monitor progress, and to adapt as necessary. Metacognition is an essential element in complex thinking.

Critical reasoning engages students in such tasks as making decisions based on evidence, forming questions to attain information, constructing arguments, and discerning biases and fallacies.

Creative thinking engages the learner's imagination and originality. The student needs to think with flexibility and fluency and be able to elaborate on ideas. When students engage in creative thinking, they use both divergent and convergent modes. First, they think of all the possibilities, and then they focus on the "best" possibility based on criteria.

Problem-solving skills engage students in a systematic process most frequently reflecting the following steps:

- Define the problem
- Identify the underlying problems and/or causes
- Generate alternative solutions
- Determine the solution most likely to solve the problem
- Implement the solution/plan
- Monitor the effectiveness of the solution/plan
- Determine whether the problem is resolved
- Repeat this process if the problem is not resolved

7 L.S. Vygotsky, *Mind in Society: The Development of Higher Psychological Processes* (Cambridge, MA: Harvard University Press, 1978).

BLOOM'S TAXONOMY

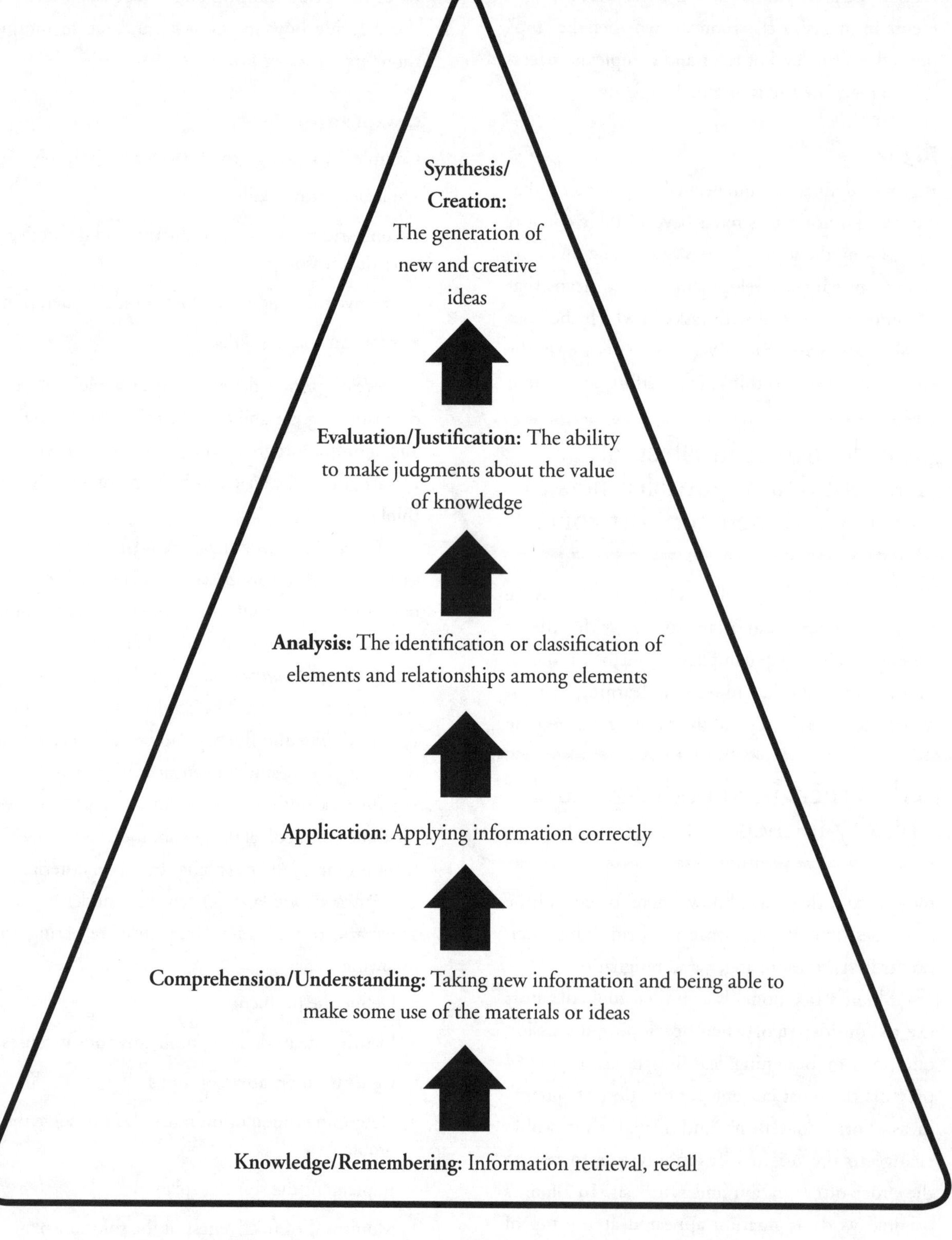

Adapted from *A Taxonomy for Learning, Teaching, Assessing: A Revision of Bloom's Taxonomy of Educational Objectives: Complete Edition* by L.W. Anderson and D.R. Krathwohl (Eds.). (New York: Longman, 2001).

Gifted learners need both rigor and complexity in their learning. Rigor is reflected in tasks that require multiple processes, more expansive knowledge bases, and greater depth or ambiguity in thinking. Complexity engages the learner in thought processes that generate and manage information.

Trigger Words

The use of trigger words[8] related to complex thinking enables you to critically reflect on the meaning of complexity, and to skillfully design a tiered task reflecting the needs of gifted learners. Trigger words help you design tasks demanding complex thinking. **Figures 89 to 94** provide trigger words for critical reasoning, creative thinking, and problem solving, as well as sample tiered assignments that use trigger words to generate ideas for differentiated tasks for gifted learners. Note that all tiered tasks are working on the same goal and efforts were made to select similar products for all tiers. In this way, the tasks differ in complexity (process), yet students do not detect the differences because the products (the ways in which the learning is presented) are similar.

FIGURE 89

Trigger Words for Critical Reasoning

Compare/Contrast	Cause/Effect
Sequence & prioritize	Point of view
Analyze arguments	Bias
Stereotypes	Relevance/Irrelevance
Deduction/Induction	Fact/Opinion
Reliable sources	Multi-faceted
Alternative perspectives	Generalizations
Intellectual risk-taking	Assumptions

8 Based on work conducted by Richard Cash and Diane Heacox, 2006–2007.

Using the critical reasoning trigger words—*compare/contrast, analyze arguments,* and *alternative perspectives*—the following tiered assignment on energy sources offers a differentiated advanced tier for gifted learners. The technology suggested for each task also increases in complexity from modified to advanced tiers.

FIGURE 90

Sample Tiered Assignment
Using Critical Reasoning Trigger Words

PHYSICAL SCIENCE
HIGH SCHOOL

KUDo: The students will be able to critically examine sources of energy: fossil fuels, nuclear fission, wind, solar, and tidal energy.

On-Target Tier for Most Students
Compare and contrast the advantages and disadvantages of each energy source. Present critical facts in a PowerPoint presentation.

Advanced Tier for Gifted Students
Analyze and evaluate the arguments for each energy source, focusing on the environmental and financial impacts of each choice. Present critical facts and your own analysis in a presentation using multi-media SMART Board technology.

Modified/Adapted Tier for Special Needs Students
Identify critical facts about each energy source that should be considered as we examine our future energy needs as a nation. Share your results on a chart or poster using words, pictures, or symbols. You may use technology in creating your presentation if you wish.

FIGURE 91

Trigger Words for Creative Thinking

Generate ideas	Use ideas in new ways
Elaborate	Innovate
Original ideas	Ambiguity
Divergent thinking	Self-expressive
Open-endedness	Less structure
Metaphorical	Imagination
Abstract	

The following advanced tiered assignment is designed using *ambiguity* as a trigger word.

FIGURE 92

Sample Tiered Assignment
Using Creative Thinking Trigger Words

SCIENCE
ELEMENTARY

KUDo: The students will understand the importance of simple machines in daily life.

On-Target Tier for Most Students
Use at least one simple machine to create an invention to make an everyday choice easier or more enjoyable. Sketch your invention and label the simple machine utilized. Describe the invention's use.

Advanced Tier for Gifted Students
Identify a design problem in a household or recreational object. Combine at least two simple machines to improve the object to make it more efficient, effective, or fun. Sketch your improved object, label the simple machines utilized in its design, and explain the problem that the redesign solved.

Modified/Adapted Tier for Special Needs Students
Given household objects, like an eggbeater, identify the simple machines that are used in the object. Sketch the object and label the simple machines.

FIGURE 93

Trigger Words for Problem Solving

Decide/Plan	Work backward
Analyze patterns	Define problem
Hypothesize	Generate alternatives
Verify/Check	Determine alternatives
Monitor	Analyze information
Summarize	Estimate
Execute	Put into practice
Select approaches	

The following advanced tiered assignment is designed using the trigger words *analyze patterns, hypothesize, and summarize.*

FIGURE 94

Sample Tiered Assignment
Using Problem Solving Trigger Words

SOCIAL STUDIES
MIDDLE SCHOOL

KUDo: The students will identify the fundamental rights of citizenship within a community.

On-Target Tier for Most Students
What are the current struggles for equality and fairness in Canada or in the United States? Describe the group and its history of equality and fairness, and discuss the group's current concerns. Create five PowerPoint slides to share information.

Advanced Tier for Gifted Students
What lessons can be learned from the European settlers' interactions with the First Nation's People (Native Americans) that inform today's struggles for equality and fairness? Create five PowerPoint slides to share your ideas.

Modified/Adapted Tier for Special Needs Students
What are the concerns related to equality and fairness of a new immigrant group? Create five PowerPoint slides to share the concerns.

Integrating Complexity and Rigor

Gifted learners benefit from both complexity and rigor. You can integrate both elements by examining rising levels of complexity along with advancing levels of rigor. **Figure 95** shows a matrix of this integration. The vertical line represents complexity. The first row on the matrix represents low levels of complexity. The middle row reflects the level of complexity appropriate for most learners, the on-target group. The top row represents high levels of complexity, as needed by gifted learners.

In examining rigor, consider Bloom's Taxonomy as the horizontal continuum line. Columns on the far left represent the knowledge level of Bloom's, the lowest level of rigor. As the continuum continues toward the right, the rigor level increases incrementally to synthesis, representing the most rigorous thinking.

Using the Complexity-Rigor Matrix

Utilizing this matrix plan, you can easily design tiered assignments that meet the criteria of rigor and complexity for gifted learners. Page 149 provides a "Template for Designing Tiered Assignments." Sample trigger words for critical thinking, creative thinking, and problem solving are listed across the top of the template. Use the following process to design tiered assignments reflecting advancing rigor at three different levels of complexity.

1. At the top of the template, record the title of your unit/theme for the tiered assignment.

2. Write the KUDo's that are the goals for the tiered assignment. This will remind you that all tasks need to work on the same goal, but in different ways.

3. Start with the on-target task, the one that will be appropriate for most of your students. Focus your planning at one of the following levels of Bloom's Taxonomy: application, analysis, evaluation, or synthesis. Consider the Bloom's verbs in the boxes across the top to help you generate ideas for a task that reflects rigorous learning.

4. Design a task that works specifically on the goal and is appropriate for most of the students in your classroom. Write this on-target task in the appropriate box in the center row.

5. Next, consider a more advanced version of this on-target task. Using the sample complexity trigger words along the top, identify how the on-target task might be modified to reflect greater complexity. Continue to focus on the most rigorous levels of Bloom's. Write this advanced task in the appropriate box in the top row.

6. Finally, examine the on-target task and consider the special needs students in your classroom. In what specific ways might the on-target task need to be adapted or modified to meet the criteria of an IEP or IPP? In what ways might it be modified in light of an RTI intervention? Write the modified task in the appropriate box in the bottom row of the template. Remember that the level of rigor (Bloom's level) is not necessarily changed as you modify the on-target task. You might simply add more scaffolding as needed to support the student's work. For example, you may maintain the same level of rigor as the on-target task, but identify a less complex product, provide a graphic organizer to trap ideas, or supply a word bank for key topics.

Figures 96 to 98 provide examples of how the energy sources, simple machines, and citizenship tiered assignments would appear on the template.

FIGURE 95

Complexity-Rigor Matrix[9]

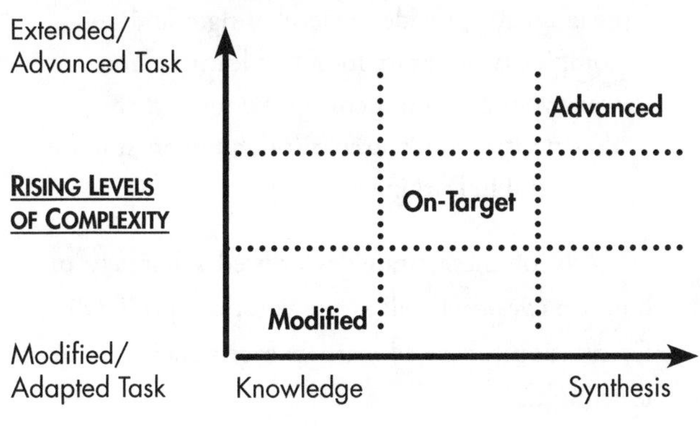

9 Based on work conducted by Richard Cash and Diane Heacox, 2006–2007.

Energy Sources Matrix

Note that the on-target task for the energy source tiered assignment reflects rigor at the analysis and synthesis levels. The advanced task is written at both of these levels as well and also at the evaluation level, reflecting the complexity trigger words: *compare/contrast, analyzing arguments,* and *alternative perspectives.* The modified task is written at the evaluation and synthesis levels as well as the application level, since its purpose is to reinforce the students' understanding of energy sources. All students are working on the same goal but doing so in different ways.

Simple Machines Matrix

The simple machines unit matrix reflects both on-target and advanced tasks written at the synthesis level. Each task engages the students in generating original ideas. However, using the sample complexity trigger words: *ambiguity, define problem,* and *put into practice,* the advanced task asks students to identify a design problem and then improve an object using at least two simple machines. These students are working from "what is" and determining ways to redesign an object to improve it. The modified task reinforces the characteristics of simple machines and asks students to identify them in everyday objects.

Citizenship Matrix

Both the on-target and modified tasks for the citizenship unit are written at the analysis level. However, the modified task targets a particular group, immigrants, for study and narrows the focus to concerns only. The on-target task broadens the content to include current struggles of all groups. Students are able to choose the group they wish to study and then explore both the history and the concerns of the group related to equality and fairness. The advanced task uses the sample complexity trigger words: *analyze patterns, hypothesize,* and *summarize.* These trigger words create a task at the evaluation level that asks students to critically analyze past interactions to determine lessons that can be applied to current struggles.

The "Template for Designing Tiered Assignments" provides a structure to assist you in creating appropriate tasks for a broader range of learners—from those needing modifications or adaptations to gifted and talented students. The use of complexity trigger words in the design of tasks for your gifted students ensures that you are applying research-based practices in meeting their needs.

Differentiation for Gifted Learners Is Different

In thinking about the gifted students in your classroom, remember that "differentiation for all" does not necessarily mean the specific needs of these learners are being addressed. Look to the national standards for gifted education to provide guidance as you consider what distinguishes "differentiation for all" from differentiation that addresses the specific cognitive and affective characteristics of gifted students.

In recognition of these differences, this chapter has provided several strategies to guide your work:

- First, closely consider the ways in which you differentiate content, process, or products for gifted learners. Make sure that your work on their behalf reflects research-based best practices for gifted students.
- Secondly, determine whether it is appropriate to develop learning goals that extend above and beyond required grade-level standards or goals. Also consider the depth and complexity of your curriculum topics. Question-posing can elicit new ideas for developing curriculum that reflects greater complexity and depth.
- Finally, question whether your tiered assignments provide the level of rigor and complexity necessary for gifted learners. You want your gifted students in the zone where they need to think, exert effort, and persist to be successful in learning.

Any of these strategies utilized separately or built on over time will assure you that specific differentiation for gifted learners meets their unique learning needs.

Template for Designing Tiered Assignments

Sample Complexity Trigger Words

Critical Thinking			Creative Thinking			Problem Solving		
Compare/Contrast	*Cause/Effect*	*Assumptions*	*Generate ideas*	*Elaborate*	*Innovate*	*Analyze patterns*	*Hypothesize*	*Verify/Check*
Point of view	*Analyze arguments*	*Generalizations*	*Divergent thinking*	*Ambiguity*	*Abstract*	*Generate alternatives*	*Monitor*	*Decide/Plan*
Relevance/Irrelevance	*Fact/Opinion*	*Sequence & Prioritize*	*Open-endedness*	*Imagination*	*Metaphorical*	*Define problem*	*Summarize*	*Put into practice*

Unit/Theme:

KUDo's:

Advancing Rigor →

↑ **Raising Complexity**

Knowledge	Comprehension	Application	Analysis	Evaluation	Synthesis
Bloom's verbs: *tell, list, define, label, recite, memorize, repeat, find, name, record, fill in, recall, relate*	**Bloom's verbs:** *locate, explain, summarize, identify, describe, report, discuss, review, paraphrase, restate, retell, show, outline, rewrite*	**Bloom's verbs:** *demonstrate, construct, record, use, diagram, revise, reformat, illustrate, interpret, dramatize, practice, organize, translate, manipulate, convert, adapt, research, calculate, operate, model, order, display, implement, sequence, integrate, incorporate*	**Bloom's verbs:** *compare, contrast, classify, critique, solve, deduce, examine, differentiate, appraise, distinguish, experiment, question, investigate, categorize, infer*	**Bloom's verbs:** *judge, predict, verify, assess, justify, rate, prioritize, determine, select, decide, value, choose, forecast, estimate*	**Bloom's verbs:** *compose, hypothesize, design, formulate, create, invent, develop, refine, produce, transform*
Extended, Advanced Task					
On-Target Task					
Adapted, Modified Task					

FIGURE 96

Template for Designing Tiered Assignments: Energy Sources

Sample Complexity Trigger Words

Critical Thinking			Creative Thinking			Problem Solving		
Compare/Contrast	*Cause/Effect*	*Assumptions*	*Generate ideas*	*Elaborate*	*Innovate*	*Analyze patterns*	*Hypothesize*	*Verify/Check*
Point of view	*Analyze arguments*	*Generalizations*	*Divergent thinking*	*Ambiguity*	*Abstract*	*Generate alternatives*	*Monitor*	*Decide/Plan*
Relevance/Irrelevance	*Fact/Opinion*	*Sequence & Prioritize*	*Open-endedness*	*Imagination*	*Metaphorical*	*Define problem*	*Summarize*	*Put into practice*

Unit/Theme: Energy Sources

KUDo's: The students will be able to critically examine various sources of energy: fossil fuel, nuclear fission, wind, solar, and tidal energy.

Advancing Rigor →

↑ Raising Complexity

Knowledge	Comprehension	Application	Analysis	Evaluation	Synthesis
Bloom's verbs: *tell, list, define, label, recite, memorize, repeat, find, name, record, fill in, recall, relate*	**Bloom's verbs:** *locate, explain, summarize, identify, describe, report, discuss, review, paraphrase, restate, retell, show, outline, rewrite*	**Bloom's verbs:** *demonstrate, construct, record, use, diagram, revise, reformat, illustrate, interpret, dramatize, practice, organize, translate, manipulate, convert, adapt, research, calculate, operate, model, order, display, implement, sequence, integrate, incorporate*	**Bloom's verbs:** *compare, contrast, classify, critique, solve, deduce, examine, differentiate, appraise, distinguish, experiment, question, investigate, categorize, infer*	**Bloom's verbs:** *judge, predict, verify, assess, justify, rate, prioritize, determine, select, decide, value, choose, forecast, estimate*	**Bloom's verbs:** *compose, hypothesize, design, formulate, create, invent, develop, refine, produce, transform*
Extended, Advanced Task				Analyze and evaluate the arguments for each energy source focusing on the environmental and financial impacts of each choice. (Analysis also)	Create a multimedia presentation using SMART Board technology.
On-Target Task			Compare and contrast the advantages and disadvantages of each energy source.		Present critical facts in a PowerPoint presentation.
Adapted, Modified Task			Examine critical facts about each energy source that should be considered as we determine our future energy needs as a nation.		Share your results on a chart or poster using words, pictures, or symbols. You may use technology in creating your presentation if you wish.

FIGURE 97

Template for Designing Tiered Assignments: Simple Machines

Sample Complexity Trigger Words

Critical Thinking			Creative Thinking			Problem Solving		
Compare/Contrast	*Cause/Effect*	*Assumptions*	*Generate ideas*	*Elaborate*	*Innovate*	*Analyze patterns*	*Hypothesize*	*Verify/Check*
Point of view	*Analyze arguments*	*Generalizations*	*Divergent thinking*	*Ambiguity*	*Abstract*	*Generate alternatives*	*Monitor*	*Decide/Plan*
Relevance/Irrelevance	*Fact/Opinion*	*Sequence & Prioritize*	*Open-endedness*	*Imagination*	*Metaphorical*	*Define problem*	*Summarize*	*Put into practice*

Unit/Theme: Simple Machines

KUDo's: Students will understand the importance of simple machines in daily life.

Advancing Rigor →

↑ **Raising Complexity**

Knowledge	Comprehension	Application	Analysis	Evaluation	Synthesis
Bloom's verbs: *tell, list, define, label, recite, memorize, repeat, find, name, record, fill in, recall, relate*	**Bloom's verbs:** *locate, explain, summarize, identify, describe, report, discuss, review, paraphrase, restate, retell, show, outline, rewrite*	**Bloom's verbs:** *demonstrate, construct, record, use, diagram, revise, reformat, illustrate, interpret, dramatize, practice, organize, translate, manipulate, convert, adapt, research, calculate, operate, model, order, display, implement, sequence, integrate, incorporate*	**Bloom's verbs:** *compare, contrast, classify, critique, solve, deduce, examine, differentiate, appraise, distinguish, experiment, question, investigate, categorize, infer*	**Bloom's verbs:** *judge, predict, verify, assess, justify, rate, prioritize, determine, select, decide, value, choose, forecast, estimate*	**Bloom's verbs:** *compose, hypothesize, design, formulate, create, invent, develop, refine, produce, transform*
Extended, Advanced Task					Identify a design problem in a household or recreational object. Combine at least two simple machines to improve the object to make it more efficient, effective, or fun. Sketch your invention, label the simple machines, and explain the problem the redesign solved.
On-Target Task					Use at least one simple machine to create an invention to make an everyday chore easier or more enjoyable. Sketch your invention and label the simple machines. Describe the invention's use.
Adapted, Modified Task	Given household objects, like an egg beater, identify the simple machines that are used in the object. Sketch the object and label the simple machines.				

FIGURE 98

Template for Designing Tiered Assignments: Citizenship

Sample Complexity Trigger Words

Critical Thinking			Creative Thinking			Problem Solving		
Compare/Contrast *Point of view* *Relevance/Irrelevance*	*Cause/Effect* *Analyze arguments* *Fact/Opinion*	*Assumptions* *Generalizations* *Sequence & Prioritize*	*Generate ideas* *Divergent thinking* *Open-endedness*	*Elaborate* *Ambiguity* *Imagination*	*Innovate* *Abstract* *Metaphorical*	*Analyze patterns* *Generate alternatives* *Define problem*	*Hypothesize* *Monitor* *Summarize*	*Verify/Check* *Decide/Plan* *Put into practice*

Unit/Theme: Citizenship Within a Community

KUDo's: The students will identify the fundamental rights of citizenship within a community.

Advancing Rigor →

↑ **Raising Complexity**

Knowledge	Comprehension	Application	Analysis	Evaluation	Synthesis
Bloom's verbs: *tell, list, define, label, recite, memorize, repeat, find, name, record, fill in, recall, relate*	**Bloom's verbs:** *locate, explain, summarize, identify, describe, report, discuss, review, paraphrase, restate, retell, show, outline, rewrite*	**Bloom's verbs:** *demonstrate, construct, record, use, diagram, revise, reformat, illustrate, interpret, dramatize, practice, organize, translate, manipulate, convert, adapt, research, calculate, operate, model, order, display, implement, sequence, integrate, incorporate*	**Bloom's verbs:** *compare, contrast, classify, critique, solve, deduce, examine, differentiate, appraise, distinguish, experiment, question, investigate, categorize, infer*	**Bloom's verbs:** *judge, predict, verify, assess, justify, rate, prioritize, determine, select, decide, value, choose, forecast, estimate*	**Bloom's verbs:** *compose, hypothesize, design, formulate, create, invent, develop, refine, produce, transform*
Extended, Advanced Task				Determine the lessons that can be learned from our interactions with First Nation's People (Native Americans) that can inform today's struggles for equality and fairness. Create five PowerPoint slides to share your ideas.	
On-Target Task			What are the current struggles for equality and fairness in the United States? Describe a group, its history related to equality and fairness and discuss the group's current concerns. Create five PowerPoint slides to share the information.		
Adapted, Modified Task			What are the concerns related to equality and fairness of a new immigrant group? Create five PowerPoint slides to share the concerns of this immigrant group.		

CHAPTER 11

Critical Element: Using Differentiation Strategies in Response to Intervention

As more and more classrooms implement Response to Intervention (RTI), it is important that we recognize the explicit connections between this classroom-based special education initiative and differentiated instruction. RTI has the potential to strengthen and deepen the practices of differentiation in the classroom, while the critical elements of differentiation serve as the very foundation of Response to Intervention. In short: *you cannot do RTI without DI.*

You cannot do RTI without DI.

Response to Intervention is a teaching and learning process using research-based instructional practices that reflect learners' needs, monitor student learning progress, and modify and adjust instruction as necessary to ensure continued growth. The 2004 reauthorization of Individuals with Disabilities Education Act (IDEA) prompted many U.S. schools to change from a discrepancy model, which relied on intelligence test scores and classroom performance to determine the presence of a learning disability, to a new more proactive and aggressive paradigm. RTI is that new paradigm. There is an underlying assumption in RTI that failure to respond to otherwise effective instruction indicates the possible presence of a disabling condition[1]. In other words, if teachers effectively and appropriately differentiate, students should learn. RTI procedures are used for students who are having difficulties academically as well as those who might be experiencing behavior issues. For purposes of discussion in this book, we will focus only on academic interventions.

The Fundamental Beliefs of RTI

Response to Intervention is primarily a general classroom initiative, rather than a special education service. However, special education professionals may be involved in planning or implementing the instructional interventions along with the classroom teacher. Particular beliefs at the foundation of RTI also connect with the fundamental beliefs of differentiation:

1. All students can learn. If they are not learning, it is our responsibility as educators to determine how to increase their success in learning.
2. Learning results from interactions between the student and our instructional methods, techniques, and strategies.

1 William N. Bender and Cara Shores, *Response to Intervention: A Practical Guide for Every Teacher* (Thousand Oaks, CA: Corwin Press, 2007).

3. Consistent use of differentiated instruction in the regular classroom enables most students to achieve learning goals.
4. When a student is struggling, early intervention is best.
5. Curriculum and instructional strategies must be research-based.
6. Research-based interventions are determined through careful analysis of student data.
7. Problem-solving methods are used by teachers and teacher teams in determining appropriate interventions for students.
8. Progress of students should be regularly monitored, and classroom interventions and student responses to these interventions should be documented.
9. Progress monitoring informs classroom instruction and plans for interventions for students.
10. Collaborative efforts of classroom teachers and special educators benefit students and enhance their learning opportunities.

A Three-Tier Model

Response to Intervention is typically represented as a three-tier model:

TIER I

In Tier I, all students are engaged in differentiated instruction in the general curriculum. Baseline data is collected on students who are having difficulties academically. Classroom teachers may design more specific interventions for these students and must monitor their progress. If instruction is appropriately differentiated using research-based best practices, RTI proponents assert that 80 to 90 percent of students will be successful in learning.

TIER II

If students do not make adequate progress in Tier I, more intensive interventions are implemented. Tier II strategies include the use of small groups and more intensive instruction that is reflective of flexible instructional groups and tiered assignments used in differentiation. Progress continues to be monitored and instruction adjusted as appropriate. RTI proponents suggest that an additional 5 to 10 percent of students can be successful with the help of the Tier II strategies.

TIER III

When students do not adequately respond to the Tier II interventions, the special education referral and due process procedures may be initiated. The school obtains parental consent and begins evaluation procedures for the student. All information available on the student from Tier I and II interventions, as well as from additional assessment related to cognitive, achievement, and adaptive behavior functioning, is reviewed. An individual educational plan may result. It is suggested that no more than 5 percent of students should need Tier III interventions.

> RTI's reflective process is used by classroom teachers in determining when and how to differentiate instruction.

In implementing RTI, teachers, as part of a team of school professionals, take the following steps:

- Identify a student's *academic difficulties*
- Determine the student's *strengths, interests, and talents*
- *Review data* on the student's learning progress
- *Design specific interventions* to increase the student's success in learning

This same reflective process—utilizing data and designing instruction based on student needs—is used by classroom teachers in determining when and how to differentiate instruction.

FIGURE 99

RTI's Reflective Process

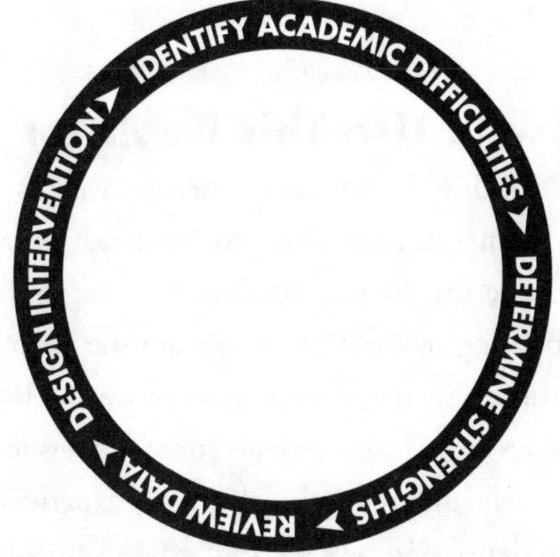

RTI's reflective process is used by classroom teachers in determining when and how to differentiate instruction.

A Problem-Solving Process

In academic interventions, specific plans result from teachers engaging in a four-step problem-solving process where learning differences are identified, teaching and learning interventions are planned and implemented, and student progress is monitored[2]. This process is outlined as follows:

1. Define the problem.
   - What specifically is the student's learning problem?
   - Is there a gap between expected and actual performance?
   - What assessment data do I have about this particular learning problem?
2. Plan an intervention.
   - What are the student's weaknesses and needs?
   - In what ways might I differentiate instruction to best meet the needs of this learner?
   - What research-based strategies can I implement to help the student learn?
3. Implement the intervention plan.
   - Is the intervention being appropriately implemented?
   - Does progress monitoring indicate that the intervention is effective?
   - Do additional instructional adjustments need to be made to the plan?
4. Evaluate the student's progress.
   - What does the collected data tell me about the student's learning progress?
   - What is the next course of action?
   - Do I develop a new intervention plan or consider the student for the next tier of interventions?

Although RTI uses the problem-solving process in a very intentional way, this is very similar to the thinking teachers engage in as they consider differentiation for all students in their classroom.

RTI's problem-solving model mirrors the thinking teachers engage in as they consider differentiation for all students in their classroom.

Universal Design for Learning

Universal Design for Learning (UDL) is the method often utilized in RTI for creating multiple pathways for student learning. The initial conceptualization of UDL resulted from concerns related to accessibility in architecture[3]. It made more sense to design a home with the needs of the occupant

2 J. Grimes and S. Kurns, "An Intervention-based System for Addressing NCLB and IDEA Expectations: A Multiple Tiered Model to Ensure Every Child Learns" (paper, National Research Center on Learning Disabilities Responsiveness to Intervention Symposium, Kansas City, MO, 2003).

3 B. Pisha and P. Coyne, "Smart from the Start: The Promise of Universal Design for Learning," *Remedial and Special Education* 22, no. 4 (2001): 197–203.

in mind, rather than to modify the house once it was built. Applied to education, UDL urges us to consider the needs of our students first and

UDL directly reflects the strategies utilized in differentiated instruction.

plan for them from the start, rather than modifying our plans later to address varying readiness needs, interests, and learning preferences. Instructional planning starts with the students in UDL.

UDL specifically responds to the needs of struggling learners in the classroom by using a variety of instructional methods, thereby differentiating process; offering students multiple ways to demonstrate their learning, thereby differentiating product; and providing opportunities for students to engage in their interests, thereby offering student choice in content, process, or product. In this way, UDL directly reflects the strategies utilized in differentiated instruction. Authentic differentiation engages students in a variety of instructional strategies, provides them opportunities to show what they have learned using a variety of learning preferences, and increases their motivation for learning through providing student choices. If you utilize universal design, you are using strategies of differentiation. The "Differentiated Learning Plan" presented in Chapter 4 on page 58 provides a process for designing lessons with your students in mind.

The RTI–DI Link

Because Response to Intervention and differentiation are so closely linked, a teacher skilled in differentiation will find it easier to implement RTI than one who is not. As RTI is implemented for an individual, differentiation is deepened because its strategies become even more specific to a learner's needs.

Proponents of RTI suggest that its implementation creates a renewed interest in research-based best practices, that teachers become more skilled and specific in responding to learning differences, and that instruction is enhanced for all students. I suggest that it is the *linkage between differentiated instruction and RTI* that will successfully create the kind of student-centered, learner-responsive classrooms we need in our academically diverse schools today.

Figure 100 outlines the links between RTI and DI.

How to Use This Book for RTI

RTI requires classroom teachers as well as special education team members to have vast knowledge and expertise in research-based strategies for differentiating instruction. These are the strategies to be utilized in the intervention process. This book provides the instructional strategies essential to effectively differentiating learning experiences for all students, and will serve to guide your planning for classroom-based interventions related to RTI initiatives. As you engage in the problem-solving process at each tier of the RTI model, review the differentiation strategies in this book and include them in your implementation plan.

In particular, Chapter 2 enables you to examine the instructional strategies currently in use in your classroom and suggests new strategies to add to your instructional repertoire. Chapter 4 presents seven ways to tier assignments and match students to "just right, right now" instructional tasks, which are essential to effective interventions. Templates and formats for both structuring and easing the preparation of differentiated experiences are abundantly provided.

All students can learn; but they don't all learn in the same way. As tempting as it might be, you can't buy prepackaged intervention activities and expect that they will work in addressing your students' individual and specific achievement issues. The authentic differentiated instruction described in this book responds to specific learning differences and needs and is the critical element in classroom interventions that produce positive results for students.

FIGURE 100

The RTI–DI Link

HOW RTI RELATES TO DIFFERENTIATION

- More frequent monitoring of student learning progress
- Broader assessment tools, including:
    - standardized assessments
    - formal and informal assessments, such as:
        - work samples
        - parent/teacher/student rating scales
        - observations of students
        - teacher logs
        - parent input
        - information about the student's physical condition
        - information about the student's social and/or cultural background
- Greater sensitivity to individual academic progress
- Interventions (a.k.a. differentiation strategies) that more specifically match skill deficits
- A more comprehensive problem-solving approach to planning interventions/differentiation strategies
- A greater adherence to appropriate implementation of best practices in teaching and learning
- Collaborative problem solving with a team of school professionals
- Consideration of appropriate growth based on expected progress for the student's grade level
- More strategic use of paraprofessionals and/or co-teachers in the classroom
- More intensive small-group instruction based on needs (Tier II)
- Data-based reflection on the success of an intervention/differentiation strategy

HOW DIFFERENTIATION RELATES TO RTI

- Preparation of teachers for RTI-like thinking
- Awareness of and implementation of research-based best practices in teaching and learning
- A recognition of the importance of assessment in informing instruction
- A broader range of instructional strategies to respond to differences
- Variety in instructional methods
- An acceptance that not all students will be doing the same thing at the same time
- Use of preassessment and formative assessment to make data-based decisions on appropriate differentiation for students
- Awareness of and planning for differences in readiness, interests, and learning preferences
- Ability to differentiate the content, the processes, and the products involved in teaching and learning
- Involvement of ALL students in respectful, engaging, and significant work
- Use of tiered assignments to match students with "just right, right now" learning experiences
- Skills in grouping students in a variety of ways for a variety of purposes
- Experience in using student choice in content, process, and products

CHAPTER 12 Critical Element: Leadership for Differentiated Classrooms

Leadership in today's schools is no longer centered in the principal's office. The influence of teachers reaches beyond their classroom walls into teaching teams, schools, and districts.[1] Many factors in the current educational environment have led to an increased need for *teacher leaders.*

Teacher Leaders

Teachers are a natural source of leadership. Many of them seek opportunities for greater responsibility and more significant challenges in their work. However, these teachers may not be interested in pursuing an administrative degree or full-time work as a school administrator. In addition, principals today are expected to be educational visionaries, competent building managers, instructional leaders, spokespersons to their school stakeholders, and state accountability point persons. Competently fulfilling all these roles may exceed the time and energy of many principals. Given these factors, teacher leaders have emerged as critical professionals in our schools.

Charlotte Danielson suggests that teacher leaders can serve either formally or informally.[2] Formal teacher leaders apply and are chosen through a selection process to fulfill particular responsibilities in the school. These leaders include teachers on special assignment (TOSA), department or grade-level chairs, and instructional coaches.

Informal teacher leaders emerge spontaneously from a faculty. They have no positional authority, but influence colleagues through their professional expertise and outstanding classroom practices. Informal teacher leaders take personal initiative to address a problem or support educational improvement plans. In the complex world of schools today, school improvement depends on the work of principals, teacher leaders, and the faculty as a whole.

In the complex world of schools today, school improvement depends on the work of principals, teacher leaders, and the faculty as a whole.

School leaders, including teacher leaders and administrators, often ask for advice on how they can support differentiation in their schools. This chapter walks you through an eight-step process for specifically examining the current level of differentiation implementation in your school. Then you will develop an action plan for extending differentiation practices into more sophisticated applications.

Administrative walkthroughs are being used more extensively as differentiation becomes something that school leaders look for in the classroom. However, specific walkthrough protocols focusing on differentiation are needed. This chapter suggests

1 C. Danielson, "The Many Faces of Leadership," *Educational Leadership* 65, no.1 (2007): 14–19.

2 Danielson, 2007.

what leaders can look for as evidence of differentiation as they visit classrooms. Finally, strategies will be offered for ways to keep differentiation initiatives alive and the energy around them positive.

Developing a School-Based Action Plan for Differentiation

The action planning form on page 160 will take you through an eight-step process that enables you to examine the current level of implementation in your school, as well as identify action steps to move the differentiation practices to higher levels of sophistication. This action-planning process can be used by teacher leaders, principals, a school leadership team including the principal and teacher leaders, or by an entire school faculty.

As you work through the process, record your thoughts on the planning form. For example, in the first box, list examples or evidence of differentiation that are brought to mind as you answer the five questions in Step 1 starting below.

You may also want to supplement your impressions by using tools provided in Chapter 2 on professional practices. The "Teacher Inventory on Differentiation Practices and Strategies" (pages 13–14) could be administered to all teachers in your school and the data analyzed to examine the practices most frequently used, as well as those in more limited application. In addition, the "Continuum of Levels of Teacher Development in Differentiation" (pages 15–18) can either be completed by teachers or used by leaders as they reflect on the practices of individual teachers they observe in the classrooms.

EIGHT STEPS TO CREATE AN ACTION PLAN

Step 1: Reflect on Current School Practices

A first step in examining the level of implementation of differentiation in your school is to critically reflect on what you know and have seen. Following are quality indicators of differentiation. Think through these questions when reflecting on the practices in your school.

Quality Indicators of Differentiation

1 To what degree do teachers have clarity about what they want their students to know, understand, and be able to do?

- If asked, are they clear about how the activities in their classrooms are connected to your state's standards or province's goals?
- Can they tell you the learning goals for particular lesson plans or is teaching for them a collection of activities around a topic or theme?

2 How well do teachers know their students?

- Are they aware of their students' readiness levels?
- Do they review, analyze, and act on any school, district, or state assessment data as they consider student learning needs?
- Do they know their students' learning preferences, interests, and whether they prefer to work alone, with a partner, or in a small group?
- Are they aware of the implications of gender and cultural and ethnic backgrounds on learning?
- Do they use this knowledge about their students as they plan curriculum and design instructional and assessment activities?

3 Do teachers actively seek information about their students' readiness needs?

- Do you see evidence of preassessment and formative assessment strategies in the ongoing work of classrooms?
- Are teachers aware of informal assessment strategies, and do they use them to quickly gather information to guide their instructional planning?

4 Do teachers use flexible instructional strategies to respond to learning differences?

- Do you see a variety of strategies for teaching and learning in use in the classrooms?
- Are teachers aware of the rigor and complexity needs of students and are learners likely to be matched with what is "just right, right now" for them?

School-Based Action Plan for Differentiation

1. Reflect on Current School Practices

In my school, I see . . .

2. Examine Teachers' Beliefs

- ☐ We are there. Beliefs are held and acted on.
- ☐ We're almost there.
- ☐ We have work to do.

3. Consider Teachers' Attitudes

- ☐ Generally positive
- ☐ Somewhat positive
- ☐ Skeptical
- ☐ Oppositional

4. Take Stock of School Initiatives

Initative:____________________________ + –

Initative:____________________________ + –

Initative:____________________________ + –

Initative:____________________________ + –

5. Estimate Change Needed

1................2................3................4

Little leap — Big change

6. Identify Obstacles to Change

List.

7. Assess Available Energy (1 = Little, 3 = A Lot)

____ School leadership

____ Teachers

____ District Administrative Team

____ Board of Education

____ Parents

8. Determine Where to Begin

We will start by . . .

- Do teachers scaffold instruction as necessary and appropriate to meet students' needs?
- Are the students offered choice in content, process, or product?
- Are multiple arrangements used to group students in a variety of ways for a variety of purposes?

5 Do teachers diagnose student learning needs and prescribe particular tasks to particular students based on their needs?

- Do you see teachers using tiered assignments and flexible instructional groups as appropriate to the needs of their students?
- Do teachers match students with particular tasks based on their readiness, interests, and learning preferences?

Differentiation does look different from one classroom to the next because the strategies teachers use are reflective of their teaching styles and the needs of their students. However, the five previous questions enable you to comment on what you have seen in your school.

Step 2: Examine Teachers' Beliefs

The next consideration is the degree to which the teachers in your school hold beliefs that form the foundation for differentiation. See "The 20 Foundational Beliefs of Differentiated Classrooms" on page 162. School leaders need to consider whether these beliefs are held and acted on in your school. Can you provide examples or evidence that these beliefs are in practice in your school?

Examine each belief and determine the degree to which the belief is reflected or rejected by your school community. Keep in mind that these beliefs form the foundation for differentiation. If these beliefs run counter to the beliefs of your school community, it is going to be difficult to move this initiative forward or have it embraced by your faculty. In the second box of the action planning form, note where your school community is with these beliefs: you are there, you are almost there, or you have work to do. If there are beliefs related to differentiation that are *not* held by community members, consider ways in which you can discuss and resolve the belief differences. Identify a variety of ways to work on these beliefs, such as doing one or more of the following:

- read and discuss relevant articles
- initiate professional book clubs
- facilitate faculty discussions
- have faculty members present testimonies or case studies
- analyze and problem-solve scenarios
- invite outside facilitators who may open up thoughtful explorations of the beliefs

Step 3: Consider Teachers' Attitudes

The attitudes of teachers toward differentiation can either support differentiation practices in the classroom or can undermine any school-wide initiative. The next step in your action plan is to consider the attitudes of teachers in your school. Ask yourself:

- What kinds of conversations are teachers having about differentiation in the teachers' lounge, at faculty meetings, or in grade-level or department planning or advisory sessions?
- Are teachers reluctant, passive, or hostile about attending professional development sessions on differentiation practices, or are they always looking for new ways to improve their classroom practices?
- Do some teachers view differentiation as not worth their time, effort, and attention, or do they see that differentiation is making a difference for the students in your school?
- Do some teachers believe that differentiation is just this year's trendy topic that will go away in time, or do they see that differentiation is a survival strategy in modern standards-based classrooms?
- Are those teachers happily engaged in differentiation accepted and sought out by colleagues, or do they quietly do their work, resisting the pressure to conform to past practices?

The 20 Foundational Beliefs of Differentiated Classrooms

1. All people share common feelings and needs.

2. Schools should help people understand and respect their commonalities.

3. All children can learn.

4. Individuals differ significantly as learners.

5. Schools should help people understand and respect their differences.

6. Intelligence is not fixed; it is dynamic.

7. There are many ways to be smart.

8. The art of teaching is maximizing our students' success in learning.

9. The central goal of schools should be to increase the likelihood that all students will learn and succeed in reaching learning goals.

10. Students are at the center of the classroom; it is not about what *we* teach, but what *they* learn.

11. Students should be actively involved in making sense of the world around them.

12. All students represent a unique profile of readiness needs, learning preferences, and interests.

13. Effective teachers know their students' readiness needs, learning preferences, and interests, and act on this knowledge as they plan for instruction.

14. Because of the unique profiles of students, not all students will do the same thing at the same time in the classroom.

15. All students require respectful, engaging, and rigorous learning experiences.

16. Students' feelings of confidence and competence in learning are enhanced through success in learning experiences at the edge of their competencies that offer challenge and require effort.

17. Learning should be about individual growth and progress and not about comparisons to others.

18. Teachers and other adults need to help students accept responsibility for their growth and learning progress.

19. Students and teachers deserve schools and classrooms that are communities of respect, safety, and learning.

20. Parents can be partners in encouraging and supporting students' success in learning.

Adapted from *Leadership for Differentiating Schools and Classrooms* by Carol Ann Tomlinson (2000). Alexandria, VA: Association for Supervision and Curriculum Development. Used with permission.

In the third box of the action planning form, consider the general attitudes of teachers in your school. Are their attitudes toward differentiation generally positive, somewhat positive, skeptical, or downright oppositional?

Step 4: Take Stock of Current School Initiatives

Next, consider the initiatives already underway in your school or district. The number of initiatives underway at any one time in a school can be truly overwhelming. You may be implementing a new reading program, working on designing and implementing an anti-bullying curriculum, and reviewing new math programs for adoption. If you are going to put an emphasis on differentiation or want to extend practices in your school, you need to consider how much else is going on. You also need to consider whether the existing initiatives are going to build on, support, or conflict with an increased focus on differentiation.

It is very important that school leaders show clearly and explicitly how district initiatives work together.

In the fourth box of the action planning form, list any current initiatives that are underway in your school and then consider whether they support (+) or conflict (-) with differentiation initiatives. For example, Response to Intervention supports efforts in differentiation. However, if you have a school initiative that discourages grouping, it conflicts with practices of differentiation since flexible groups are an important management strategy. Any initiative you note as a conflict needs to be considered carefully. Is there a way you can get around it, get through it, or go over it? Or does this initiative need to be closely examined or modified to enable both initiatives to flourish?

It is very important that school leaders show clearly and explicitly how district initiatives work together. Chart them out and share them or present the connections at a faculty meeting. Failure to make the connections between school initiatives result in teachers assuming any new initiative is nothing more than the next educational bandwagon leaving past initiatives forgotten. Remember that differentiation is a collection of research-based best practices in teaching and learning, thus almost any school improvement initiative should be able to be clearly connected to one of its elements.

Step 5: Estimate How Much School-Wide Change Is Needed

Consider the degree of change that is required to more fully implement differentiation in your school.

- Do you have a base of teachers to work with?
- Are there individual teachers, clusters of teachers, or particular grade levels or departments who are taking the lead in differentiation in your school?
- Are most of your teachers "there" but need some refinement or extension of the strategies they are already using?
- Is differentiation a major change in practices in your school, or do you already have a solid group of teachers embracing and implementing its strategies?
- Do you have some teacher leaders to work with as an implementation team?

In the fifth box of the action planning form, note your impressions about the degree of change required in your school. Is moving into greater levels of implementation or higher degrees of sophistication a little leap or a big change? Rate your school from 1 (little leap) to 4 (big change).

Step 6: Identify the Obstacles to Change

In any school change, obstacles can stand in the way of progress. Consider what obstacles you will face in implementation.

- Is there a budget shortfall that will hamper opportunities for professional development or curriculum planning?

- Are attitudes of teachers, administrators, parents, or community members going to impede progress?
- Are there other curriculum or program initiatives or revisions that need attention and time?
- Are curriculum materials or resources unable to be funded?

In the sixth box of the action planning form, list any major obstacles that you believe may impede your progress.

Step 7: Assess Available Energy

In your professional life, you have only so much energy to give to your work. Both teachers and administrators can be stretched too thin with obligations and job responsibilities. Consider honestly how much energy can be expected of your school community members in moving differentiation into more sophisticated applications. Consider how much energy is available from you, the teachers in the school, the administrative team members, the board of education, and the parent community. In the seventh box of the action plan, rate the level of energy each of the school "stakeholders" has available to commit to implementation or extension of differentiation practices. Rate each from 1 (little energy left for this) to 4 (lots of energy can be depended on from this group).

Step 8: Determine Where to Begin

Finally, you are ready to consider how to start in putting your plan into action. You have critically reflected on important issues related to the change, and you have entered your perspectives on the action planning form. Consider the list of next steps below, and enter a brief summary in the eighth box.

Your next steps:

- Review the data represented on the action planning form.
- Based on the data, consider where your school is in implementing differentiation. Are you *beginning?* Are you *emerging?* Or are you *refining* your practices?
- Determine what is "doable" given the factors represented on the action planning form.
- What is doable yet this school year?
- What will be your focus for next year?
- How will the classrooms "look" by the end of the first year?
- How will you facilitate the change? Alone? With a team?
- Where will you start?

The action planning process used by a teacher leader, a principal, a school leadership team, or an entire school faculty enables you to examine the current level of implementation of differentiation in your school and to consider next courses of action to extend or refine practices.

Reflecting on Teaching Practices

Looking for evidence of differentiation in classrooms is often a perplexing problem for school leaders. The realities of differentiation are such that two teachers can be equally adept and yet using completely different strategies. You may wish to review the "25 Formats for Differentiation" in Chapter 7 (pages 116–117) to bring to mind the multitude of strategies that may be used in differentiation. In addition, use the indicators of differentiation used in Step 1 of the action planning form to reflect on individual teachers' practices.

WALKTHROUGHS

Many administrators use walkthroughs to gain perspectives about classroom practices. The three- to five-minute unannounced strolls through the classroom offer a snapshot of the classroom environment, grouping arrangements, learning activities, instructional strategies, and levels of student engagement. Post-walkthrough conferences provide opportunities for discussions between leaders and teachers about teaching and learning. Walkthroughs and the post-conferences also enable leaders to coach teachers to new levels of professional practice.

What might be observed during a walkthrough that indicates differentiation is taking place? Page 166 provides indicators of differentiation in action.

The indicators of differentiation can also be used by principals as they formally observe a teacher's lessons as part of a performance review. Teachers may note which strategies they will use in a lesson prior to the observation, or principals may check off what they see during the observation. The indicators can also be used post-observation in a discussion with the teacher about additional ways they may have differentiated the lesson.

REASONABLE GROWTH TARGETS FOR TEACHERS

As school leaders consider differentiation as part of their coaching practices or a component in supervision or evaluation of classroom teachers, professional growth targets may result. Following are some examples of growth targets that are both reasonable and doable for classroom teachers to accomplish over a designated period of time. Remember, teachers should add one new strategy at a time to avoid becoming overwhelmed!

- Choose one new differentiation strategy to implement over a grading period.
- Implement a new strategy or format for student choice. If you have used choice in products, try offering students a choice in content or process.
- Try out a new way to tier an assignment. If you have tiered tasks based on challenge level, try tiering them in a new way such as by degree of structure or abstractness.
- Group for instruction in a new way. If you have grouped by readiness, try creating groups based on interests or learning preferences.
- Use formative assessment data to plan and implement a differentiated lesson.
- Differentiate workstations by purposefully assigning particular students to specific stations or specific tasks within a station.
- Assign students to particular books or articles based on reading-readiness scores, and provide appropriate tasks based on student needs.
- Select a curriculum unit that you have used previously. Analyze the level of rigor, the relevance of instructional activities, the variety exhibited in student tasks, and your teaching strategies. Modify the activities in the unit to reflect the needs of your current students.
- Gather information about your students' interests or learning preferences, and use that data to plan differentiated activities for a curriculum unit or series of lessons.
- Try new informal assessment strategies and use the data to adjust your plans for a lesson or modify the next day's activities.

Strategies for Keeping Differentiation at the Forefront

Professional development in your school should be ongoing. However, the "Continuum of Levels of Teacher Development in Differentiation" in Chapter 2 (pages 15–18) made clear that teachers in a single school are as diverse as students in their classrooms. Each teacher is in a particular and personal stage of her or his professional development in differentiation. Therefore, when considering professional development plans, you need to consider the specific needs of individual teachers in your school and plan for them.

Professional development doesn't necessarily mean major commitments of time and dollars. Page 167 shows strategies for keeping differentiation initiatives alive and the energy around them positive.

School leaders—both teacher leaders and principals—are critical in supporting the efforts of teachers in differentiation. It is important that teachers view you as knowledgeable about and interested in their classroom practices. Honor the work all teachers are currently doing to help students succeed, yet encourage continued professional growth.

Walkthrough Indicators of Differentiation in Action

- ☐ Teacher uses a variety of instructional strategies to engage the students in learning.
- ☐ Teacher purposefully responds to student differences as they appear during the lesson by reteaching, reinforcing, or extending learning.
- ☐ Students are engaged in different tasks but are working on similar goals.
- ☐ Students are engaged in the same task but are using readiness-based resources.
- ☐ Students are engaged in different tasks at different levels of challenge or complexity.
- ☐ Students are engaged in tasks representing different degrees of scaffolding.
- ☐ Some students are engaged in tasks that have been modified or adapted for their needs.
- ☐ Student activities reflect differences in readiness, interest, or learning preference.
- ☐ Technology is being used to provide different learning experiences for some students.
- ☐ Teacher is using an informal or formal preassessment strategy (e.g., check-in slips).
- ☐ Teacher is gathering formative assessment data (e.g., exit slips).
- ☐ Students are purposefully grouped for activities.
- ☐ Students are given a choice in content, process, or product.
- ☐ Students are given a choice to work alone, with a partner, or in a small group.
- ☐ Resources within the classroom reflect differences in depth or sophistication of content.
- ☐ Resources within the classroom reflect differences in reading-readiness levels.
- ☐ Teacher is appropriately utilizing anchor activities for students who complete work early.
- ☐ Students are able to move to independent work when they are ready.
- ☐ Workstations represent a range of skill progressions.
- ☐ Workstations present print resources reflecting different readiness levels.
- ☐ Students are assigned to particular workstations or particular tasks within a workstation.

Tips for Keeping Differentiation Alive in Your School

- Spotlight a strategy or share an application at each faculty meeting.
- Convene problem-solving groups. Bring together teachers who have had success with a strategy and those who are finding it difficult to implement.
- Do school mailbox or email professional development. Share an article or contribute a new idea or strategy by duplicating and delivering it to teachers' mailboxes or forwarding an article or link via email.
- Share ideas and differentiated activities by placing a hanging file by the copy machine or in the teachers' lounge or workroom.
    - Organize file folders by grade or department.
    - Ask teachers to share their differentiated activities by putting an extra copy in the file folder for others to review as they have time.
    - Agree to a practice that if you modify someone's idea or activity based on the needs of your students, you put your new version in the file. This way the ideas grow.
    - Alternately, post a share file for each grade level or department on your school's intranet site.
- If such requirements are possible, require a professional growth target related to differentiation.
- Hold a question and answer session with an outside differentiation expert or an active practitioner in your district or school or neighboring school district.
- Establish a book study group on a differentiation text.
- Set up expert groups for each differentiation strategy. Determine who to go to for advice about tiering, for using a particular choice format, for using informal assessment strategies, etc.
- Discuss an article or piece of research related to differentiation at a coffee and dessert "happy hour" or a brown bag lunch session.
- Set up a make-and-take work session to create differentiated classroom materials.
- Commit a grade-level or department meeting agenda to discussing ideas for differentiation or for collaborative planning.
- Encourage and provide opportunities for teachers to observe colleagues using a particular differentiation strategy in their classrooms.
- Identify teachers who could be coaches for colleagues as they try out new differentiation strategies. Allow time for them to visit the classroom, observe a lesson, and provide feedback, ideas, and coaching to enhance practices.
- Determine times when teachers can do specific topic-alike planning. For example, all primary teachers can get together to work on literacy ideas, or all social studies teachers can meet to work on service learning activities.

CONCLUSION

Making Differentiation a Habit

This book has walked you through the critical elements of differentiated instruction in academically diverse classrooms. In applying these elements, you can be confident that the work you do in differentiation is based on a solid foundation of research and best practices in teaching and learning.

Remember, it is only authentic differentiation when you:

1. Integrate strategies for differentiation and RTI into your classroom practices.
2. Identify learning goals, or KUDo's (what your students need to **K**now, **U**nderstand, and be able to **Do**).
3. Examine your professional practices in light of your students' needs.
4. Apply practical, doable, and valid assessment strategies.
5. Create differentiated learning plans.
6. Use choice opportunities to motivate student learning.
7. Prescribe tiered assignments and use flexible grouping as necessary and appropriate.
8. Maintain flexibility in your planning and teaching.
9. Develop student responsibility and independence.
10. Use ethical grading practices.
11. Differentiate instruction for gifted students with their particular and specific learning differences in mind.
12. Commit to a leadership framework for differentiated classrooms in your school.

Differentiation done well becomes the way you think about teaching and learning in your classroom. It becomes a habit, an almost automatic response in how you engage in the art and science of teaching. The ways of thinking presented on page 169 are examples of the habits of differentiation.

The habit of differentiation results in students enthusiastically engaged in learning, experiencing increasing levels of success, and gaining confidence in themselves as learners.

It results in teachers who welcome and celebrate the diversity of lives, talents, interests, and passions in their students. The habit of differentiation creates schools that take pride in being a learning community where everyone from the office secretary to the principal, from the custodian to the teacher, shares a commitment to their students' success in learning. Differentiation becomes the way we do the work in today's academically diverse and increasingly challenging classrooms. It's a habit worth developing.

The Habits of Differentiation

- Survey, watch, listen, and ask in order to find out more about your students as individuals and as learners.
- Use quick informal preassessments one to two weeks before you start a unit.
- Act on both formal and informal formative assessment data as it comes in.
- Determine your KUDo's before you plan student activities.
- Discard activities that are not directly related to the goals established by your KUDo's.
- Sort activities into two groups: those that need to be done by all students and those that should only be done by some students. Be selective about activities in the "all" group.
- Use the "some" activities as a level of a tiered assignment or on a choice board.
- Use generic rubrics whenever possible.
- Provide opportunities for student choice of content, process, or product.
- When the need arises, tier an assignment by content, process, or product, and prescribe "just right, right now" tasks.
- Use multiple print or technology resources matched to students' reading readiness or prior knowledge about a curriculum topic.
- Grade less, remark more.
- Grade less, use peer- or self-assessment more.
- Pay attention to the balance of learning preferences in your teaching and in the products of your students.
- Always maintain or increase the rigor of learning tasks as you differentiate.
- Try new ways of grouping for instruction: by readiness, by challenge/complexity, or by learning preference.
- Set up structures for and expect more independence and responsibility on the part of your students.
- Remember the key to motivation is interest. Use "hooks" to interest students in new topics and motivate them to do the work.

References and Resources

Anderson, Lorin W., and David R. Krathwohl, eds. *A Taxonomy for Learning, Teaching, Assessing: A Revision of Bloom's Taxonomy of Educational Objectives.* Boston: Allyn & Bacon, 2000.

Armstrong, Thomas. *Multiple Intelligences in the Classroom.* Alexandria, VA: Association for Supervision and Curriculum Development, 2000.

Bender, William N. *Teaching Students with Mild Disabilities.* Boston: Allyn & Bacon, 1996.

——. *Differentiating Instruction for Students with Learning Disabilities: Best Teaching Practices for General and Special Educators.* Thousand Oaks, CA: Corwin Press, 2002.

——. *Differentiating Math Instruction: Strategies That Work for K–8 Classrooms!* Thousand Oaks, CA: Corwin Press, 2005.

Bender, William N., and Cara Shores. *Response to Intervention: A Practical Guide for Every Teacher.* Thousand Oaks, CA: Corwin Press, 2007.

Blaz, Deborah. *Differentiated Instruction: A Guide for Foreign Language Teachers.* Larchmont, NY: Eye On Education, 2006.

Bloom, Benjamin, et al. *Taxonomy of Educational Objectives: Handbook of the Cognitive Domain.* New York: Longman, 1984.

Brookhart, Susan M. "Teachers Grading: Practice and Theory." *Applied Measurement in Education* 7, no. 4 (1994): 279–301.

——. *Grading.* Upper Saddle River, NJ: Pearson, 2004.

——. *How to Give Effective Feedback to Your Students.* Alexandria, VA: Association for Supervision and Curriculum Development, 2008.

Butler, R. and M. Nisan. "Effects of No Feedback, Task-Related Comments, and Grades on Intrinsic Motivation and Performance." *Journal of Educational Psychology* 78 (1986): 210–216.

Clayton, Marlynn K. and Mary Beth Forton. *Classroom Spaces That Work.* Greenfield, MA: Northeast Foundation for Children, 2001.

Cummings, Carol. *Winning Strategies for Classroom Management.* Alexandria, VA: Association for Supervision and Curriculum Development, 2000.

Danielson, C. "The Many Faces of Leadership." *Educational Leadership* 65, no.1 (2007): 14–19.

Denton, Paula and Roxann Kriete. *The First Six Weeks of School.* Greenfield, MA: Northeast Foundation for Children, 2000.

Diller, Debbie. *Literacy Work Stations: Making Centers Work.* Portland, ME: Stenhouse Publishers, 2003.

——. *Practice with Purpose: Literacy Work Stations for Grades 3–6.* Portland, ME: Stenhouse Publishers, 2005.

Earl, Lorna M. *Assessment as Learning: Using Classroom Assessment to Maximize Student Learning.* Thousand Oaks, CA: Corwin Press, 2004.

Fisher, Douglas and Nancy Frey. *Checking for Understanding.* Alexandria, VA: Association for Supervision and Curriculum Development, 2007.

Forsten, Char, Jim Grant, and Betty Hollas. *Differentiating Textbooks: Strategies to Improve Student Comprehension & Motivation.* Peterborough, NH: Crystal Springs Books, 2003.

Frayer, Dorothy Ann, W. C. Frederick, and H. J. Klasmeier. *A Schema for Testing Level of Concept Mastery.* Technical Report No. K16, University of Wisconsin, 1969.

Gipps, Caroline, Bet McCallum, and Eleanore Hargreaves. *What Makes a Good Primary School Teacher? Expert Classroom Strategies.* London: Routledge Falmer, 2000.

Grimes, Jeff and Sharon Kurns. "An Intervention-Based System for Addressing NCLB and IDEA Expectations: A Multiple Tiered Model to Ensure Every Child Learns." Paper presented at the National Research Center on Learning Disabilities Responsiveness to Intervention Symposium (Kansas City, MO, 2003).

Guskey, Thomas R. and Jane M. Bailey. *Developing Grading and Reporting Systems for Student Learning.* Thousand Oaks, CA: Corwin Press, 2001.

Hayes-Jacobs, Heidi, ed. *Getting Results with Curriculum Mapping.* Alexandria, VA: Association for Supervision and Curriculum Development, 2004.

Hayes-Jacobs, Heidi. *Mapping the Big Picture: Integrating Curriculum & Assessment K–12.* Alexandria, VA: Association for Supervision and Curriculum Development, 1997.

Heacox, Diane. *Up from Underachievement: How Teachers, Students, and Parents Can Work Together to Promote Student Success.* Minneapolis: Free Spirit Publishing, 1991.

——. *Differentiating Instruction in the Regular Classroom: How to Reach and Teach All Learners, Grades 3–12.* Minneapolis: Free Spirit Publishing, 2002.

Hill, Jane D. and Kathleen M. Flynn. *Classroom Instruction That Works with English Language Learners.* Alexandria, VA: Association for Supervision and Curriculum Development, 2006.

Kaplan, Sandra. *Differentiating Core Curriculum and Instruction to Provide Advanced Learning Opportunities.* Sacramento, CA: California Association for the Gifted, 1994.

——. "Layering Differentiated Curriculum for the Gifted and Talented." In *Methods and Materials for Teaching the Gifted,* edited by Frances A. Karnes and Suzanne M. Bean, 107–132.Waco, TX: Prufrock Press, 2005.

King-Shaver, Barbara and Alyce Hunter. *Differentiated Instruction in the English Classroom: Content, Process, Product, and Assessment.* Portsmouth, NH: Heinemann, 2003.

Kitano, Margie, Diane Montgomery, Joyce Lenore VanTassel-Baska, and Susan K. Johnsen. *Using the National Gifted Standards for PreK–12 Professional Development.* Thousand Oaks, CA: Corwin Press, 2008.

Kohn, Alfie. *What to Look for in a Classroom: And Other Essays.* San Francisco: Jossey-Bass, 2000.

Krashen, Stephen D. and Tracy D. Terrell. *The Natural Approach: Language Acquisition in the Classroom.* Oxford: Pergamon Press, 1983.

Kuzmich, Lin. *Data Driven Instruction: A Handbook.* Longmont, CO: Centennial Board of Cooperative Services, 1998.

Landrum, Mary S., Carolyn M. Callahan, and Beverly D. Shaklee, eds. *Aiming for Excellence: Annotations to the NAGC PreK–Grade 12 Gifted Program Standards.* Waco, TX: Prufrock Press, 2000.

Maker, C. June. *Curriculum Development for the Gifted.* Rockville, MD: Aspen Systems Corporation, 1982.

Marzano, Robert J. *Transforming Classroom Grading.* Alexandria, VA: Association for Supervision and Curriculum Development, 2000.

——. *Classroom Assessment & Grading That Work.* Alexandria, VA: Association for Supervision and Curriculum Development, 2006.

——. *The Art and Science of Teaching.* Alexandria, VA: Association for Supervision and Curriculum Development, 2007.

Marzano, Robert J., Debra Pickering, and Jay McTighe. *Assessing Student Outcomes: Performance Assessment Using the Dimensions of Learning Model.* Alexandria, VA: Association for Supervision and Curriculum Development, 1993.

Marzano, Robert J., Debra J. Pickering, and Jane E. Pollock. *Classroom Instruction That Works: Research-Based Strategies for Increasing Student Achievement.* Alexandria, VA: Association for Supervision and Curriculum Development, 2001.

Moon, Tonya R. "The Role of Assessment in Differentiation." *Theory Into Practice* 44, no. 3 (Summer 2005): 226–233.

Northeast Foundation for Children. *Responsive Classroom.* Turners Falls, MA: Northeast Foundation for Children, 2003.

O'Connor, Ken. *How to Grade for Learning: Linking Grades to Standards.* Thousand Oaks, CA: Corwin Press, 2002.

Opitz, Michael E. *Flexible Grouping in Reading: Practical Ways to Help All Students Become Better Readers.* New York: Scholastic Inc., 1999.

Passow, A. Harry. *The Gifted and the Talented: Their Education and Development.* Chicago: University of Chicago Press, 1979.

Pavelka, Patricia. *Create Independent Learners: Teacher-Tested Strategies for All Ability Levels.* Peterborough, NH: Crystal Springs Books, 1999.

Pisha, B. and P. Coyne. "Smart from the Start: The Promise of Universal Design for Learning." *Remedial and Special Education* 22, no. 4 (2001): 197–203.

Popham, W. James. *Transformative Assessment.* Alexandria, VA: Association for Supervision and Curriculum Development, 2008.

Rogers, Karen B. *Re-forming Gifted Education: Matching the Program to the Child.* Scottsdale, AZ: Great Potential Press, 2002.

Smutny, Joan Franklin and S. E. von Fremd. *Differentiating for the Young Child: Teaching Strategies Across the Content Areas (K–3).* Thousand Oaks, CA: Corwin Press, 2004.

Stiggins, Richard J. "Assessment, Student Confidence, and School Success." *Phi Delta Kappan* 81, no. 3 (Nov. 1999): 191–198.

——. *Student-Involved Classroom Assessment.* Upper Saddle River, NJ: Prentice Hall, 2000.

Stiggins, Richard J., Judith A. Arter, Jan Chappuis, and Steven Chappius. *Classroom Assessment for Student Learning: Doing It Right—Using It Well.* Portland, OR: Assessment Training Institute, 2004.

Strickland, Cindy. *Tools for High Quality Differentiated Instruction: An ASCD Action Tool.* Alexandria, VA: Association for Supervision and Curriculum Development, 2007.

Strong, Richard W., Harvey F. Silver, and Matthew J. Perini. *Teaching What Matters Most: Standards and Strategies for Raising Student Achievement.* Alexandria, VA: Association for Supervision and Curriculum Development, 2001.

Thomas, Ed. *Styles and Strategies for Teaching Middle School Mathematics.* Ho Ho Kus, NJ: Thoughtful Education Press, 2003.

Tishman, Shari and Albert Andrade. *Critical Squares: Games of Critical Thinking and Understanding.* Englewood, CO: Teacher Ideas Press, 1997.

Tomlinson, Carol Ann. *The Differentiated Classroom: Responding to the Needs of All Learners.* Alexandria, VA: Association for Supervision and Curriculum Development, 1999.

——. *How to Differentiate Instruction in Mixed Ability Classrooms.* Alexandria, VA: Association for Supervision and Curriculum Development, 2001.

——. *Fulfilling the Promise of the Differentiated Classroom: Strategies and Tools for Responsive Teaching.* Alexandria, VA: Association for Supervision and Curriculum Development, 2003.

——. "Differentiation and the Issue of Quality." Paper presented at the National Association for Gifted Children Annual Conference (Indianapolis, IN, November 2003).

——. *Common Sense of Differentiation: Meeting Specific Learner Needs in the Regular Classroom.* DVD and book. Alexandria, VA: Association for Supervision and Curriculum Development, 2005.

Tomlinson, Carol Ann and Susan Demirsky Allan. *Leadership for Differentiating Schools & Classrooms.* Alexandria, VA: Association for Supervision and Curriculum Development, 2000.

Tomlinson, Carol Ann and Caroline Cunningham Edison. *Differentiation in Practice: A Resource Guide for Differentiating Curriculum.* Alexandria, VA: Association for Supervision and Curriculum Development, 2003.

Tomlinson, Carol Ann and Jay McTighe. *Integrating Differentiated Instruction & Understanding by Design: Connecting Content and Kids.* Alexandria, VA: Association for Supervision and Curriculum Development, 2006.

The University of Chicago School Mathematics Project. *Everyday Mathematics: Student Math Journal, Volume 1 (Grade 5).* Chicago: Everyday Learning Corporation, 2001.

VanTassel-Baska, Joyce and Catherine A. Little, eds. *Content-Based Curriculum for High-Ability Learners.* Waco, TX: Prufrock Press, 2003.

Vygotsky, L. S. *Mind in Society: The Development of Higher Psychological Processes.* Cambridge, MA: Harvard University Press, 1978.

Wiggins, Grant and Jay McTighe. *Understanding by Design.* Alexandria, VA: Association for Supervision and Curriculum Development, 1998.

Winebrenner, Susan. *Teaching Gifted Kids in the Regular Classroom: Strategies and Techniques Every Teacher Can Use to Meet the Academic Needs of the Gifted and Talented.* Minneapolis: Free Spirit Publishing, 2001.

——. *Teaching Kids with Learning Difficulties in the Regular Classroom: Ways to Challenge & Motivate Struggling Students to Achieve Proficiency with Required Standards.* Minneapolis: Free Spirit Publishing, 2006.

Witherell, Nancy L. and Mary C. McMackin. *Graphic Organizers and Activities for Differentiated Instruction in Reading.* New York: Scholastic Inc., 2002.

Wormeli, Rick. *Summarization in Any Subject: 50 Techniques to Improve Student Learning.* Alexandria, VA: Association for Supervision and Curriculum Development, 2005.

——. *Fair Isn't Always Equal: Assessing & Grading in the Differentiated Classroom.* Portland, ME: Stenhouse Publishers, 2006.

——. *Differentiation: From Planning to Practice, Grades 6–12.* Portland, ME: Stenhouse Publishers, 2007.

Wrubel, Ronit W. *Great Grouping Strategies: Dozens of Ways to Flexibly Group Your Students for Maximum Learning Across the Curriculum.* New York: Scholastic Inc., 2002.

INDEX

Note: Page references in italics refer to figures; those in boldface refer to reproducible templates.

Q

R

S

T